BONHOEFFER AS BIBLICAL INTERPRETER

T&T Clark New Studies in Bonhoeffer's Theology and Ethics

Series Editors
Jennifer McBride
Michael Mawson
Philip G. Ziegler

BONHOEFFER AS BIBLICAL INTERPRETER

Reading Scripture in 1930s Germany

Jameson E. Ross

LONDON · NEW YORK · OXFORD · NEW DELHI · SYDNEY

T&T CLARK
Bloomsbury Publishing Plc
50 Bedford Square, London, WC1B 3DP, UK
1385 Broadway, New York, NY 10018, USA
29 Earlsfort Terrace, Dublin 2, Ireland

BLOOMSBURY, T&T CLARK and the T&T Clark logo are trademarks of
Bloomsbury Publishing Plc

First published in Great Britain 2021
Paperback edition published 2023

A catalogue record for this book is available from the British Library.

Library of Congress Cataloging-in-Publication Data
Names: Ross, Jameson, author.
Title: Bonhoeffer as biblical interpreter : reading scripture in 1930s
Germany / Jameson Ross.
Description: London ; New York : T&T Clark, [2021] |
Series: T&T Clark new studies in Bonhoeffer's theology and ethics |
Includes bibliographical references and index. |
Identifiers: LCCN 2021001506 (print) | LCCN 2021001507 (ebook) |
ISBN 9780567693051 (hardback) | ISBN 9780567702241 (paperback) |
ISBN 9780567693068 (pdf) | ISBN 9780567693082 (epub)
Subjects: LCSH: Bonhoeffer, Dietrich, 1906–1945. | Bible–Hermeneutics. |
Theology, Doctrinal–Germany–History–20th century. | Germany–Church history–1933–1945.
Classification: LCC BX4827.B57 R666 2021 (print) | LCC BX4827.B57 (ebook)
| DDC 220.6092–dc23
LC record available at https://lccn.loc.gov/2021001506
LC ebook record available at https://lccn.loc.gov/2021001507

ISBN: HB: 978-0-5676-9305-1
PB: 978-0-5677-0224-1
ePDF: 978-0-5676-9306-8
eBook: 978-0-5676-9308-2

Series: T&T Clark New Studies in Bonhoeffer's Theology and Ethics

Typeset by Newgen KnowledgeWorks Pvt. Ltd., Chennai, India

To find out more about our authors and books visit www.bloomsbury.com
and sign up for our newsletters.

CONTENTS

FOREWORD

Dr. Joel Lawrence

Executive Director, The Center for Pastor Theologians

"Bonhoeffer as Biblical Interpreter" explores a disarmingly simple thesis, that Bonhoeffer was a biblical interpreter, with surprising and important effect. It is not a radical claim to state that Bonhoeffer was a biblical interpreter, nor does this claim take us into previously unexplored territory in Bonhoeffer scholarship. But, as executed by Ross, it is a thesis that provides original insight into the nature of Bonhoeffer's theological method and engagement with the Scriptures through its claim that Bonhoeffer was first and foremost a biblical interpreter. For Ross, Bonhoeffer as biblical interpreter is a claim that Bonhoeffer is best understood as a hermeneutician, and that his theology is best understood through close attention to Bonhoeffer's method and practices of interpreting the Bible. While the thesis that Bonhoeffer is a biblical interpreter is simple, Ross's exploration of that thesis is important for seeing Bonhoeffer's theology in fresh light, and the method that Ross employs, a close reading of Bonhoeffer's interpretation of biblical texts, offers Bonhoeffer scholarship a new vista into the construction of Bonhoeffer's theology.

While others have written about Bonhoeffer's hermeneutics, this book stands out for the way in which Ross charts the construction and execution of Bonhoeffer's theory and practice of interpretating the Bible. Rather than engage with Bonhoeffer's hermeneutics at a theoretical or comparative level and then offer examples, Ross takes us through close readings of various writings in Bonhoeffer's *corpus*, inviting the reader to observe Bonhoeffer in the practice of interpreting actual texts and seeing, from the ground up, the process of biblical interpretation that Bonhoeffer employs. From his days as a student in 1925, to lectures given at the University of Berlin, to sermons given in London, and culminating in Bonhoeffer's most direct work of biblical interpretation, *Nachfolge*, Ross invites us on a journey to see Bonhoeffer construct and execute his interpretive vision, and does so with tremendous attention to detail that yields rich insight.

This approach provides a new appreciation of Bonhoeffer as a theologian by walking us carefully through the very construction of his theology. Because Bonhoeffer was a biblical interpreter, his theological vision can only be properly understood as a construction built on biblical texts. Ross's work gives us access to Bonhoeffer's interpretive journey with the Bible in a way that is both delightful and enlightening, helping us to trace the contours of Bonhoeffer's well-known ideas from a different perspective, an approach that in itself allows us to see those ideas in a new and fresh way. By doing this, we see Bonhoeffer's main ideas in process. In a sense, this book is something of a "behind-the-scenes" approach to Bonhoeffer, approaching his theology not as a completed edifice (if I may be allowed to mix my metaphors) but as a building under construction. Through this, we see the choice of materials with more clarity, giving us a renewed appreciation for both the construction process as well as the completed structure.

But perhaps the most delightful aspect of the book is the surprising way in which the close reading of texts, which in the hands of many writers might yield a rather colorless account of the subject, becomes in Ross's hands an invitation into Bonhoeffer's study, as Bonhoeffer sits with the biblical text, writing a student paper in his parents' home, composing sermons in a London parsonage, authoring a book while seated at his desk. Reading this book is like being invited to pull up a chair alongside Bonhoeffer, to converse with him as he reads the Bible and prays, as he wrestles with the prophets, and Paul, and God. In doing this, Ross achieves something important: a scholarly and richly detailed engagement with Bonhoeffer, focused on a close reading of Bonhoeffer's original texts, that opens up a new vista into the life of this man who has become familiar, perhaps too familiar, to so many. Grappling with the Bible, we see Bonhoeffer, like many of us, trying to understand how God has spoken and is speaking to us through the text of the Bible, learning with him how to best attune our ear and our soul to hear the Holy Spirit proclaim to us, here and now, the revelation of God in and through Jesus Christ, and in that revelation to hear the voice of the shepherd who calls us, like he called Bonhoeffer, to follow.

So, as you read this book, I invite you to pull up a chair alongside Bonhoeffer in his study, to sit with him as he exegetes the Scripture, to learn with him about the call to discipleship, and, through this, to view Bonhoeffer's theology with fresh eyes.

ACKNOWLEDGMENTS

This book is a slightly revised version of the PhD thesis I submitted to Durham University in early 2019. In the two years since I first expressed gratitude to so many for supporting that initiative, I have only grown more thankful.

I now have the opportunity to add thanks to the editors of this series, *New Studies in Bonhoeffer's Theology and Ethics*, Phil Ziegler, Michael Mawson, and Jennifer McBride, as well as the team at T&T Clark.

Many thanks to Professors Francis Watson and Mike Higton, my PhD supervisors. Their commitment to reading primary texts in their original languages, their love of learning, and their commitment to me and the project—expressed to a large degree in their careful reading of and incisive comments on draft chapters, comments that, time and again, made it much better—were the greatest gifts of the postgraduate process.

Without any question I have spent more time talking with friends about this project than actually writing it. I am so grateful to have had the opportunity to dialogue with the following colleagues: Josh Mobley, Andy Byers, Nathan White, Jon Bentall, Madison Pierce, Richard Rohlfing, Justin Allison, Stephen Campbell, and Ben White (the last four made up the 50 N. Baily PG8 Crew). Special thanks also to John and Christina Castling, Martin and Rachel Smith, Matt Williams, Sam Tranter, Peter Baker, and Tim Escott.

A group of what must be some of the most generous people on the planet got behind us, giving all the money we needed for tuition, travel, and living expenses for three years in England. The Ministry and Education Foundation offered to serve us by administering these funds for us, and they, specifically Joanne Erickson and Nancy Singer, did a wonderful job on our behalf. Thank you all so much.

We are very thankful for the way our families cared for us from a distance and sometimes in Durham. My parents-in-law, Jim and Sue Nicodem, have been very involved and supportive at each stage. Additionally, my brothers-in-law and sisters-in-law, Adam and Emily Hendrix and Andrew and Marianne Nicodem, came to visit us and cheered me on constantly.

I'm grateful that my kids, Charlotte Grace, Winston Graham, and Adler Gray, were around to interrupt the writing process, the first two during the PhD thesis phase in England and the final one as the book was nearing completion at the end of 2020. If, as I argue in the book, biblical interpretation is a matter of engaging biblical texts for the benefit of others, then chief among those "others" would be my kids. I look forward to continuing to read with and for them.

In his book *The Edge of Words: God and the Habits of Language*, Rowan Williams says (recalling the words from Dewi Philips) that saying "I can't tell you how grateful I am" is precisely the way we tell someone how grateful we are. To my wife Rachel: I can't tell you how grateful I am. I hope that you will take these words as the way that I tell you how exceedingly grateful I am for you and your support on this journey. I dedicate this to you with love, gratitude, and affection.

A NOTE ON TRANSLATION

Unless otherwise indicated, Scripture quotations are from the Holy Bible, New International Version, copyright 2011 by the International Bible Society. Used by permission of Zondervan. In rare instances I have found it necessary to amend the NIV, and where this has been the case I have indicated it in a footnote.

Translations of Hebrew and Greek are my own.

I will quote from DBW and provide my own English translations. I do this for two reasons. It is important for me, as an English-speaking scholar, to interact with Bonhoeffer's texts in his own language so that I am enabled to hear him rather than his translators. In addition, I have found the translations of the volumes in DBWE to vary significantly in quality. At times, some are unreliable and unidiomatic, which has the tendency to give the impression that Bonhoeffer's German prose is idiosyncratic in style. At other times, they are simply unhelpfully misleading.

Translating the texts myself meant making decisions about Bonhoeffer's use of language regarding gender. I have sought to use gender-inclusive language where possible, but it is often the case that I stayed with Bonhoeffer's use in order to honor him in his own time and place and to avoid using cumbersome or awkward phrases to render his usage gender-inclusive. For example, the archaic use of "Er" will be translated with the masculine pronoun in English in order to respect Bonhoeffer's own choice of words in the 1930s context in which he was writing, a time when no one was concerned with these issues. However, "der Mensch" will be translated with the more general "person" (unless it refers back to a singular, masculine noun or pronoun) because a general meaning is consistent with Bonhoeffer's own usage. Having noted this here, I will not draw attention to each decision of this type as the book unfolds. There is simply too much material quoted for this to be realistic. Instead, I will note instances where my translation is significant for the interpretation of the passage in question.

ABBREVIATIONS

DBW   Dietrich Bonhoeffer Werke, German edition
DBWE   Dietrich Bonhoeffer Works, English edition
NIV   Holy Bible, New International Version

All other abbreviations adhere to the forms found in the SBL Handbook of Style, 2nd ed. (Atlanta, GA: SBL Press, 2014).

INTRODUCTION

1. Listening in on Bonhoeffer Reading Scripture

While in America on June 26, 1939, Dietrich Bonhoeffer jotted down some reflections on the closing verses of Apostle Paul's second letter to Timothy. Here is the relevant portion:

> Heute las ich zufällig aus 2. Tim. 4[,21] „komme noch vor dem Winter"—die Bitte des Paulus an Timotheus. Timotheus soll das Leiden des Apostels teilen und sich nicht schämen. „Komme noch vor dem Winter"—es könnte sonst zu spät sein. Das geht mir den ganzen Tag nach. Es geht uns wohl so wie den Soldaten, die vom Feld in den Urlaub kommen und trotz allem, was sie erwarteten, wieder ins Feld zurückdrängen. Wir kommen nicht mehr davon los. Nicht als wären wir nötig, als würden wir gebraucht (von Gott!?), sondern einfach weil dort unser Leben ist und weil wir unser Leben zurücklassen, vernichten, wenn wir nicht wieder dabei sind. Es ist gar nichts Frommes, sondern etwas fast Vitales. Aber Gott handelt nicht nur durch fromme, sondern auch durch solche vitalen Regungen. „Komm[e] noch vor dem Winter"—Es ist nicht Mißbrauch der Schrift, wenn ich das *mir* gesagt sein lasse. Wenn mir Gott Gnade dazu gibt.[1]

> Incidentally, I read today from 2 Tim. 4:21 "come before the winter"—Paul's plea to Timothy. Timothy is to share the suffering of the apostle and not be ashamed. "Come before the winter"—otherwise it might be too late. That is getting to me the whole day. We are like soldiers on leave from the field of battle, who, despite all that awaits them, push to return to the front. We cannot get away from it. Not as if we were necessary, as if we were needed (by God!?), but rather simply because our life is there and because we leave behind or destroy our lives if we are not part of things there. It is not at all a pious thing, but something almost vital. But God acts not only through feelings of piety, but also

---

1. DBW 15:234, emphasis original. The journal entry, running to a total of only twenty sentences, also contains a note about a letter received from Bonhoeffer's parents, the fact that he was in the library all day, and the books he read while there, with book review comments included.

through such vital impulses. "Come before the winter"—it is not a misuse of the Scripture if I allow this to be said *to me*. If God gives me the grace for that.

This is an unexceptional occurrence in his American diary. Bonhoeffer reflected on Scriptural passages in his journal and thought explicitly about the way in which the biblical text related to his life. This journal entry does stand out, though, because this reflection served, alongside a number of other compelling factors, to support the decision to return to Germany rather than stay in the safety of the United States even as war seemed imminent.[2] There is an additional reason to dwell on this short record. In the second to last line of the journal entry, he quotes the words, "Komme noch vor dem Winter" [Come before the winter] for the third time, writing, "Es ist nicht Mißbrauch der Schrift, wenn ich das *mir* gesagt sein lasse" [It is not a misuse of the Scripture if I allow this to be said *to me*]. At this point, what he chooses to include in his private journal is quite telling. To whom is this comment directed? Why is this necessary? Is his judgment right? This reassuring comment, it seems, is meant for Bonhoeffer himself.[3] In these few words he signals an awareness of an interpretive dynamic, a struggle in which he feels the need to defend his interpretation to himself.

What does that interpretation consist of?[4] He reads with attentiveness to context. As seen above, he begins by quoting Paul's words, "Komme noch vor dem Winter," and notes the context within which the words are found.[5] The line comes in the final greetings, 2 Tim. 4:19-22, where Paul names specific individuals that he wishes Timothy to greet or from whom he sends greetings; this is the section in which Paul's request is made to Timothy. This is not the only relevant context though. Bonhoeffer rightly sees this request as connecting to the movements of

---

2. According to Eberhard Bethge, that decision was made on June 20. See Eberhard Bethge, *Dietrich Bonhoeffer: A Biography*, rev. ed., ed. Victoria Barnett and trans. Eric Mosbacher, Peter Ross, Frank Clarke, and William Glen-Doepel (Minneapolis, MN: Augsburg Fortress, 2000), 653. Chronologically considered, that decision provided a framework or hermeneutical lens for Bonhoeffer as he engaged everything else he did while in America. Also of interest is an excerpt of a letter Bonhoeffer sent to Reinhold Niebuhr about this decision (cf. DBW 15:210; DBWE 15:210).

3. There is another possibility. Bonhoeffer very closely associates personal Bible reading with praying, especially of the intercessory sort, so it is possible that this is conceived in terms of a dialogue with God. If this were the case though, one would think his references to God would take on a more direct form rather than the indirect form it takes in the final sentence.

4. What follows does not imply that Bonhoeffer intentionally set out "to interpret" in a formal, programmatic sense. He did not employ steps one, two, and three in a methodologically aware way. The descriptions are simply helpful devices for explanation.

5. In accordance with Bonhoeffer, who does not comment in the context of this journal entry on the authorship of the letter he is reading, I refer to Paul as the author of 2 Timothy throughout.

coworkers and Paul's imprisonment, as well as the context of the letter as a whole, which has been about Timothy's share in Paul's suffering and lack of shame (cf. 1:8; 2:3).

After quoting the line for the second time, Bonhoeffer underscores Paul's urgency. This aspect has intensified throughout Chapter 4, so that the final of three such requests is found in 2 Tim. 4:21. Paul's request is urgent and so is the need for an immediate response from Timothy. Bonhoeffer reads here with an empathetic awareness, recognizing the complicated interpersonal dynamics at play in Paul's communicative act.

On the basis of his observations, which, again, are the result of attention to Paul's words and the letter as a whole, Bonhoeffer reads in relation to his own situation. It is not difficult to notice some of the parallels between Bonhoeffer and Timothy. Both are brought to a point of decision. Both will, assuming a Roman imprisonment for Paul, need to embark on a sea voyage. Both will endure suffering. And in both scenarios the stakes are life and death. The words "Komme noch vor dem Winter" are read as Paul's plea for urgent action on Timothy's part in order to share in suffering. Paul covered a lot of ground in the letter, but in essence he has said to Timothy, "Get here quickly." Interpreted by Bonhoeffer, the words exchanged between Paul and Timothy become a plea, direct address, from members of the Confessing Church (Paul) for Bonhoeffer (Timothy) to "Get here quickly," to urgently join them in their suffering, the life and death situation they face in Germany.

This episode serves as a particularly helpful point of focus for thinking about Bonhoeffer's biblical interpretation because, as this study will seek to show, this interpretive activity is of a piece with substantive theological convictions that were formed in the decade that preceded it. Stepping back a bit from the details, a personal element is discernable here. He reads the Bible and fully expects that what he reads will importantly shape his actions. But there is an ecclesial, corporate element as well. His reading is in reference to and in concert with other people, the Confessing Church in Germany. Bonhoeffer is also attentive to a communicative element as he reads Scripture. In very general terms, he recognizes that someone is speaking to someone else about something.[6] This allows the something said to be directed, as he says, *mir* [to me]. This points, additionally, to a past–present dynamic, since he attends to the uniqueness of the past act and only then does he place himself analogically in the position of the recipient of the speech act. This accounts for his ability to read himself as Timothy. And all of this takes place within a specific construal of the Bible.[7] He considers this act of reading to be *Vitale* [vital]

6. This way of describing discourse is indebted to various formulations of a point made by Kevin Vanhoozer. For one such formulation, see Kevin Vanhoozer, "Lost in Interpretation? Truth, Scripture and Hermeneutics," *Journal of the Evangelical Theological Society*, 48:1 (2005), 89–114.

7. I am relying on David Kelsey's discussion of construals of Scripture here. See David Kelsey, *Proving Doctrine: Uses of Scripture in Modern Theology* (Harrisburg, PA: Trinity Press International, 1999), 2.

rather than *Fromme* [pious] because his lifeline is the Bible as a witness to God's action in Jesus Christ and as communication from God through Jesus Christ to the disciple. It is this final element that unites his biblical interpretation, whether in the form of theologizing, preaching, or, as here, personal meditation.

In short, Bonhoeffer *interprets* the Bible. He pays attention to words and phrases and contexts and meanings. He uses a variety of means at his disposal to draw out meaning, to interpret it for the sake of appropriating it, even as he is addressed and appropriated by it.[8] This study is about that interpretive dynamic in Dietrich Bonhoeffer's reading of the Bible, focusing both on the hermeneutical point—what he actually does as he reads texts—and the biographical point—how he came to do so.

2. *The Argument in Conversation with Bonhoeffer Scholarship*

The argument I make in this book is, simply put, that Dietrich Bonhoeffer was an interpreter of the Bible. It is important to attend to the interpretive dynamic in his work in detail because it illumines the character of his theology as a whole. I want to demonstrate the *biblical* character of his theology in the 1930s by analyzing his explicit reflections on hermeneutics; describing his interpretive practice as he engaged in preaching, writing, reading, and lecturing; and synthesizing his main interpretive concerns.[9]

---

8. For two different renderings and evaluations of this scene in Bonhoeffer's life, see Richard Hays, *Echoes of Scripture in the Letters of Paul* (New York: Yale University Press, 1989), 178–9, 184, 226–7; Stephen Westerholm and Martin Westerholm, *Reading Sacred Scripture: Voices from the History of Biblical Interpretation* (Grand Rapids, MI: Eerdmans, 2016), 389–90.

9. This project is, then, a partial fulfillment of a research proposal outlined by Philip Ziegler, but an accidental one since I only came across the following comments after completing most of this book. Ziegler profiles how prominently Pauline apocalyptic functions in Bonhoeffer's theology during the 1930s and asks a couple of important and probing questions:

> If this biblical *Denkform* (pattern of thought) is an important aspect of Bonhoeffer's own theological constitution, then can the question of continuity and development be properly assessed without attending *in particular* to the wide array of scriptural expositions authored as sermons, letters, lectures, and so forth during these years? And if texts such as these—rather than, say, the earlier dissertations or the final *Letters and Paper from Prison*—were adjudged to represent the center of gravity in the whole corpus, how might our understanding of the whole be affected?

See Philip Ziegler, *Militant Grace: The Apocalyptic Turn and the Future of Christian Theology* (Grand Rapids, MI: Baker, 2018), 184 (emphasis original).

The basic claim of this study—that Bonhoeffer was an interpreter of the Bible—is fairly straightforward.[10] He was, after all, a *Protestant*, and a *Lutheran* Protestant, and a Lutheran Protestant *theologian* at that; of course he was a biblical theologian.[11] Scholarly entries on the theme "Bonhoeffer and the Bible" confirm the importance of this commonsense observation. The studies consist of a couple of full-length dissertations, several articles or chapters in books, and a number of sections within books and can be categorized as follows: (1) summary articles,[12]

10. The situation is similar to a recent statement made by Michael DeJonge on the relationship between Bonhoeffer and Luther in broader Bonhoeffer scholarship. He writes, "In Dietrich Bonhoeffer's writings, Martin Luther is ubiquitous. Too often, however, Bonhoeffer's Lutheranism has been set aside with much less argumentative work than is appropriate in light of his sustained engagement with Luther. As a result, Luther remains a largely untouched hermeneutic key in Bonhoeffer interpretation." See Michael DeJonge, *Bonhoeffer's Reception of Luther* (Oxford: Oxford University Press, 2017), back cover. In this section, I am making a similar claim. Bonhoeffer's interpretation of the Bible is ubiquitous, so much so that it often remains in the background, an assumption that, when critically conceived, could open up new angles of vision.

11. Agreeing at this level of generality is not very fruitful if the purpose is to *understand* Bonhoeffer. A number of questions can complicate the picture: What does the word biblical mean in this statement? Of what does Bonhoeffer's interpretation (recognizing that it is not monolithic) consist? How does he move from text to interpretive claim, specifically? What is "interpretation" for Bonhoeffer? To what is it contrasted? How did this interpretive activity change as Bonhoeffer lived through the church struggle and moved from the university to the pastorate and to training pastors in a seminary? How reflective was Bonhoeffer about what he was doing with the Bible? In other words, the obvious character of this fact needs explication; that is the task of subsequent chapters.

12. Richard Grunow, "Dietrich Bonhoeffers Schriftauslegung," in *Die Mündige Welt* 1 (Munich: Kaiser, 1955), 62–76; Walter Harrellson, "Bonhoeffer and the Bible," in *The Place of Bonhoeffer*, ed. Martin E. Marty (London: SCM Press, 1963), 115–42; Jay C. Rochelle, "Bonhoeffer and Biblical Interpretation: Reading Scripture in the Spirit," *Currents in Theology and Mission*, 22:2 (1995), 85–95; Nadine Hamilton, "Dietrich Bonhoeffer and the Necessity of Kenosis for Scriptural Hermeneutics," *Scottish Journal of Theology*, 71:4 (2018), 441–59; Stephen Westerholm and Martin Westerholm, *Reading Sacred Scripture: Voices from the History of Biblical Interpretation* (Grand Rapids, MI: Eerdmans, 2016), 389–408; Michael Mawson, "Scripture," in *The Oxford Handbook of Dietrich Bonhoeffer*, ed. Michael Mawson and Philip G. Ziegler (Oxford: Oxford University Press, 2019); Jonathan D. Numada, "Dietrich Bonhoeffer's Lutheran Existentialism in Theological Interpretation," in *Pillars in the History of Biblical Interpretation: Prevailing Methods after 1980*, vol. 2, ed. Stanley E. Porter and Sean A. Adams (Eugene, OR: Pickwick, 2016), 71–95; Sean F. Winter, "Word and World: Dietrich Bonhoeffer and Biblical Interpretation," *Pacifica*, 25 (2012), 137–50; Sean F. Winter, "Bonhoeffer and Biblical Interpretation: The Early Years," *Bonhoeffer Legacy: Australasian Journal of Bonhoeffer Studies*, 1 (2013), 1–15; Sean F. Winter, " 'Present-ing the Word': The Use and Abuse of Bonhoeffer on the Bible," *Bonhoeffer*

(2) treatments of Bonhoeffer and the Bible in the context of explicating either his theology as a whole or other theological topics informed by engaging with his theology,[13] and (3) specialized studies, focused on a piece in his corpus or a broad theme concerned with interpretation.[14] Each of these makes a helpful contribution toward understanding this aspect of Bonhoeffer's theology, focusing on his attitude toward the Bible.

So the claim is an obvious one and significant work has been done to draw attention to its importance for Bonhoeffer scholarship, but despite all this

---

Legacy: Australasian Journal of Bonhoeffer Studies, 2:2 (2014), 19–35. These pieces—though helpful—can have a tendency to abstract aspects of Bonhoeffer's relation to the Bible from the shifting contexts that were so important for how he was reading the Bible and remain very important for analyzing his interpretation.

13. In the first group, one can find: Frits de Lange, *Waiting for the Word: Dietrich Bonhoeffer on Speaking about God*, trans. Martin N. Walton (Grand Rapids, MI: Eerdmans, 2000); Ernst Feil, *The Theology of Dietrich Bonhoeffer* (Philadelphia, PA: Fortress, 1985); John D. Godsey, *The Theology of Dietrich Bonhoeffer* (London: SCM Press, 1960), 119–94; J. A. Phillips, *The Form of Christ in the World* (New York: Collins, 1967); James W. Woefel, *Bonhoeffer's Theology: Classical and Revolutionary* (Nashville, TN: Abingdon Press, 1970); Philip G. Ziegler, "Dietrich Bonhoeffer: A Theologian of the Word of God," in *Bonhoeffer, Christ and Culture*, ed. Keith L. Johnson and Timothy Larsen (Downers Grove, IL: Intervarsity Press, 2013), 17–37; Jens Zimmermann, "Reading the Book of the Church: Bonhoeffer's Christological Hermeneutics," *Modern Theology*, 28:4 (2012), 763–80.

In the second group: Brian Brock, *Singing the Ethos of God: On the Place of Christian Ethics in* Scripture (Grand Rapids, MI: Eerdmans, 2007); David F. Ford, *Self and Salvation: Being Transformed* (Cambridge: Cambridge University Press, 2009); Stephen Fowl and Gregory Jones, *Reading in Communion: Scripture and Ethics in Christian Life* (London: SPCK, 1991); Nadine Hamilton, *Dietrich Bonhoeffers Hermeneutik Der Responsivität: Ein Kapital Schriftlehre im Anschluss an 'Schopfung und Fall* (Göttingen: Vandenhoeck & Ruprecht, 2016); John Webster, "Reading the Bible: The Example of Barth and Bonhoeffer," in *Word and Church: Essays in Christian Dogmatics* (New York: T&T Clark, 2001), 87–110. These works cannot be faulted for their treatment of the theme in question; they are simply interested in something else and only comment upon the relation of Bonhoeffer to the Bible while moving to their real concern.

14. Stephen J. Plant, "Uses of the Bible in the 'Ethics' of Dietrich Bonhoeffer" Ph.D. Cambridge University, 1993; Stephen J. Plant, *Taking Stock of Bonhoeffer: Studies in Biblical Interpretation and Ethics* (Farnham: Ashgate, 2014); Brad Pribbenow, *Prayerbook of Christ: Dietrich Bonhoeffer's Christological Interpretation of the Psalms* (Lanham: Rowman and Littlefield, 2018); Martin Kuske, *The Old Testament as the Book of Christ* (Philadelphia, PA: Westminster Press, 1976); Derek Taylor, *Reading Scripture as Church: Dietrich Bonhoeffer's Hermeneutic of Discipleship* (Downers Grove, IL: IVP Academic, 2020). These books deal with Bonhoeffer's interpretation in detail. Still, the focus is more on synthesis with respect to the manner of constructing explicitly Christian ethics (Plant), a Christological interpretation of the Old Testament (Kuske, Pribbenow), and ecclesiology (Taylor).

Bonhoeffer is still not often thought of as a biblical interpreter, a descriptor that has a tendency to shift one's expectations and to open up new avenues of reflection.[15] In other words, it is one thing to consider him a theologian who engages with Scripture and another thing to think of him as a biblical interpreter. This study is intended to supplement existing scholarship on Bonhoeffer and the Bible, suggesting that Bonhoeffer was indeed a biblical interpreter by attending to the way in which he interpreted biblical texts in the 1930s.[16]

One of the distinctive contributions of this book is the way the argument proceeds. Form is determined by content: the genre most suited to attending to Bonhoeffer's "commentaries" is commentary. Showing what he does as he moves from biblical text to comment demands attention to his texts. Two important implications arise from this, both of which can help to manage expectations moving forward. First, Bonhoeffer's texts must take the lead in the exposition that follows, so his text will be encountered page after page in large quotations, and since it is his text it will be in his language, German. Second, since each chapter is hyper-focused on excerpts from Bonhoeffer's texts and my commentary on his texts, they are not focused on wide-ranging engagement with the work from which they are excerpted (though some connections are drawn in the body and the footnotes), nor are they focused on synthetic reflections (though, again, each chapter does have a short, by comparison with the body of the chapter, section of "synthesis," and the conclusion is largely devoted to the task of reflecting on implications that arise from the detailed treatment that precedes it), nor are they focused on the contributions of other scholars on these same texts (though, again, some such conversations can be found in the footnotes).[17] The chief purpose

---

15. This is an admittedly limited piece of evidence, but it is still worth pointing out that in *The Cambridge Companion to Dietrich Bonhoeffer*, ed. John W. de Gruchy (Cambridge: Cambridge University Press, 1999), there are many valuable essays devoted to a number of aspects of Bonhoeffer scholarship: history, theology, and contemporary appropriation. Not included in the section on Bonhoeffer's theology is an essay on his engagement with the biblical text; it is addressed in one or two paragraphs on other topics. In comparison to other volumes in the series devoted to theologians, those focused on Thomas Aquinas, Augustine, Martin Luther, John Calvin, Friedrich Schleiermacher, and Karl Barth all have a chapter concerned with their engagement with the Bible. As referenced in note 13 above, *The Oxford Handbook of Dietrich Bonhoeffer* does include an entry on "Scripture," indicating recent interest in the question of Bonhoeffer's relation to Scripture.

16. Of his published books, *Schöpfung und Fall* [Creation and Fall], *Nachfolge* [Discipleship], *Gemeinsames Leben* [Life Together], and *Das Gebetbuch der Bibel* [The Prayerbook of the Bible] were written in the 1930s. As is widely recognized, these works are marked by their thoroughly *biblical* character.

17. One should rightly wonder if my commentary can be rightly distinguished from "synthetic reflections," as if my summarizing act is not always already a matter of restatement, and thus a matter of my own interpretation or synthesis. It would be naïve to think it was

of each chapter is to display Bonhoeffer's texts, leaving other, albeit important, discussions to the side (or, as I have indicated, to the footnotes).

It is important for me to admit the main strength and weakness of this approach. The strength is that the details of Bonhoeffer's texts and his language are displayed, allowing for rich insights and observations about the patterns of his thought and expression, underlining nuances here and there that can be neglected by higher level treatments; that is, this approach can put us as readers of Bonhoeffer's texts in contact with a living dynamic in those texts. Sticking closely to his texts in their irreducibility, though, can also mean, and this is the weakness, that it is hard to keep hold of the central thread or argument throughout most of this book. In the hopes that it does not get lost, here is a restatement of it: I am demonstrating that Bonhoeffer should be thought of as a biblical interpreter by displaying his interpretive practice in a number of key texts throughout the 1930s.

3. Scope and Plan

The guiding presupposition of this project is that a sound interpretation of Dietrich Bonhoeffer's theology will only take shape by thinking biography and theology together. As a result, careful attention must be given to the specific contexts within which Bonhoeffer was operating. This not only highlights the fact that his social location is vital for understanding how he was interpreting the Bible (as each new location—University, Church, Seminary—changes his interaction with the Bible) but also keeps the study in touch with the historical context within which he worked, hopefully guarding against interpretive mistakes as well as hagiography.[18] Also, by connecting theology and life together a limit can helpfully be determined for actually executing the study. The sheer amount of material relating to the Bible available in the new critical edition of the Bonhoeffer works is staggering, so a limit will help to define some parameters. It has been determined that the 1930s give us the best area of focus for Bonhoeffer's biblical interpretation. This is the period when Bonhoeffer produced the most biblical interpretation, was the most stable and vocationally satisfied, and a period that is understudied in comparison to the emphasis put on *Ethik* [Ethics] and *Widerstand und Ergebung* [Letters and Papers from Prison] in the 1940s.[19]

---

not, but my hope is that since the text itself will be on display the reader will be able to judge whether the relation between my summary and Bonhoeffer's text is one of fidelity or not.

18. Theologians approaching Bonhoeffer without proper awareness of the history is a main issue for Andrew Chandler in his article, "The Quest for the Historical Bonhoeffer," *Journal of Ecclesiastical History*, 54:1, 2003: 89–96.

19. After completing the first session of seminary training at Finkenwalde, Bonhoeffer wrote, "Der Sommer 1935 ist für mich, glaube ich, die beruflich und menschlich ausgefüllteste Zeit bisher gewesen" [The summer of 1935 was, I believe, the most fulfilling period in my entire life thus far both professionally and personally] (DBW 14:97; DBWE 14:119).

Chapter 1 will serve as sort of a prelude to the interpretive practice undertaken in Chapters 2 and 3. It is important to start at the beginning of Bonhoeffer's theological trajectory because, at least in relation to the Bible, it is at the beginning that Bonhoeffer sets the stage for what is to come. As a result, Chapter 1 will provide an in-depth analysis of an early student paper from 1925. It will be argued that Bonhoeffer determines the main contours of his future interpretation of the Bible at this stage, even though he does not really begin to practice it until early in the 1930s. Here we see his dependence upon both Martin Luther and Karl Barth, speaking as he does about the Bible as the testimony to God's revelation of himself in Jesus Christ. This way of talking about the Bible and interpretation will provide a consistent and coherent point of reference throughout his life, sustaining all the various contexts within which he works in the 1930s. This initial hermeneutical statement develops a deep continuity that lives within situational discontinuity.

Chapter 2 will begin the process of actually observing Bonhoeffer perform acts of biblical interpretation. As a *Privatdozent* [unsalaried lecturer] at Berlin University, he uses the Bible to make theological claims. On the surface this is an uninteresting and commonplace observation. Upon further investigation though it will become clear that the interest lies in *how* Bonhoeffer moves from the biblical text to a theological claim. One main source will be studied from Bonhoeffer's time in Berlin, *Schöpfung und Fall*. In this work, he interprets the Bible, thus differentiating his theological approach in this period from his previous work.

Chapter 3 will continue the focus on interpretive performance, but in a very different social location. In 1933, Bonhoeffer moved from the lectern in Berlin to the pulpit in London. Here the Bible becomes the resource through which Jesus encounters his people in the sermon as the pastor interprets Scripture for his congregation. Two sermons will be examined in order to discern the shifts in interpretive practice that take shape as he is primarily concerned with pastoring a congregation. In addition, while Bonhoeffer is serving as a pastor in London, the Confessing Church is solidified at Barmen and Dahlem, producing significant implications for the ecclesial and confessional framework within which he carried out his interpretive work.

Chapter 4 will be an interlude, a moment to break from the action in order to reflect again on the theory that supports the action and is informed by it. The chapter will survey a lecture given after Bonhoeffer returned from London in order to direct one of the Confessing Church's five seminaries. The incomplete lecture, entitled "Vergegenwärtigung neutestamentlicher Texte" [Contemporizing New Testament Texts], is his most sophisticated hermeneutical statement, standing in as it does for a book he wished he could have written on the subject. We will find that there is significant continuity between his student paper from 1925, studied in Chapter 1, and this piece delivered in 1935. Again, there is also discontinuity, but it arises this time from greater sophistication, the years of experience teaching in the University and preaching in the Church, and the debates—on display throughout the lecture—with the German Christians. This interlude will allow time not only to collect a number of themes present in the first three chapters but also to prepare for the most formative and important time in Bonhoeffer's biblical interpretation.

Chapter 5 will reengage with Bonhoeffer's interpretive performance, this time at Finkenwalde. Bonhoeffer's Bible in the seminary is used for forming pastors who can preach, pray, resist, do theology, and serve. It will be argued that the years when he was training pastors, thus blending his roles as professor and pastor in the previous two social locations, were his most satisfying years and the best place to see his mature interpretive activity with the Bible. This will be seen in his published book, *Nachfolge*. The Bible is at the center of the pastor's life because it attests Jesus; making this plain for the members of the Confessing Church was Bonhoeffer's abiding preoccupation and the focus of his own personal example. Finkenwalde is the place to see Bonhoeffer as a seasoned interpreter of the Bible.

Finally, in the conclusion I will suggest that the best way to characterize Bonhoeffer's interpretation—taking into consideration the evidence assembled throughout the book, both theoretical and practical—is through a notion of dependence, a blend of activity and passivity that is established and sustained by the Spirit. In addition, some synthetic reflections on Bonhoeffer's hermeneutic will be offered in order to consider what an eclectic and expansive form of biblical interpretation can look like today.

Chapter 1

PRELUDE: FRAMING INTERPRETATION

The claim advanced in this chapter is that Dietrich Bonhoeffer's student essay of 1925, entitled "Läßt sich eine historische und pneumatische Auslegung der Schrift unterscheiden, und wie stellt sich die Dogmatik hierzu?" [Can One Distinguish between a Historical and Pneumatological Interpretation of Scripture, and How Does Dogmatics Stand to This?], anticipates the various ways he engages the Bible in the 1930s, whether for theological work, preaching, or the training of seminarians. The theological and hermeneutical framework developed in the paper from 1925 serves as a constant for Bonhoeffer's biblical interpretation. Confirmation of this claim will, in the nature of the case, have to wait until further chapters can demonstrate the relationship of specific interpretive decisions to these more fundamental theological and hermeneutical convictions; what is necessary at this stage is to unfold the character of these convictions, carefully attending to the issues as Bonhoeffer addresses them so that the relationship to what follows can be more clearly seen. This chapter will proceed, then, first by setting up the context within which Bonhoeffer's paper was written and presented (Section 1). The next sections will consider the content of the paper through an exposition (Section 2) and synthetic summary of some key relations (Section 3), and finally some of the expectations this paper creates for what Bonhoeffer's engagement with the Bible should look like within the framework he sets out will be forecasted (Section 4).

1. The Setting of Bonhoeffer's 1925 Paper

After one year at the University of Tübingen, 1923 to 1924, Bonhoeffer began his studies at Berlin University. Preeminent among his professors, both from the standpoint of the university faculty at large and from Bonhoeffer's perspective, were Adolf von Harnack, Karl Holl, and Reinhold Seeberg (his future doctoral supervisor). These three feature prominently on the course list from the summer semester of 1925, five of seven curriculum items relate to them: Bonhoeffer enrolled in Holl's "Church History I" and his Seminar in Church History, Seeberg's "Ethics" and Seminar in Systematics, and Harnack's "History of the Development of the

New Testament and the Apocryphal Gospels."[1] Seeberg's seminar in systematic theology gave Bonhoeffer his first opportunity to launch out into his chosen field: the product was the subject matter of this chapter, the paper on interpreting Scripture; the grade was simply, "Genügend" [Satisfactory], a bad mark and the worst he would receive during his time at Berlin University.

The reasons the paper did not succeed, as his previous academic attempts had and future ones would, are not difficult to discover. As a 19-year-old student he was overly confident, biting off more than he could possibly chew. The essay ranges from a critique of historical–critical scholarship to an outline of the chief problems with several centuries of Scripture reading to various elements of a doctrine of Scripture to engagement with contemporary issues of dogmatic and exegetical work. The scope is simply too much, leaving sections sparse and clipped in terms of explanation and argumentation. In addition, his confidence at times results in nearly heroic (brash?) claims. For instance, he writes the following in a footnote that seems less likely to actually state his position vis-à-vis the canon but rather as a defense of Luther: "Wir wissen, daß Luther einen sehr kühnen Schritt tut, aber wir wissen auch, daß es im Interesse evangelischen Glaubens liegt, ihn mitzutun" [We know that Luther is taking a very bold step, but we also know that it is in the interest of Protestant faith for us to take it with him].[2] At times, he is loose, downright sloppy even, in his formulations, which in certain moments provides the impetus for Seeberg's attempts to rein him in with some exasperated marks in the margins (Nein! Was heißt das? also!).[3] There is no question that the paper is, in a sense, an excellent piece of work completed and presented to the seminar by a bright and independently minded young scholar, but a young and inexperienced scholar nonetheless.

One of the other major reasons the paper did not succeed in academic terms is that Bonhoeffer demonstrated his recent acquaintance with Karl Barth. According to Bethge, in the preceding semester, winter 1924–5, Bonhoeffer started to read Barth's work.[4] Whether it was the result of his cousin Hans-Christoph von Hase sending him Barth's lecture notes from Göttingen or from the continuing effects of the 1923 Barth-Harnack debate,[5] he started to gain a sense of an alternative theological vision, articulated especially in Barth's second edition of the *Römerbrief* (1922) and *The Word of God and the Word of Man* published in 1924.[6] Bonhoeffer cites Barth a few times in the essay and is certainly influenced by Barth's thinking about dogmatics and its relationship to Scripture, but Seeberg was

---

1. DBW 9:640; DBWE 9:585.

2. DBW 9:320-321; DBWE 9:297.

3. DBW 9:308, footnote 19. See also DBW 9:319, footnotes 79 and 83.

4. Bethge, *Bonhoeffer*, 73.

5. James M. Robinson, ed., *The Beginnings of Dialectical Theology*, vol. 1, Eng. trans. K. R. Crim, L. De Granzia (Louisville, KY: John Knox Press, 1968), 163–87.

6. Karl Barth, *The Epistle to the Romans*, Eng. trans. Sir E. Hoskyns (Oxford: Oxford University Press, 1933); Karl Barth, *The Word of God and Theology*, Eng. trans. Amy Marga (New York: T&T Clark, 2011).

not impressed by his student's new fascination. On balance though, it seems that Seeberg may have missed the degree to which Bonhoeffer was able to maintain his independence in important places in the essay, demonstrating just how much his Berlin teachers had made their mark on him and anticipating some significant differences between Bonhoeffer and Barth on the Bible as well as some of the most enduring disagreements these two theologians had from 1925 through to 1945.

This is a fascinating relationship and the beginning of many dramatic ups and downs for both men, but it is possible that—at least in regard to the paper from 1925—if it receives too much attention it can distort Bonhoeffer's own emphasis. Most of the comments made on the 1925 essay focus on Barth's influence and Bonhoeffer's negotiating of Barth and Berlin.[7] There is no doubting the fact that he is trying to develop something of a *via media* between these very influential theological paradigms (though it is certainly anachronistic to describe Barth's project as a "paradigm" at this stage), but the importance of this essay can be seen not exclusively in concert or contrast with Barth but in respect of Bonhoeffer's theological development itself. The main concern here is what Bonhoeffer says in the essay and how what he says anticipates his future biblical work.

2. The Content of Bonhoeffer's 1925 Paper

The essay consists of nineteen pages in DBW, containing a brief introduction, four main parts, a conclusion, a bibliography, and a table of contents.[8] What follows is an exposition that attempts to unfold the logic and concerns of each section. This is followed by a synthesis that outlines the key relations that inform Bonhoeffer's conception of the doctrines of revelation and Scripture as well as the shape interpretation should take in their light.

2.1. Exposition

2.1.1. Introduction and Historical Interpretation After an introduction to the subject of his essay, which helpfully and economically serves to anticipate the main themes—revelation, Spirit, and the historical grounding of revelation— Bonhoeffer offers a somewhat polemical description of an approach to interpreting Scripture concerned solely with history. On his reading, the historian, lacking theological interests, still privileges the Bible because of the significant role it has played through the centuries, but at the same time constantly underscores that it is a book among others since it was written by humans who adapted and edited

---

7. Editor's Afterword to the German Edition, translated in DBWE 9:573-574; Bethge, *Bonhoeffer*, 79–80; Clifford Green and Michael DeJonge, eds., *The Bonhoeffer Reader* (Minneapolis, MN: Fortress Press, 2013), 9; Charles Marsh, *Strange Glory: A Life of Dietrich Bonhoeffer* (New York: Alfred A. Knopf, 2014), 54.

8. DBW 9:305-323; DBWE 9:285-300.

traditions in a variety of historical settings. The historian, as a subject examining a distinct object, begins the work of criticism—textual, literary, form, etc.—leading to comparisons with other religious texts and figures and the identification of preexisting, adopted forms underlying the biblical texts.

Bonhoeffer does affirm a number of aspects of this approach—the validity of leaving dogmatic commitments aside because it is possible they could lead one to misconstrue the research, the recognition that humans wrote the texts and as a result historical means are necessary to understand them, and that the Bible should receive careful attention in the light of its historically significant place in culture—but his problem with an approach that is solely historical is less about these various rationale and more about result. The less than charitable bits arise as asides rather than as a full-frontal attack on the entire historical approach. In the section on various critical methods applied to the Bible, he says:

> Nach dieser vollkommenen Zertrümmerung der Texte verläßt die Kritik den Kampfplatz, Schutt und Splitter zurücklassend, ihre Arbeit scheint erledigt.[9]

> After this utter destruction of the texts, criticism leaves the arena: rubble and fragments are left behind; its work is, it seems, finished.

And, to conclude the section:

> Aber die Historik bleibt hier stehen und hält ihre Arbeit für beendet.[10]

> However, historical work ceases at this point; it holds its work as completed.

The rhetorical force of the battle metaphor in the first quotation says quite a bit, but it can possibly obscure his actual point made in both of these sentences, which is that the result of a strictly historical approach is that it does not go far enough; it does not do anything after it has applied the various forms of criticism. According to Bonhoeffer, the problem with an approach to interpreting Scripture simply historically is the devastation that is caused and the fact that there are no resources left over to put it all back together again. This section shows his familiarity with the all-conquering discipline associated with his university but also that he has a conception of interpretation—yet to be spelled out in the essay—that assumes a purpose broader than simply demonstrating historical causes, effects, similarities, differences, precedents, and patterns. He writes, "Nun, wir werden weiter sehen" [Not content to remain there, let's move forward], both to the next section of the essay and also to his real concern for historical *and* theological interpretation.[11]

2.1.2. Pneumatological Interpretation The first short section on historical interpretation is followed by a much longer one devoted to pneumatological

---

9. DBW 9:307.
10. DBW 9:308.
11. DBW 9:308.

interpretation, of which there are two forms: one appropriate and the other, according to Bonhoeffer, inappropriate. These two types, though distinct, are united and thus rightly called pneumatological, insofar as both agree on a crucial point: the Bible is God's word. He writes:

> Die erste Aussage aller Pneumatik ist, daß die Bibel nicht nur Wort über Gott, sondern Wort Gottes selbst ist, d. h. irgendwie ist hier der entscheidende Begriff der Offenbarung einzuschalten.[12]

> The first thing to say about all pneumatic interpretation is that the Bible is not only a word about God, but is itself God's word, that is, in some form or other here the decisive concept of revelation is introduced.

Interpreting the Bible is an activity that puts one into a context in which the Spirit of God—this is *pneuma*-tological interpretation after all—is at work to make God known. In a telegraphed form, developed to a slightly greater extent in later sections of the paper, Bonhoeffer says that the past is made present: interpretation on the basis of the Spirit is concerned with the past, as is historical interpretation, but it is concerned with it for a specific, present purpose. This kind of interpretation desires to make something of the past in the present or, better, to be shown something of the important and involving relation of God's past and present. He nods here to a relationship between revelation, its relation to Scripture, and the concrete place of the interpreter. This is the key dynamic in dogmatics, preaching and church life, and getting this key dynamic out of balance leads to an inadequate type of pneumatological interpretation. That inadequate form is treated first. It is insufficient because it fails to discern the right relation between revelation and Scripture: revelation, a divine activity, is wrestled into the human sphere and put to work for various interpretive purposes.

In this section of the essay it is difficult at times to follow the structure of the argument. Bonhoeffer does have a point to make, resources to draw on in making it, and specific negative examples and some implications, but the organization has a tendency to obscure his central insight. To be fair, his paper is not meant to be a history of interpretation so one should not have high expectations of a detailed engagement with much of this material, but it remains a weakness of the paper that topics are introduced extremely briefly, leaving the reader who does not already share the perspective of the author to do quite a bit of work to get up to speed.

The scope of his indictment begins with the early centuries of the church and moves through to his own context (conveniently leaving Luther's sixteenth century as well as Barth's and his own century out of the story). The culprits, presented with no citations and little-to-no expansive explanations of their positions or the various historical contingencies that produced them, include the Catholic Church, the (non-specified) Mystics, the Anabaptists, seventeenth-century Protestant Orthodoxy, and, closer to home, Protestant liberalism. The by-product of their inadequate relation of revelation and Scripture ranges from the establishment

---

12. DBW 9:308.

of the canon, the principle of verbal inspiration, allegorical interpretation, various spirit experiences, typological interpretation, the fourfold sense and the psychological interpretation evidenced in, for instance, Wilhelm Dilthey and Friedrich Schleiermacher. It is important to note that, in a sense, the historical examples and implications do little to advance the argument he is seeking to make. His point, described below, could stand on its own, abstractly articulated in terms of revelation and Scriptural interpretation, but, positively, he recognizes the need to ground his own positive proposal, which comes in the next section, in contrast to some concrete and very influential alternatives.

The single point that unites these otherwise enormously diverse movements and approaches to interpretation is that, in Bonhoeffer's own words, they

> Alle suchen von außen einen Maßstab zur Auffindung und Auslegung des positiv Offenbarungsmäßigen in der Schrift an diese heranzutragen, weil man diesen in der Bibel selbst nicht finden konnte.[13]

> all seek in this way to bring an external standard for retrieval and interpretation of positive revelation in Scripture because one cannot find this in the Bible itself.

He makes this point repeatedly—four times in this section—and it is valuable to note each of the other three iterations of the point.

> die Offenbarung in der Schrift zu verdinglichen, festzulegen, d. h. mit menschlichen von außen hergebrachten Mitteln faßbar zu machen begannen, von den Mystikern, Wiedertäufern bis zur Orthodoxie und weiter.[14]

> Revelation in Scripture is reified, set, that is, using human means from outside they—everyone from the mystic, the Anabaptist and up until Orthodoxy and onwards—began to make it into a conventional, comprehensible instrument.

> Immer sucht man Offenbarung von außen her festzulegen, zu verdinglichen, d. h. man trennt Wahrheitsquelle und deren Bestätigung.[15]

> One seeks to establish revelation from the outside, to reify, that is, one isolates the source of truth and its confirmation.

> überall müssen wir eine Vermenschlichung, d. h. eine oberflächliche Verkürzung des Offenbarungsbegriffes konstatieren: man versucht Göttliches durch Menschliches zu begreifen, indem man es nicht streng scheidet und vergißt das alte: finitum incapax infiniti.[16]

> We find everywhere a humanization, that is, a superficial reduction of the concept of revelation: one tries to apprehend the divine through the human, and

---

13. DBW 9:309.
14. DBW 9:309.
15. DBW 9:309.
16. DBW 9:310.

thus one fails to make a strict distinction and forgets the old adage: the finite is incapable of the infinite.

Bonhoeffer's problem with this strand of relating Scripture and revelation throughout church history is that in each instance what is known on other grounds (tradition, authority, experience, a conception of truth)—all grounds which are in his view removed from God's revelation of himself as attested in Scripture—is utilized to demarcate where and in what way revelation can be found and appropriated. This amounts to two revelations, that which God gives and that which humans give to confirm God's revelation. He wonders, appealing to Calvin, if such a picture really works: is God in the business of making himself known only to wait for humans to confirm the validity of his self-communication on other grounds already possessed in the human sphere? Bonhoeffer responds with a strong negative. He thinks it should be sufficient that God speaks. If God endeavors to make himself known then he will do so effectively and on his own terms. In addition, Bonhoeffer criticizes this view because the external standard, not derived from the Bible itself, has the unfortunate effect of causing the interpreter to read that previously determined standard everywhere rather than reading what God himself says in the Bible. Avoiding the hermeneutical circle might be harder than his critique here assumes, but at least he recognizes that the necessity and sufficiency of Scripture demand that the interpreter responds to its own internal standard rather than creating or importing one from elsewhere, leading to a humanly controlled Scripture. Shifting to his positive proposal, he writes in a slightly dramatic tone:

> Der energische Gegenschlag muß vollführt werden durch Verselbständigung im Sinne der Vertiefung des Offenbarungsbegriffes im Verhältnis zur Schrift.[17]

> A decisive counter-attack is necessary: the independence of revelation must be established by deepening its relation to Scripture.

What is the *Vertiefung* [deepening] to which he refers and does he actually provide the deeper relation between Scripture and revelation that he suggests is needed? In this crucial section of the essay, Bonhoeffer seeks to steer clear of the error outlined in the previous section, an error that too closely identified Scripture and revelation and continues to produce various problems, while trying to relate them closely to one another. It is not an easy task since on the basis of outward appearance not much will look different. The substance, however, is indeed significantly different. It is this surface similarity obscuring difference that leads to the dialectical form of argument employed throughout. He gives something only to quickly redefine or qualify it.

---

17. DBW 9:310.

He starts this next section, as he did at the beginning of this part of the paper, with agreement, noting a shared element in both kinds of pneumatological interpretation:

> Nur in der Schrift ist für uns noch Offenbarung zu finden.[18]

> Revelation is for us still to be found only in Scripture.

The place or location or field of God's revelatory work is in some way found in the Bible. This is a conviction Bonhoeffer and his opponents share, and it is a statement that may also be recalling an important sixteenth-century Reformation emphasis.[19] The immediate query he addresses to this is, "Why?" Harkening back to one of his two critiques in the preceding part of the paper, he responds that reasons cannot be given if they in some way seek to domesticate God's decision and desire. It is—in the nature of the case, that is, when dealing with God—enough to affirm that God chose to reveal himself through Scripture. This is the kind of reality that cannot be explained or given grounding in some typical kind of human argument. It is, rather, the sort of thing that once it has happened, which it has, can only be talked about retrospectively.

Once he has linked revelation and Scripture in this way, the challenge is describing the link so that the two terms do not become strictly identified. This is where the dialectical work begins to take shape. Revelation is included in Scripture, but, very importantly, Scripture is not revelation without remainder. If it were, then Scripture as revelation would be humanly possessed and controllable again. Instead, God has made himself known through "einen großen Offenbarungskomplex" [a great complex of revelation], which includes much more than simply Scripture, though Scripture as a "Zeugnis gebende Urkunde" [testimony-giving document] witnesses to this broader revealing activity of God. When Scripture does its witnessing work, presumably through human engagement with it by reading (though this is not spelled out), the revealing activity of God, that is, God making himself known, is what is experienced. Scripture is the field or context set apart by God for this encounter:

> dort Offenbarung ist, wo der Mensch sie hört, wo Menschenwort Gotteswort, wo Zeit Ewigkeit wird.[20]

> Revelation is there—where the human hears it, where man's word is God's word, where time becomes eternity.

It is at this stage in the argument that he introduces the Spirit. Pneumatological interpretation gets its name from the agent of revelation, the Holy Spirit, and it

---

18. DBW 9:311.

19. Bonhoeffer may at times envisage himself following in Luther's steps, a point strengthened slightly by the way he employs Luther at key points in this paper.

20. DBW 9:311.

is the Spirit that makes the understanding of Scripture possible. Revelation, the Spirit making God known, *happens* through Scripture's witness. If one is going to understand Scripture, then one must understand that Scripture can only be understood *as the Spirit reveals* what Scripture is about since what Scripture is about is God. A human being cannot get at what Scripture is about, God, through an external, humanly derived means of interpretation. Again, if revelation—as *God's* revelation of himself—through the means that he has chosen is going to have any integrity then it is the kind of thing that human beings cannot make happen at will or once it has happened control on their own terms. Humans are dependent upon God to make himself known and to give them the proper means for appropriating that revelation. They have no in-built resources for such. He writes:

> Das ist das Problem der konsequenten pneumatischen Auslegung, das die Exegese der katholischen Kirche, der Täufer, d. h. derer, die willkürliche Maßstäbe von außen an die Schrift herantragen, gar nicht kennt. Das *Auslegungsprinzip* muß aus der schon verstandenen Schrift kommen. Spricht Gott wirklich in der Schrift, so kann nicht der Mensch hören, sondern wieder nur Gott. Geist aus dem Wort und das Wort aus dem Geist.[21]

> This is the problem of consistent pneumatological interpretation; it is that which the exegetes of the Catholic Church and the Anabaptists, that is, those who bring in arbitrary standards from outside Scripture, do not know at all. The *principle of interpretation* must come out of an already understood Scripture. If God really speaks in Scripture, then human hearing is not automatic, but rather God must make it so. Spirit accompanied by the word and the word accompanied by the Spirit.

To this point, Bonhoeffer has been talking notionally or theoretically about the concept of revelation in such a way as to retain its integrity as divine rather than human revelation. In the paragraphs that follow he particularizes this, both by making the notional challenge an actual existential problem for real human beings and by elucidating some of the implications of thinking in these terms. If revelation is as dependent upon God as he has indicated, then is there any way, any possibility that revelation can actually happen in the human sphere? His answer is affirmative because God does in fact reveal himself and he does provide the necessary equipment to appropriate it.

> Die Lösung ist, daß in unbeschreiblichen unvorherbestimmbaren Augenblicken Gott dem Menschen in diesem oder jenem Worte die Augen öffnet für die Offenbarung; d. h. das Objekt des Erkennens schafft dem Subjekt Organe für das Erkennen im Akte der Erkenntnis; d. h. das Objekt muß Subjekt werden, Gott wird heiliger Geist.[22]

---

21. DBW 9:312, emphasis original.
22. DBW 9:312.

The solution is that in indescribable, unpredictable moments God opens the eyes of humans in this or that word for revelation; that is, the object of knowledge creates for the subject organs for recognition in the act of knowing; that is, the object must become subject, God becomes the Holy Spirit.

The dynamic of the Spirit revealing through Scripture and its reception in the newly created organs—eyes for seeing and ears for hearing—given by the Spirit to the human is labeled "inspiration," because here God is comprehended or understood by means of God. The human being is caught up in a dynamic happening: Spirit, Scripture, and interpreter all belong together, and more to the point, no revelation takes place if they are not. Bonhoeffer makes the point most clearly in the following words:

> der konsequente Offenbarungsbegriff nicht substantiell, sondern funktionell gedacht ist, d. h. er ist nicht so sehr ein Sein, sondern ein Urteil, ein Wille Gottes in der Schrift.[23]

> The radical concept of revelation is not to be conceived substantially, but rather functionally, that is, it is not so much a fixed entity, but rather a judgment willed by God in Scripture.

Before he moves on to relate this brand of pneumatological interpretation to the form of historical interpretation described in part one of the paper, he touches on some positive implications of this way of thinking about revelation as attested in Scripture and guards against some possible misunderstandings. As was the case noted above, his strength does not lie in helpfully fleshing out exactly what he has in mind when employing illustrations or profiling other positions. Here he briefly comments that the kind of knowledge in play with this construct of revelation and Scripture is such that past and present are closely linked because the past action of God and the present action of God are unified in his act of revealing. In other words, revelation is not a past action that is then ensconced in a textual deposit that is accessible in the future by people, but is witnessed to then and now as God uses Scripture to so witness. This picks up again briefly on the point he made earlier in the paper about God's word in the Bible being a supratemporal reality. The one example provided to make this point is Barth's translation of "Israel" in Romans 9-11 as "church" throughout, which Bonhoeffer thinks is justified in precisely this kind of linking of past and present in dialectical or analogical ways.

With respect to possible misunderstandings, he tries to differentiate the picture he has been drawing from two other notions, what he labels "intuitiven historischen" [intuitive-historical] interpretation and a kind of interpretation based on an axiom or religious a priori. In each case respectively, what is needed for the sake of understanding is some common point already available in the interpreter, a link between the "I" who interprets and the alien "I" that is being

23. DBW 9:313.

interpreted, or some universal element available to all thinking people, as in the axioms of mathematics (e.g., 2 + 2 = 4). The problem with both of these is that the ground is sought from within the human, solely from that shared horizon. In contrast, Bonhoeffer's vision of pneumatological interpretation relies exclusively on God's ability to create what is necessary and previously unavailable inside humans for revelation to be received.

The bottom line drawn out in the conclusion of this section is that without the Spirit of God making Godself known in the act of interpreting Scripture, an adequate notion of pneumatological interpretation cannot take shape. Being initiated by God into the revelation-dynamic puts one in touch with the Spirit who enables the efficacy of all future interpretive attempts. In Calvin's words, quoted at this juncture by Bonhoeffer, "Sine spiritus illuminatione verbo nihil agitur" [Without the illumination of the Spirit the word can do nothing].[24]

2.1.3. Relationship of Historical and Pneumatological Interpretation He begins the project of relating the two types of interpretation that have been his focus by drawing out how the words on the page, words written, produced, and edited by people in specific historical circumstances and thus the primary area of concern to the historian, can relate to the field of revelation sketched in the previous section. One could easily have gotten the impression that a reader of Scripture gains access to revelation by no human agency at all. It seems that God speaks and gives ears to hear and understand, and that is the whole story. This part of the paper is meant to fill out the relation between divine and human agency in interpretive acts. To accomplish this, he sets out a phenomenology of the *Wortbegriff* [concept of word] proceeding, again, in dialectical fashion.

On his account, a word spoken using the normal human means of speech, that is, vocal chords, tongue, lips, is isolated from the infinite options of what could be said using the features of the human brain to make selections. There are lots and lots of words from which one could choose, and against that background one makes a choice in order to speak. Simply selecting a word, though, does not mean communication is taking shape yet. Using relatively complicated philosophical jargon, he makes the pretty common distinction that a word has both a semantic aspect and a pragmatic aspect. When considering its semantic aspect, one is underscoring the fact that the word is about an object or an idea, that it is readily accessible to competent language users, and as such it looks a certain way when written and sounds a certain way when spoken and signifies certain things. In that sense, it is a clearly demarcated entity when it is used in normal speech events. It has a semantic range and semantic potential. Its pragmatic aspect, though, is the word in actual usage, the way it is employed in speech contexts to actually communicate something. When used for a specific purpose, the word is open-ended because it bounces off the other words in the sentence as well as the receptivity of the hearer or reader. Bonhoeffer is suggesting a way of understanding the relationship between

24. DBW 9:314, quoting Calvin, Institutes 3.2.33.

historical and pneumatological interpretation by observing the relationship between a word standing, so to speak, by itself and that same word employed by a speaking agent. The act of speaking takes what is already there and employs it for a purpose.

Bringing things slightly closer to the idiom of the paper to this point, Bonhoeffer tries to express this in another way. He says the word chosen in a specific context by a specific speaker bears a relation to the topic upon which the speaker is speaking and can be understood by a hearer because the speaker and hearer share a common language and frame of reference. In this case, the word bears a relation to the subject matter, but that is not the same thing as saying that the word bears a relation to the Spirit, since the Spirit's activity of picking up and employing words can only be discerned if one has the Spirit's activity revealed by that same Spirit. How does this explanation draw out the relation between historical and pneumatological interpretation? They are related, not in terms of *Voraussetzung* [foundation] and *Folge* [consequence], but rather both kinds of interpretation presuppose speakers and hearers that are competent to use a shared language. For Bonhoeffer this means that although interpretation of Scripture is a revelation-oriented activity, it nevertheless takes place within the human sphere. Revelation through Scripture means real human acts of interpretation, acts that consist of the things all must do to speak and hear in human language contexts.

The link from philosophy to theology is made through the word "word," but this time by borrowing the "Word of God" from Jn 1:1 and Heb. 1:2. The same dialectical tensions on display in the previous paragraph of the paper, fragment and infinitude, closed and open, are present here, but the object of concern is Jesus Christ, or better, Jesus *and* Christ, the unified Word of God. In a bold and imaginative move, he notes that God's speech and action in the Gen. 1 creation narrative are unified: God's speaking is acting. This is the same with Jesus Christ. He is the Word of God unified in his word (Jesus) and act (Christ). In some ways, this is simply a variation of a two-natures Christology because Bonhoeffer wants to underscore that the humanity of Christ (throughout the paragraph glossed as "Jesus") and the divinity of Christ (throughout the paragraph glossed as "Christ") are unified but not simply the same thing. The Word of God consists of the historical Jesus, the *gewordene* [has been] who is no longer here but also the Christ who is always present. Jesus is the entity selected (the semantic aspect), but Christ is the communication of the Spirit (the pragmatic aspect). He writes:

> wird Christus durch Jesus erfaßt, so wird aus Vergangenem Gegenwärtiges, nicht als Einzelheit die Lehre, das Wunder, sondern durch Einzelheit als Totalität. Aus einem Worte kann der ganze Christus ergriffen werden; *so* ist jedes Wort von unendlicher Tiefe. Aber nicht Fleisch und Blut offenbaren den Menschen Christus als Sohn Gottes, sondern der Geist des Vaters durch den heiligen Geist.[25]

---

25. DBW 9:316, emphasis original.

If Christ is realized through Jesus then the past becomes present, not as a particular—the "teaching," the miracle—but rather through the particular as a totality. The entire Christ can be grasped from a single saying; *thus* every saying is infinitely deep. However, it is not flesh and blood that revealed to humans Christ as the Son of God, but rather the Spirit of the Father through the Holy Spirit.

These sentences accomplish a few important things. Negatively, they differentiate Bonhoeffer's conception of Christology from his Berlin teachers, particularly Adolf von Harnack's perspective. For, whereas von Harnack recognizes the significance of Jesus in particular aspects of his teaching, Bonhoeffer sees the whole of Jesus in his historical particularity as constituting the divine Word. And this has implications for conceiving the unity of Scripture, since, as he spells out concisely, every statement picked up by the Spirit gets to Christ, a point developed in the following paragraph of the paper. Positively, he brings home the Spirit-letter hermeneutic that has been developing, but does so by grounding it in the deep nature of Christology and a biblical text about the Spirit. Matthew 16:17 emphasizes that divine revelation by the Spirit is the source of Peter's ability to see and understand who Jesus is, and this conception of revelation and interpretation, based on this text, has been at work in this paper since the opening sentence.

In these brief, but complex paragraphs, Bonhoeffer moves from phenomenology to Christology to pneumatology and now, before proceeding to show how this all works out by tackling some specific issues regarding interpretation, he brings it all back around to Scripture. Scripture is caught up in the revelation dynamic of the Spirit because it is written in human language and in history, and, precisely as such, it is picked up by the Spirit for the purpose of revealing God:

> In diesem Sinne ist von der Pneumatik die Schrift zu verstehen und auszulegen, als von solchen geschrieben, denen es der Geist offenbart hatte, daß in dieser geschichtlichen Person Jesu, ganz menschlich, ganz im Rahmen des gewöhnlichen Geschehens aufgetreten, da grade deshalb Offenbarung zu finden war.[26]

> In this sense, on the basis of Pneumatology, Scripture is to be understood and interpreted, as written by such, to whom the Spirit has revealed it, that in this historical person, Jesus—entirely human, appearing entirely in the frame of common events—there precisely as such revelation was to be found.

The authors of Scripture, the Prophetic (i.e., Old Testament) and Apostolic (i.e., New Testament) writers, were inspired (the theological term that can stand as a shorthand for revelation about Jesus Christ by the Spirit in these texts) so that their human speech, written and heard in a shared and normal speech context, is also God speaking and creating hearing. The reason Bonhoeffer can draw such a close

---

26. DBW 9:316.

analogy between the authors of Scripture and readers of the Scripture they write is the unified action of the Spirit. Pneumatology and Christology make up the key resources for a doctrine of Scripture and its interpretation. His summary helpfully blends the preceding elements:

> Jedes dieser Worte aus dem Geist, der Verständnis der Tatsachen vermittelt, geschrieben, ist leibhaftiges Abbild der Person Jesu Christi selbst, mit der ganz geschichtlichen, unbedeutsamen unauffälligen Schale und dem andern dahinter, „was Christum treibet", wo Christus wirklich lebendig, gegenwärtig ist, wie beim Katholiken im Meßopfer, d. h. aber nicht als Substanz, sondern als Offenbarung, als Urteil und Wille.[27]

> Each of these words, having been written from the Spirit, who mediates the understanding of the facts, is an embodied image of the person of Jesus Christ himself, with the entire historical, insignificant, inconspicuous husk and behind it, the other element—"what promotes Christ"—where Christ is really alive, present … not as substance, but rather as revelation, as judgment and will.

Completely normal human words are employed by the Holy Spirit in order to make God known in Christ. This is the notion that sets one up to rightly coordinate the concerns of historical interpretation within the broader frame of pneumatological interpretation. The relation, then, that he is after is not two equal approaches but rather the historical limited and subsumed under the pneumatological, because the latter is made open to the telos of the former. So, the minute he speaks of "eine ganz korrekte Einordnung" [a proper coordination] he also speaks of qualifications and limits. The pneumatological interpreter cannot be dependent on the methodology of historical criticism not only because the results are regularly shifting in that field but also because the theological conviction of these interpreters concerns the Word who became flesh. In a similar way, the historian cannot be told what to do by the convictions and theological formulations of the pneumatological interpreter. Bonhoeffer's idea of coordination is that "sind beide Methoden nebeneinander vorhanden" [the two methods coexist side by side] in tension, in an asymmetrical way in the interpreter who seeks to interpret by the Spirit.

What does this look like in the actual concrete acts of interpretation? Both methods have the Bible in front of them so that what is on the page, human words in specific historical contexts, is the shared element:

> Für Historik und Pneumatik ist die Bibel zunächst Schrift, Text, Menschenwort. Jeder Sinnzusammenhang wird von beiden auf seine reine äußere Sachbezogenheit, d. h. buchstäblich, geprüft. Sind hier schon Schwierigkeiten, so tritt nach exaktem Handschriftenlesen Textkritik in Funktion.[28]

27. DBW 9:316-317.
28. DBW 9:317.

For historical and pneumatological interpretation the Bible is—in the first instance—writing, text, human words. For both each context of meaning will be studied for its pure, external reality, that is, literally. If there are already difficulties here, then after an accurate reading of the manuscripts the task of textual criticism comes into operation.

Bonhoeffer does not hold a naïve picture of the biblical text. He recognizes that the literal meaning is not fixed because the text has gone through a long and complicated process of transmission. This fact gives validity to textual criticism. Hebrew and Greek texts need to be compared in order to establish, to whatever degree is possible, the text that constitutes Scripture. Here already though, at an early stage in the interpretive process, the agreement is qualified with respect to the end or purpose of interpretation:

Nach Herstellung des ursprünglichen Textes geht jedes seine eigenen Wege.[29]

After establishing the original text, each [method] goes its own way.

Both approaches go on to consider the form of the established text and the material content of that established text in that specific form, but they do so in slightly different ways. It will be remembered that in the first part of the paper he left the historical critic's field covered in debris, at that stage only nodding to the fact that something must be done with that which historical criticism has destroyed. He affirms that genuine findings about various underlying traditions, or set-forms, or sources that editors utilized to construct the final form of the biblical text should be acknowledged *restlos* [completely, fully, without exception]. Having said that though, he quickly adds that the difference is that the pneumatological interpreter is enabled by the Spirit to see "die Offenbarung, auf die die Texte Anspruch erheben" [the revelation to which the texts lay claim].[30] Like textual criticism, form criticism is trying to get to what the text is, and insofar as this is the case it is useful for the pneumatological interpreter since it allows him or her to see that unified activity of the Spirit in the production and the interpretation of the text of Scripture. Getting at the origins or genesis of the text—what is behind the text—in no way hinders but can only help in being able to see through to the subject matter. There is an interesting dynamic unfolding here: he wants to say that *revelation* is what is *hidden*; revelation is hidden from ordinary eyes, but not to those who have had their eyes opened by the Spirit to see.

Patterned on the presentation of the historical approach in part one of the paper, he moves from a consideration of the form of the text to the content of the text. How can pneumatological interpretation and historical interpretation be allies if the historian's method often serves as the impetus to conclude that the

---

29. DBW 9:317-318.
30. DBW 9:318.

biblical text is one among many such texts from the ancient world and that Jesus is a parallel figure to other first-century rabbis? He writes:

> Schwieriger erscheint dem ersten Blick die Stellungnahme zu den inhaltlichen Kritiken zu sein. Wir dürfen der Historik nicht verbieten, nach den hinter der Schrift liegenden Tatsachen zu suchen, d. h. sie als Quelle zu betrachten … Fallen nun hier die Ergebnisse negativ aus, so daß selbst Jesu Person den sicheren Händen entgleitet und im Dunkel verschwindet, so scheint zunächst damit die Pneumatik gänzlich abgetan.[31]

> At first sight, the situation appears to be more difficult with respect to a critique as regards content. We may not forbid historical interpretation to search for the underlying facts behind the text, that is, to look at it as a source … If the findings turn out to be negative here, so that the person of Jesus himself slips out of reliable hands and vanishes in the dark, then it seems for the time being that pneumatological interpretation is completely to be dismissed.

His response is threefold. First, he underscores the fact that for both the historical interpreter and the pneumatological interpreter the task at hand is interpretation, which is to say that each approach is employed in order to offer *a way* of making sense of the text. If one sets out to understand what a biblical author is saying, then that person is interested in drawing out the links and questions and concerns that the text is meant to address. The end product of that endeavor is a "reading" of the material. The upshot of this is that each interpreter, offering an *interpretation* of the tradition, a way of putting the pieces together, is not able to produce a final statement about the historicity of this or that person or event encountered in the Scriptural text. Interpretation does not allow that kind of totalizing perspective for either interpreter. So, for example, the historian studying the Gospels may plausibly claim that the Jesus encountered in the Gospel of Mark bears no relation to the Jesus of history. In fact, the Jesus in the text could simply be a fiction, a textual product, created by the evangelist. Though historical criticism may claim to have the resources to make this judgment, Bonhoeffer says this is still no less than one interpretive option among others.

Second:

> Das vollständige Untergehen in der Zeitgeschichte für den rein geschichtlich eingestellten Blick ist symptomatisch für den christlichen Offenbarungsbegriff: Der Gott, der in die Geschichte einging, machte sich unkenntlich vor den Kindern dieser Welt, von der Krippe bis zum Kreuz.[32]

> Complete immersion in contemporary history for the pure, historically oriented perspective is symptomatic for the Christian concept of revelation: God, who

---

31. DBW 9:318.
32. DBW 9:318-319.

entered into history, made himself unrecognizable to the children of this world, from the manger to the cross.

The historical approach retains its importance for Bonhoeffer (i.e., it has validity and thus should not be repudiated but instead utilized) because underlying the historical approach is one side of the very concept of revelation, Christianly understood: God is present among us in actual, palpable, tangible, real history, but he is so in a hidden way. The historical actuality of Jesus' life means that various challenges can be put to the presentation of Jesus, the interpretation mentioned above, but Jesus cannot, on the basis of the terms set by historical study, be challenged as God's Son. The claim that Jesus is the Son of God lies beyond historical proof.

Finally, since a Christian concept of revelation takes the historically contingent so seriously, he offers a further way in which pneumatological interpretation is linked to history. Since God communicates through the witness of historical revelation, the Bible, then he must also have been speaking in the historical events. That is, revelation takes place in the historical events that make up Jesus' life and death, and this historically real life and death are witnessed to in the Gospel accounts, and these Gospel accounts make ongoing revelation possible as the Spirit makes God known through Scripture. In this formulation, Bonhoeffer makes it clear that history and theology are both necessary for the interpretation of Scripture.

Before moving on to his final word on the relation of historical and pneumatological interpretation, Bonhoeffer, prompted by his reflections on historicity, raises the question of miracles and the resurrection. This becomes something of a case study because what is found in the Gospel texts, for example, the various miracle stories and the resurrection, can either be questioned in order to prove that it did or did not happen or it can be questioned in order to understand what role it is playing in the text itself. For Bonhoeffer, the Bible simply presents a miracle to us, that is, what is given to us and it is not the interpreter's job to wonder about whether it happened or not. The interpreter's job, since he or she is interpreting the Bible given to them, rather than another one, is to understand what the miracle story is for. He writes:

> Unsere Frage bei der pneumatischen Auslegung ist mithin nicht: Ist das Wunder faktisch geschehen?, sondern: Was soll es in diesem Zusammenhange des Zeugnisses der Offenbarung? Das ist durchgängig, die Schrift ist nur für die Historie *Quelle*, für die Pneumatik ist sie *Zeugnis*.[33]

> Our question with pneumatological interpretation is therefore not: "Did the miracle actually happen?" but rather: "What is its function in the context of witness to revelation?" It is always the case that Scripture is only a *source* for history, but for pneumatological interpretation it is a *witness*.

33. DBW 9:320, emphasis original.

The reason this is the case—that the interpreter of Scripture can only ask how the story serves to witness revelation—is that the inspiration of the authors of the Bible applies solely to their interpretation of what they have received and not to knowledge of the historical factuality of any specific miracle. For example, an exegesis of Jn 2:1-11, where Jesus turns water into wine at the wedding at Cana, is not undertaken in order to show that Jesus certainly did turn water into wine or how it is possible for Jesus to have turned water into wine. Rather, taking the miracle seriously as it is presented by the author of the Fourth Gospel the exegete is concerned to understand how the action of turning water into wine is a parable of the theologically significant revelation of Jesus. In other words, the exegete has the task of showing how this particular miracle story fits into John's Gospel as a whole and what role it is playing in this particular context to witness to what is revealed in Jesus. Here the "historical" element of historical interpretation is seen to coordinate with pneumatological interpretive interests because the revelation witnessed to can only come through a careful, literal reading of the historically composed and situated text that the interpreter has received.

At this point Bonhoeffer has sketched an account of the sort of relation he envisages between historical and pneumatological interpretation. The most succinct statement of this relation is provided as a conclusion and is as follows:

> Also in diesen Rahmen wird die historische Kritik eingespannt. Die entstandene Spannung ist das notwendige Charakteristikum pneumatischer Auslegung, d. h. daß einmal durchaus das Ungleichzeitige, Historische, Zufällige erkannt und anerkannt werden muß, zugleich aber das Gleichzeitige als das Wesentliche immer herausgestellt wird.[34]

> Therefore, in this framework, historical criticism can be included. The tension that arises is the necessary characteristic of pneumatological interpretation, that is, that at one moment the non-contemporaneous, historical, contingent must be completely recognized and accepted; however, at the same time the contemporaneous is proven always to be the essential.

This is a tension he claims exists not only for the interpreter who acts on the basis of the Spirit but also for the writers of Scripture, because again, the same Spirit links the authoring of the books of Scripture and the interpretation of them. He finds warrant for this similarity in the prologue to the Gospel of Luke. Though he does not spell out exactly how this warrants his conclusion, it is plausible to assume that in the same way that Luke went about compiling his sources, sorting through them, and putting together an interpretation on the basis of them for the benefit of instructing Theophilus in spiritual things, so it is for the theologian who interprets the biblical text. One difference is that Luke shares the context of his sources, whereas the modern interpreter encounters alien features of the text, perhaps even alienating features that are hard to accept but still bear witness in

34. DBW 9:320.

the present.[35] In any case, on Bonhoeffer's reading, as it was for those to whom the Spirit revealed the truth about Jesus, so

> Unbedingt müssen wir uns der Fallibilität der Texte versichern und damit das Wunder erkennen, daß wir doch immer Gotteswort aus diesem Menschenwort hören.[36]

> we must unconditionally accept the fallibility of the texts and thereby recognize the miracle that we nevertheless always hear God's word out of this human word.

This is the position from which he is able to consider a number of issues that arise for the interpretation of Scripture. He touches on interpretation of the Synoptics, the relationship of "canon" and interpretive criteria, in which he revisits the discussion from part two on faulty versions of pneumatological interpretation, and finally affirms the equality of both Old and New Testaments for interpreting Scripture. In reality, he does not actually say too much about any of these, partly because he does not spend too much time on any of them (there are only a few sentences devoted to each) and probably because he does not have too much interpretive practice under his belt to say anything that would demonstrate anything more than an acquaintance with the details of actually interpreting texts; that will change in the years to come. What these concluding paragraphs of part three accomplish though is to signal his interest in thinking holistically about a central theme throughout the paper, that is, "what promotes Christ." This, following Luther, is the internal standard presented by the Bible for affirming the status of one text as Scripture over another; that which promotes Christ, which by definition is revelatory, is canonical.[37] This also brings unity to the diversity encountered in Scripture, a unity extending to Old Testament and New Testament, as well as specific disparate texts within books. Paul serves as his model of an interpreter who has a way of holding the various pieces of the traditions about Jesus together while still seeing the singular event of God sending Christ. Paul sees

---

35. To anticipate: this is precisely how Bonhoeffer treats the various issues that arise when reading Gen. 1–3. In *Schöpfung und Fall*, he seeks to take the text seriously as the witness to revelation but also wants to take seriously the scientific knowledge available to him in the 1930s. The alien worldview of the biblical writers still bears witness to God as he reveals himself there.

36. DBW 9:320.

37. Against Calvin and Barth, Bonhoeffer follows Luther here, and it is in this context where he makes the confident statement about what Protestant faith demands as noted above on page 12. His perspective on canon articulated here is not consistent with his practice of interpretation. He does not ever function as if the canon were open. For a good discussion of this issue, and one of the only in-depth studies of the 1925 paper, see Edward van 't Slot, "The Freedom of Scripture—Bonhoeffer's Changing View of Biblical Canonicity," in *God Speaks to Us: Dietrich Bonhoeffer's Biblical Hermeneutics*, ed. Ralf K. Wüstenberg and Jens Zimmermann (Peter Lang: Frankfurt am Main, 2013), 101–22.

a unified character, articulated as his decision "to know nothing among you except Jesus Christ and him crucified" (1 Cor. 2:2). This is the Christian theologian's task and thus the guiding principle for engaging in the interpretation of Scripture.

2.1.4. Dogmatics and Conclusion In the final section of the paper the reader is finally able to see where the reflections have been heading. Bonhoeffer has been seeking to provide legitimation for the task of Christian dogmatics, the existence of particular, empirical church communities, and the act of preaching. It must be said, though, that his act of legitimization is counterintuitive because it has no basis in human forms of argument or justification. In other words, it is solely given by God and received through God's Spirit. It is also here, in his concluding remarks, that the up-to-now underdetermined interpreting subject comes into view. He has been envisaging an interpreter as one who speaks for the benefit of others, which is, in the purest form, a preacher. The theologian and the preacher (or the theologian *as* preacher) both have God's revelation in history as the object of their reflections, and this entails a proper relation of that revelation to Scripture as witness. Dogmatics undertaken apart from these pneumatological interests would simply become a project in the history of religions. Dogmatics and preaching affirm that the historical elements cannot be eliminated but rather are situated by the concerns of revelation, the concerns represented by Bonhoeffer's version of pneumatological interpretation. He concludes, in reference explicitly to preaching, that

> Ihr Schicksal ist das der Auslegung, das der Schrift selbst, der Versuch, mit Menschenworten Gotteswort zu reden, der nie über den Versuch hinauskommt, wenn nicht Gott sein Ja dazu spricht. Hier sind wir beim Letzten, Tiefsten, es lag in allem Vorhergesagten verborgen: jeder pneumatische Auslegungsversuch ist Gebet, ist Bitte um den Heiligen Geist, der sich allein Gehör und Verständnis schafft nach seinem Gefallen, ohne den auch geistvollste Exegese zu nichts wird. Schriftverständnis, Auslegung, Predigt, d. h. Erkenntnis Gottes ist beschlossen in der Bitte: „Veni creator spiritus"[38]

> its goal is that of interpretation, that of Scripture itself, of an attempt to speak God's word with human words, which never gets beyond the attempt unless God speaks his "Yes" to it. Here we are at the end, the deepest point, which lies hidden in everything that has been said previously: every pneumatological interpretive attempt is a prayer, it is a request for the Holy Spirit, who alone— as he wills—creates hearing and understanding, without which even the most brilliant exegesis comes to nothing. Scriptural understanding, interpretation, preaching, that is, the knowledge of God, is incorporated in the request: "Come, Creator Spirit."

---

38. DBW 9:322.

3. Synthesis

Bonhoeffer's main point in his paper is that, when rightly conceived, revelation as attested in Scripture is central for Christian dogmatics, preaching, and the congregation. He secures this conception by underscoring three important relations: the relation of revelation and Scripture, the relation of theology and history, and the relation of the Spirit and the interpreter.

3.1. A Proper Relation of Revelation and Scripture

Revelation. Dependent to a large degree on Mt. 16:17, Bonhoeffer receives as well as constructs revelation as *God manifesting himself* by the Holy Spirit and with special reference to Jesus Christ. Revelation is not strictly concerned with epistemology, obsessed with knowledge of God and norms for securing it, but instead a happening in which God makes himself present. As such, revelation can never be an entity, but must always be construed as an encounter, an event, or happening. It is divinely initiated, orchestrated, and oriented from start to finish. On the human side, there is no capacity internal to humans that would allow revelation to be received. As a result, God must provide eyes to see and ears to hear so that revelation can happen. This miraculous provision is invisible, since it is concerned with spiritual organs for perception and reception, but that which is invisibly provided is tangibly and contingently activated through human processes of reading, thinking, and speaking. Revelation is not abstracted from the context of normal, material human life. It is a divine action with a human correlate, and as such, revelation takes shape in time and history. Revelation is a trinitarian event that happens through interpreting Scripture in the context of the church.

Scripture. The Bible—made up of Old and New Testaments, the canon of Christian Scripture—is historically situated human speech that, when interpreted, is caught up by the Holy Spirit in order to make God known. It is, in this context, God's word because the Spirit makes God *erlebbar* [experience-able] and known as one seeks the language in which to talk about God. Scripture is inspired and fallible: inspired because the Spirit revealed God to the authors of Scripture, but fallible because the authors of Scripture are historically contingent human beings who employed the normal conventions of human language and communication. These authors and their words bear witness to God's revelation, and when these words are interpreted on the basis of the Spirit that same Spirit illuminates them in order for inspiration (which is synonymous with revelation) to happen in new historical circumstances. This being the case, Scripture is necessary and sufficient to serve as a witness to revelation.

Relation. Revelation is not Scripture and Scripture is not revelation; they are not to be identified. Revelation, God manifesting himself, is the broader framework within which Scripture makes the sense that it does and plays the role that it has been given. Scripture is a witness to revelation, and its subject matter, God, is encountered when it is read according to the Spirit. Bonhoeffer is sensitive to the ways that Scripture and revelation are brought under human control, domesticated, and tamed, so he does not define the relationship of Scripture and revelation any more than is absolutely necessary. It is sufficient to keep them distinct but closely related.

3.2. A Proper Relation of Theology and History

Theology. Dogmatics is a discrete academic discipline with its own structures of thinking, forms of language, norms, and sources. Its similarity to other disciplines should never obscure the fact that there is a fundamental difference: theology is focused on the "word of God," that is, the entire complex of divine revelation in history as attested in Scripture and read on the basis of the Spirit in the context of the church's preaching. This conception of dogmatics entails a complex and sophisticated view of temporality. Time is unified by the action of God as he reveals himself in the past, present, and future, and time is the condition within which the events that make up revelation took shape and the condition for appropriating it, reading and preaching and living in the church. This way of thinking about theology also underscores the fact that God is active to judge in an ongoing way. There is, therefore, a critical function built in which it has implications for a chastened form of theological language. Dogmatics is rigorous and disciplined since it holds to a radical or intense vision of what has been revealed, but this firm conviction is constantly put in question by the object or, better, the Subject of that revelation.

History. God makes himself known to his creatures in the world in which he has placed them. What is more, God became a human who lived in that very world, a historical existence lived in time in the life and death of Jesus of Nazareth. The aftermath of his life, death, and resurrection has reverberated for centuries, producing prayer and liturgy and preaching and dogmatics. History is important because it is within history that God has revealed himself and continues to reveal himself. History matters, so the discipline of historical study matters as well. Like theology, history has its own structures of thinking, forms of language, norms, and sources. All of this potentially bears fruit, producing insight, and, perhaps most of all, in allowing the past to remain strange or foreign.

Relation. The genuinely historical element of the task of dogmatics forces the question of the relationship of theology and history, both in general terms and in disciplinary terms. In general terms, theology, as noted above, is concerned with revelation *in history*, which means theology cannot operate in abstraction and interpreters of Scripture will be concerned to immerse themselves in the literal sense and the historical setting of authors and recipients. This implies that theologians will be interested in the work of biblical scholars and will benefit greatly from what they produce, often recognizing in an intellectually honest way that the putative early traditions or redaction history or historical reconstructions offered by those scholars are helpful to fill out what revelation in history precisely means. What theology will not do is become biblical scholarship. Theology's concern with the findings of historical scholarship is to understand in what way those findings further clarify the subject matter of revelation. Theology's aims, questions, and interests set a limit for historical scholarship, receiving that which is helpful from it while resisting the temptation to believe that its totalizing claims, whether about historicity and facticity or plausible reconstructions or parallels, must be assimilated wholesale. In theological work, the relation of theology and history is one of integration, even if the relation of the disciplines of systematic theology (or dogmatics) and historical scholarship is asymmetrical, coordinated in an ad hoc manner. Bonhoeffer sometimes confuses this distinction, and in addition, his dialectical approach in the paper can give the impression that he is down on history, affirming it in one moment only to take it all back the next. On a more charitable reading, there is quite a bit more subtlety here than that.

3.3. A Proper Relation of Spirit and Interpreter

Spirit. The Holy Spirit is the agent of revelation, the Spirit that makes God in Christ known to creatures. The Spirit was at work in the life, death, and resurrection of Jesus, as the Prophets and Apostles wrote Scripture and the same Spirit is at work in the interpreters who read and preach Scripture. In the latter two instances, the work of the Spirit is to create receptacles for revelation, eyes to see and ears to hear. The "Creator Spirit" of the paper's concluding invocation is the only agent capable of creating hearing and understanding, and the Spirit does so according to his will and in response to the request to "Come." As such, the Spirit, as the Spirit who creates through revelation, inspiration, and illumination, is not possessed or controlled by individuals or the church community. The Spirit is the Lord who graciously acts to underwrite human action and employ it in his service.

Interpreter. The result of the Spirit's work in the Prophets and Apostles through various centuries is Christian Scripture, the canon of Old and New Testaments. This is a product of material culture because it took time to write, edit, compile, and produce in the diverse forms it has taken in both the past and present. Since it is a human product formed of human speech acts, interpreters must employ the normal procedures of reading and thinking in order to understand what is being said. Equally though, since these human speech acts are Scripture inspired and illuminated by the Spirit they are not transparent apart from the revelation-oriented eyes and ears that the Spirit gives. Additionally, interpretation of Scripture happens in and for the church, which means that the acts of reading and thinking about Scripture have not fulfilled their purpose until what is revealed therein is spoken for the benefit of others. Interpreters are theologians and preachers, concerned with the subject matter of revelation, God himself as he makes himself known on his own, gracious terms.

Relation. Pneumatological interpretation is perhaps more helpfully described as interpretation on the basis of the Spirit because this draws out just how essential the resources of Pneumatology are for the type of Scripture interpretation that is taking shape. It is based on the Spirit in at least two ways. Concrete, human, historical action has its source in the Spirit because to be concrete, human, historical action is to be creaturely action, that is, action that has its source in the Creator, and related to this, in a slightly more specific way, interpretation of Scripture, which attests revelation, is only accomplished by the creation of the proper organs to receive revelation, thus demarcating another more precise sphere in which the Spirit is source. The Spirit's work does not subtract from what could be attributed to human interpretive agency, but rather enables the proper functioning of human interpretive agency. This results in a posture of interpretation on the basis of the Spirit that is humble and prayerful. Interpretation, on this view, is meant to become increasingly a matter of deep recognition of dependence, reliant upon God's present activity.

4. The Trajectory from Bonhoeffer's 1925 Paper

The claim with which this chapter began is that Bonhoeffer's 1925 paper on the interpretation of Scripture is the proper starting point for a consideration of his theological hermeneutics. What takes shape in that paper provides the framework for how he engages the Bible in the major period considered in this study, the 1930s. Before moving on to the chapters that follow, chapters that analyze Bonhoeffer's key texts that engage the Bible in order to see how this framework is in fact in play, it is important to step back and take stock, both of how this paper engages the Bible—is there anything already present here that we can see as an outworking of the hermeneutical framework?—as well as what expectations this paper creates as the investigation enters the 1930s—if this is what is constructed at this stage, then what anticipatory hints can be perceived about what is to come as he engages the Bible?

4.1. What Role Does the Bible Play in This Paper?

Is there anything already present here that we can see as an outworking of the hermeneutical framework? In a paper devoted to the theme of interpreting Scripture, one might think some interpretation of biblical texts would take place. In one sense, that is clearly not the case. The purpose of the paper is to develop a relation between historical and pneumatological interpretation, and that is not undertaken simply to show that such a relation can be achieved, but to underwrite his dogmatic enterprise. But in another sense, it might be the case that he is engaging in biblical interpretation. Recalling the fourfold typology developed in the introduction, Bonhoeffer employs various biblical texts that he may or may not cite even though they are at work under the surface, playing a very important role in shaping what is said. He also offers explicit expositions of biblical passages, most often taking the form of commentary or preaching. At times biblical texts are used to authorize theological proposals. When he does this, various citations of Scripture provide warrants for claims he is making. Finally, Bonhoeffer meditates on texts in public, so to speak, resulting less in an exposition and more in an indwelling wherein imaginative connections are made and existential implications are explored. The purpose of drawing attention to these four kinds of biblical interaction is not to suggest that he is doing one or more of exactly these things or that he must have done one or more of these things to count as interpretation. The point is rather to recognize that biblical interpretation is diverse and once that diversity is recognized a lot of interesting connections can be made.

With respect to this paper from 1925, in reading Scripture Bonhoeffer finds examples of Scripture readers. Though he does not fill out either example with much by way of explanation, he finds the examples of Luke and Paul compelling. Paul, as noted above, is able to see the whole picture, constituted by its parts but still more than simply the sum of those parts, by focusing on Christ alone. 1 Corinthians 2:2 is not cited in this connection, but this text helpfully encapsulates the single-minded quality he finds in Paul, since in that context Paul commits to know nothing but Christ and him crucified. As for Luke, the prologue is cited and serves to ground both the way in which contemporary interpreters and biblical authors are related to one another and to make a statement about Scripture's fallible but miraculous character.[39] Both Paul and Luke can see through (enabled by the Spirit) to what the text in all its variety is really about, that it witnesses to the subject matter which concerns God. One learns how to interpret Scripture by paying attention to Scripture's interpreters.

One also learns how to interpret Scripture by attending to the form Scripture itself takes. One of the major conceptualities operative in Bonhoeffer's thinking is the shape of the canon, that it is comprised of both Old and New Testaments. This does surface not only in the brief paragraphs near the end of the paper where he talks explicitly about it but also in his way of talking about the Spirit's work in *both* Prophets and Apostles. This twofold construction mirrors the shape of the Bible. Following in the footsteps of Luther and Barth, he is convinced that the Old and New Testaments relate in terms of law and gospel or promise and fulfillment. The Prophets look forward to Christ and the Apostles look back to Christ, and it is this central focus, that which Paul and Luke so helpfully model, that drives to or promotes Christ. The shape of the canon of Scripture sets expectations for how one reads Scripture.

The transition from a phenomenological consideration of human language and communication to a Pneumatology and Christological grounding of historical and

---

39. Luke also serves to supply some evocative language. In a beautifully written sentence on pages 318–19, Bonhoeffer writes, "Der Gott, der in die Geschichte einging, machte sich unkenntlich vor den Kindern dieser Welt, von der Krippe bis zum Kreuz" [God, who entered into history, made himself unrecognizable to the children of this world, from the manger to the cross]. It is possible that the phrase "vor den Kindern dieser Welt" is an allusion to Lk. 16:8; this exact German phrase is found in the Luther Bible. In the parable of the shrewd manager, a contrast is drawn between the children of this world and the children of light. Interestingly, the children of the world are affirmed in this text for seeing what must necessarily be done, that is, they see what the children of light do not see. It seems Bonhoeffer borrows the language but is not intending to call to mind some of the potential associations.

theological interpretation marks a moment in which a cluster of biblical texts play a role. Bonhoeffer finds the identification of God's speech and action in Gen. 1:1 mirrored in two New Testament claims about Jesus Christ as the "Word of God," Jn 1:1 and Heb. 1:2. In the order of presentation the neutral or general consideration of the concept "word" comes first, but after these dogmatic resources are put on display one can rightly assume that the theological argument, with its terminology and conceptualities borrowed from these biblical texts, is taking the lead. These texts are not employed lightly. They are doing the heavy lifting at this stage of the argument but they are not the focus; the focus is that to which they point.

The same can be said for the use of Mt. 16:17, which also shows up in this context, veiled as it is. The verse from Matthew is crucial since it provides the theme of revelation, that God is interested in revealing himself to humans, the object of revelation, Jesus Christ as he is attested in the Gospel texts, and the subject of revelation, the Holy Spirit, who, in contrast to flesh and blood (standing in here for surface level, bare historical description), reveals Christ as Son of God. This verse, never cited and never quoted, is the argument of the paper in a nutshell. Anticipating much of what will be on display in his future biblical work, Bonhoeffer does not talk about the text in its context in Matthew's Gospel, or about authors and recipients, or about anything else that comprises the concerns of conventional biblical interpretation. Instead, understanding the shape of many of these issues, but not feeling compelled to exaggerate their importance, he points to what he thinks the text itself points to or witnesses to, that is, Christ as revealed by the Spirit to Peter and hopefully, prayerfully revealed in the moment of interpretation as Bonhoeffer himself is encountered by God in making the text known to others.

4.2. If This Framework Is What Is Constructed in 1925, Then What Expectations Arise about What Is to Come as He Engages the Bible in the 1930s?

On the basis of this paper, Bonhoeffer's interpretive practice should, if at all consistent, do a number of things. It is a mode of interpretation that is ambivalent about historical criticism, emphasizing the historical situatedness of the setting within which Scripture was written and produced as well as the setting and time of the interpreter, but not engaging much in the standard fare of biblical scholarship. This is not the case because he thinks historical criticism has an unimportant role to play, but because he thinks it is a distraction for theologians (especially theologians who are also preachers as most Lutheran theologians were) to highlight what the historical critic's research uncovers, let alone for a theologian to transform his or her discipline into historical critical scholarship. Historical criticism will be employed to help the theologian understand what the Bible is and to take it seriously as a foreign and fallible human product, but a limit is set at that point.

The limit is meant to serve the second important element of the direction in which his biblical interpretation should tend. Biblical interpretation is dogmatically and homiletically oriented. The Christian theologian needs the Bible in order to do theology at all because rather than creating from scratch theologians are responding to a prior word or summons that calls them to reflect and speak. This is why the Bible is as central as it is in Bonhoeffer's theology. Also, Old *and* New Testaments need to be the field of engagement since they stand only in relation to one another as they both witness to Christ. Finally, whatever interpretive effort follows on from this framework it will, to be consistent, need to take seriously the difficulty and hard work of interpreting texts, and the need for the Holy Spirit to illuminate Holy Scripture's subject matter, that which drives to Christ. The following chapters seek to demonstrate that the framework developed in 1925 leads to expectations much like these.

5. *Conclusion*

Dietrich Bonhoeffer is an interpreter on the basis of the Spirit, which means he carefully attends to the Bible because there is found Prophetic and Apostolic speech about God. He, as a theologian interpreting the Bible, is asking God the Holy Spirit for illumination, that the Spirit would open his eyes and ears in order to apprehend God as he is revealed here through the interpretation of these inspired texts. Since these are ancient texts that talk in historically situated ways about real, palpable historical events and people, then he as an interpreter on the basis of the Spirit must pay attention to these things insofar as they direct his attention to the subject matter, God making himself known in Jesus Christ by the Holy Spirit. The centrality of the Bible in this theological construal is the reason the Bible is on such prominent display in the 1930s.

Chapter 2

BERLIN: PRACTICING INTERPRETATION
IN THE ACADEMY

This chapter, the one that follows, and Chapter 5 are all concerned to show what Bonhoeffer's pneumatological interpretation of Scripture looks like in particular, when he moves from talking about Scripture and interpretation to actually working with and through various texts of Scripture for the benefit of others. One rightly wonders what the program described in the student essay of 1925 would look like in practice, and though the final main section of Chapter 1 began to imagine what it could look like on the basis of various hints, many questions still remained about what could be said specifically about it, beyond general statements concerned with the shape of things, and whether Bonhoeffer himself could pull off the kind of interpretive efforts he describes. In this chapter I argue that the embodiment of the 1925 vision came to fruition in 1932 in a set of lectures that eventually became the book *Schöpfung und Fall*.

To make that argument it will be necessary to say a few words about some methodological matters, namely, the relationship assumed here between theory and practice, the procedure utilized of providing close readings of texts, and the process by which the selected texts were chosen (Section 1.1). In addition, the conditions within which the lectures were produced and delivered will be described, hopefully providing a greater context for understanding what Bonhoeffer, a systematic theologian, was doing by offering a careful interpretation of the first chapters of the Old Testament's first book (Section 1.2). After situating the lectures historically and biographically, a close reading of two sections of *Schöpfung und Fall* will be offered (Section 2), followed by some big picture reflections that will serve to sum up what this analysis contributes to the evolving picture of Dietrich Bonhoeffer as a theologically interested biblical interpreter (Section 3).

1. Preliminaries

1.1. Methodological Matters

1.1.1. Theory and Practice From what can be discerned from student notes from the beginning of the lecture series and from the short introduction to the published lectures written sometime after the lectures concluded, Bonhoeffer was not interested in burdening his theological exposition of Scripture with much theoretical discussion in advance. It was necessary to say something about what it was he thought he was doing, but that something should not unduly delay the practice of actually interpreting the text. This observation signals a danger in the structure of my argument, since one could get the impression that, having read Chapter 1 immediately preceding this chapter, Bonhoeffer has a clear theory of interpretation just waiting to be worked out. It is important at this stage to point out that this both is and is not the case. It *is* the case, in the sense that as a student he had a set of instincts and impulses that were organized at what could be called a theoretical level that could only be worked out when the concrete contexts arrived within which to see how they took on a life of their own, as a professor, pastor, and seminary director. It is *not* the case, though, in the sense that the tasks of theorizing and practicing are never too precisely divided, and because biographies, as will be shown below, are much less straightforward than a clean sequence of theory to practice assumes.

This all serves as a reminder that this is a chronologically ordered argument, which means that, though attention is directed to actual concrete contexts as they were lived in through time, an element of abstraction is bound to surface here and there. The texts selected from *Schöpfung und Fall* demonstrate the practice that fulfills the theory advanced earlier, but that is not meant to flatten out the messiness that exists between theory and practice or the concrete realities of history and biography. It is meant, instead, to underscore the importance of the practice of actually interpreting texts rather than just talking about how to do so. This is where Bonhoeffer's real interest lies, concerned as he is more with what the text of Scripture is about than he is with talking about how one would begin to approach the text in order to discern what it is about.[1]

1.1.2. Close Readings and Selection of Texts The procedure taken up in what follows adheres to Bonhoeffer's concern with what the text of Scripture is about by devoting the bulk of the chapter to two close readings of his comments on specific biblical texts rather than seeking to talk of Bonhoeffer's biblical interpretation primarily through the bigger picture, thematic descriptions about the book as

---

1. Another way of making the point is to say that the "case study" chapters (2, 3, and 5) could have been presented before the "theory" chapters (1 and 4), so that, as Ben Quash has written of the structure of his book, "an extended case study will be followed by the exploration of a theoretical resource that seems to me to help make sense of the case study—not exhaustively, but usefully. The case study should give body to the theoretical material, and the theoretical material distil and clarify some key issue raised by the case study." See Ben Quash, *Found Theology: History, Imagination and the Holy Spirit* (London: T&T Clark, 2013), 55. Ordering the chapters of this book in this way would not have substantially changed the material; the decision defended in the introduction to present Bonhoeffer's biblical interpretation from the beginning, that is, from 1925 forward, demands the current shape the study has taken.

a whole. The key task is to trace the relation between the text of Scripture and Bonhoeffer's comments in particular sections of *Schöpfung und Fall*. This means, to repeat a point made in the introduction, that a lot of German text and English translation will be included in what follows, and this is necessary because part of what makes Bonhoeffer's biblical interpretation so interesting is the way in which it is done, that is, the force and style of his German as well as the structure of his thinking as it unfolds sentence by sentence. For Bonhoeffer, form and content hang together, so a detailed analysis through extensive quotation and comment on his work is fitting.[2]

A practical issue arises from this commitment: what texts from *Schöpfung und Fall* should be selected? Two sections have been chosen using the following criteria: first, it seemed important in a book devoted to both aspects of the Genesis account—creation and fall—to carefully read Bonhoeffer's comments on a section of the biblical texts concerned with both parts of his title. So, his commentary on Gen. 2:7, a "creation" text, and his commentary on Gen. 3:8-13, a "fall" text, were selected not only to respect the symmetry of the shape of the book but also to see how he treats texts concerned with the heart of his dual theme. Second, a passage needed to be long enough to trace the relation between text and comment, but short enough to be dealt with in detail.

One downside of picking only two passages from the whole book is that a lot of very interesting material will not be considered. Though this is the case, engaging two sections in close detail still necessitates the broader context of the book, since Bonhoeffer, as he lectures/writes, depends on his own analysis elsewhere in making various points. His lectures follow the text's sequence and flow, and since the text's

2. One of the chief benefits of the approach employed here, tracing the relation of biblical text to comment in detail and in particular, is that the biblical character of *Schöpfung und Fall* comes to the surface, and this helps when considering judgments made by others about Bonhoeffer's biblical interpretation. For instance, John Webster suggests that this text is significantly different from the writings of the later 1930s because the philosophical idiom from Bonhoeffer's student days remains too much in view for this to be a straightforward interpretation of Scripture. He writes, "for all its genuinely theological character, *Creation and Fall* does not simply restrict itself to repeating or applying the text. With the slightly later biblical writings, we are in a different world." Setting aside the fact that the goal of interpreting Scripture is here referred to as simply repeating or applying it, the way Bonhoeffer interprets Scripture in *Schöpfung und Fall*, as will become clear below, is to closely engage with the biblical text, allowing it, in terms of both the structure and content of his exposition, to provide the shape of each chapter of his book, which means that, albeit with variations due to context, situation, and time, it is similar to what he does in the Finkenwalde period. The idiom here is no doubt different at points, especially early in the book, but the *way* of interpreting the biblical text is consistent from the early to the later 1930s. The differences certainly do not constitute different worlds. See John Webster, "Reading the Bible: The Example of Barth and Bonhoeffer," in *Word and Church: Essays in Church Dogmatics* (Edinburgh: T&T Clark, 2001), 100-1.

own narrative, in the nature of the case, builds on what precedes it, it is important to allow the context of the whole book to bear on the interpretation of the parts that have been selected. As a result, where, in the sections under consideration in this chapter, Bonhoeffer comments on something he has helpfully developed elsewhere in the book but has not developed that same point to the same degree, the other passages will be brought in to clarify his point. In this way, the close reading of particular texts, which is the primary agenda of the chapter, will be enriched by what the book as a whole was meant to achieve.

1.2. The Context of Lectures

In the summer of 1930 Bonhoeffer qualified for a teaching position as lecturer at the University of Berlin with his second dissertation, eventually published as *Akt und Sein*.[3] Before fully committing to that task, though, he decided to spend a year as a postgraduate student at Union Seminary in New York, matriculating there from September 1930 through May 1931. On his way back to Berlin in the summer of 1931, before starting his post as a *Privatdozent*, he stopped in Bonn in order to have a face-to-face meeting with Karl Barth, who up to that point had been a theological mentor only from a distance. Around this period he also found himself more and more in ecclesial contexts, having his first foray into the world of ecumenism by attending a conference in Cambridge, England; being appointed a chaplain at the Technical College in Charlottenburg, Berlin; and receiving his ordination in November 1931, which was accompanied by the oversight of a confirmation class.

When he finally entered the lecture hall in the winter semester of 1931–2, he was determined to stake out his own position within the ever-developing theological world around him by delivering a course of lectures entitled "The History of Systematic Theology in the Twentieth Century." While lecturing through that interesting history, he also conducted a seminar on "The Concept of Philosophy in Protestant Theology." The following semester, the summer of 1932, was caught up with the question "Is There a Christian Ethic?," discussed in a seminar that ran alongside the lecture course, "The Nature of the Church." Following more ecumenical meetings in July and August of 1932, the winter semester of 1932–3 included three items: a series of lectures on "Schöpfung une Sünde" [Creation and Sin], which were eventually published as *Schöpfung und Fall* in the autumn of 1933, a lecture series on "Recent Theology," and, finally, a seminar on "Problems of a Theological Anthropology." Bonhoeffer's final months in the university before leaving Germany for a pastoral position in London, months marked by the rise of Adolf Hitler as Chancellor of Germany in early 1933, included his radio address on the Führer concept, an article "The Church and the Jewish Question," a related pamphlet entitled "The Aryan Clause and the Church," his final lecture series at Berlin University on "Christology,"

---

3. For broader biographical information on this period, see Bethge, *Bonhoeffer*, 125–255; for specific information on *Schöpfung und Fall*, see 215–17 in the same volume.

and his initial engagement with the Pastors' Emergency League, a connection that would remain very significant for the rest of his life.

The lectures "Schöpfung une Sünde. Theologische Auslegung von Genesis 1-3" [Creation and Sin. Interpreting Genesis 1-3 Theologically] started on November 8, 1932, and ran for one hour a week on Tuesdays through February 21, 1933.[4] It is difficult to discern the exact reasons why Bonhoeffer chose to lecture on the first chapters of the book of Genesis, but it is at least enough to recognize that he was engaged in seeking to discern answers to complicated questions about ethics, conscience, theological anthropology, and the so-called "orders of creation," which, as a theological, practical, political, and ethical topic, was getting a lot of attention in various ecclesial and academic settings.[5] In fact, the previous academic term was concerned with the question, "Is There a Christian Ethic?," and the answer was sought, at least in part, by some contact with the first three chapters of Genesis. In addition, the seminar running simultaneously on Theological Anthropology would have been raising similar questions. For whatever reasons, he decided to engage in the act of interpreting the Bible theologically in order to elucidate a way forward through the various complexities of the period.

The popularity of the lectures led to the participants' enthusiastic request that Bonhoeffer publish the lectures. The published version retains the feel of the oral delivery, since he decided not to undertake the work necessary to turn the lectures into an academic book like he had his previous dissertations. He left the text unadorned, so, for example, the book lacks close engagement with secondary sources and does not contain any footnotes.[6] As a result, the style of the book is related more to the sermon genre than to the academic lecture, which however independent and original, especially in the academic context of the University of Berlin, likely could not have existed without a precursor in Barth's *Römerbrief*. For the published edition, he wrote a very brief preface, indicating his dependence on the German translations of the Bible by Martin Luther and Emil Kautzsch, and a short introduction, slightly expanding the way he started the series of lectures that November.

His desire as expressed in the introduction to the published version was to present an exposition of Gen. 1-3 as Christian Scripture. Reminiscent of some of his words from the 1925 essay, he writes:

> die Kirche ... gegründet ist auf dem Zeugnis der heiligen Schrift. Die Kirche der heiligen Schrift—und es gibt keine andere „Kirche"—lebt vom Ende her.

---

4. For a helpful introduction to the material, see the editor's introduction in DBWE 3:1-17.

5. See Bethge, *Bonhoeffer*, 214-19; DBWE 3:12.

6. The footnotes that exist in DBW 3 are all editorial footnotes, many of which have been coordinated with secondary sources. The editors think Bonhoeffer may have drawn on in the production of his lectures and subsequent book. See DBWE 3:15 for a description of how the editors accomplished this.

Darum liest sie die ganze heilige Schrift als das Buch vom Ende, vom Neuen, von Christus. Was kann die heilige Schrift, auf der die Kirche Christi steht, dort wo sie von Schöpfung, vom Anfang redet, anderes sagen, als daß allein von Christus her wir wissen können, was der Anfang sei. Die Bibel ist doch eben nichts als das Buch der Kirche. Sie *ist* dies ihrem Wesen nach, oder sie ist nichts. Darum will sie ganz vom Ende her gelesen und verkündigt sein. Darum ist die Schöpfungsgeschichte in der Kirche allein von Christus her zu lesen und erst dann auf ihn hin; auf Christus hin kann man ja nur lesen, wenn man weiß, daß Christus der Anfang, das Neue, das Ende unserer ganzen Welt ist.

Theologische Auslegung nimmt die Bibel als das Buch der Kirche und legt es als solches aus. Ihre Methode ist diese ihre Voraussetzung, ist fortwährendes Zurücklaufen vom Text (der mit allen Methoden philologischer und historischer Forschung zu ermitteln ist) zu dieser Voraussetzung. Das ist die Sachlichkeit der Methode der theologischen Auslegung. Und in dieser Sachlichkeit allein ist ihr Anspruch auf Wissenschaftlichkeit begründet.[7]

The church … is founded on the witness of Holy Scripture. The church of Holy Scripture—and there is no other "church"—lives from the end. Therefore it reads the whole of Holy Scripture as the book of the end, of the new, of Christ. When Holy Scripture, upon which the church of Christ stands, speaks of creation, of the beginning, what else can it say other than that it is only from Christ that we can know what the beginning is? The Bible is after all nothing other than the book of the church. It *is* this in its very essence, or it is nothing. It therefore needs to be read and proclaimed wholly from the end. That is why the story of creation can, in the church, only be read from Christ, and only then to him; indeed one can only read about Christ when one knows that Christ is the beginning, the new, the end of our whole world.

Theological interpretation takes the Bible as the book of the church and engages it as such. Its method is this presupposition, that is, a continuous returning from the text (which is established by all the methods of philological and historical research) to this presupposition. That is the objectivity in the method of theological interpretation. And on this objectivity alone is its claim to be a disciplined approach grounded.

These words from the introduction to the published version of *Schöpfung und Fall* serve as a summary of the kind of interpretive effort Bonhoeffer envisaged in his student days. Helpfully bridging the concerns of Chapter 1 and this chapter, he is, in language borrowed but adapted from our previous analysis, an interpreter on the basis of the Spirit, carefully attending to the Bible because he seeks to find Prophetic and Apostolic speech about God there. He, as a theologian interpreting Gen. 1–3 in the lecture hall, is asking God the Holy Spirit to open his eyes and

---

7. DBW 3:22-23, emphasis original.

ears in order to apprehend God as he is revealed through the interpretation of these inspired texts. Since these are ancient texts that talk in historically situated ways about real, palpable historical events and people, then he as an interpreter on the basis of the Spirit must pay attention to these things insofar as they direct his attention to the *Sache* [subject matter], God making himself known in Jesus Christ by the Holy Spirit.[8]

2. Close Readings

Bonhoeffer interprets the text of Genesis by closely following the structure of the text, the way the words run. The task of this chapter, as stated above but helpfully reiterated before launching into this section in particular, is to trace the relation between the text of Genesis and his comments on the basis of it. In order for this close reading procedure to bear fruit it is necessary to provide Bonhoeffer's version of the Scriptural text, which often differs slightly from the text he has received from Luther and Kautzsch, his commentary on the Genesis text, and my own English translation of his German text. My comments will then seek to elucidate the links, draw out the logic, flesh out the relation between specific parts and the whole, both the part-to-whole relation of these specific pages and also in relation to the book, and to draw attention to the subtlety of what Bonhoeffer does when he interprets this biblical text within his theological and hermeneutical framework.

2.1. Creation: Gen. 2:7—Der Mensch aus Erde und Geist [The Man of Earth and Spirit]

2.1.1. Biblical Text Bonhoeffer acknowledged his debts in the preface to the published version of the lectures. He followed, as noted above, Luther and Kautzsch. Interestingly and significantly, putting secondary literature more or less to the side, two translators of the Bible served as his main sources. His dependence upon them was not absolute, however. He writes, "Der Text schließt sich so eng, wie es zulässig erschien, an Luther an; die Abweichungen sind im wesentlichen von Kautzsch übernommen" [The translation of the biblical text conforms as closely to Luther's version as the original seemed to allow; where it diverges from this, it essentially follows the version by Kautzsch].[9] Though the text of the lectures provides very little evidence of Bonhoeffer's engagement with the Hebrew text,

---

8. The language used here about real historical events and people applies only very loosely in the case of Gen. 1–3. I am retaining it here in order to underscore the close links between his interpretive practice when dealing with this part of Scripture and his thinking about interpretation more broadly as described in the previous chapter. For the precise way in which the concerns of this sentence—authors, people, and events—relate to Genesis as Scripture, see Bonhoeffer's comments in footnote 24 below.

9. DBW 3:19; DBWE 3:19.

it seems as though he had access to the Hebrew original, Luther, and Kautzsch, making it his practice to determine the best way of rendering the text for his purposes. This conclusion is confirmed by analyzing each citation of the biblical text at the heading of each chapter in *Schöpfung und Fall*, since slight variations are visible from the translations with which he was working. That is the case with the text under consideration in this section. Here is Bonhoeffer's rendering of Gen. 2:7:

> Da bildete Jahwe Gott den Menschen aus Staub vom Ackerboden und blies in seine Nase Lebensodem; so wurde der Mensch ein lebendiges Wesen.[10]

> Then Yahweh God formed man out of dust from the ground and blew in his nose the breath of life; so the man became a living being.

The text here follows Kautzsch rather than Luther. The reason for this decision is that whereas Luther translates Yahweh as *HErr* [LORD], Kautzsch sticks with *Jahwe* [Yahweh], a feature of the text that Bonhoeffer makes theologically interesting in his comments.

Before beginning an analysis of the specific relation between text and comment in Gen. 2:7, it is important to note a structural feature of each section of the commentary. It is Bonhoeffer's practice to make the biblical text central, by always starting with the text and then re-presenting it throughout his exposition. He will quote part of the text and then focus on certain aspects of that quotation, then cite another section and comment upon it, and so on. The section he cites clues the hearer/reader into what is coming, the themes one can expect to engage. In doing this he makes good on his intention, noted above, to interpret by a continual return to the text.

2.1.2. Bonhoeffer's Commentary "Man ist früh darauf aufmerksam geworden, daß hier eine zweite, von der ersten ganz verschiedene, wesentlich ältere Schöpfungsgeschichte vorliegt. Wie ist das zu beurteilen? Was bedeutet das für unsere Auslegung?" [It was long ago realized that what we have here is a second creation story that is quite different from, and substantially older than, the first. What are we to make of that? What does it mean for our exposition?].[11] This is Bonhoeffer's transition statement as his interpretation moves from Gen. 1 to 2. He highlights eight ways in which the two chapters can be contrasted, recognizing that *together* the two form a unified whole. They are talking about the same thing from two different sides.[12] With this contrast in mind, he begins his exposition of Gen. 2:7:

---

10. DBW 3:69.

11. DBW 3:67; DBWE 3:71. The final question is structurally similar to Bonhoeffer's treatment of miracles in the student essay from 1925, in which he sought to understand the significance of the miracle insofar as it witnesses to revelation. Here, the hard-won and established historical–critical consensus on the relation between Gen. 1 and 2 is taken for granted, but moves from there to a question about the theological significance of this observation, that is, how does it, precisely as this two-source reality, witness?

12. DBW 3:67-68; DBWE 3:71-73.

Mit ganz anderer Deutlichkeit und Ausschließlichkeit als bisher sind wir hier auf die Erde gewiesen. Es interessiert hier zunächst gar nicht das Kosmische, sondern unsere Erde und der Mensch.[13]

With a completely different clarity and exclusivity as previously, we are here directed to the earth. In the first instance, the concern here is not at all with the cosmos, but rather our earth and humanity.

In Gen. 1 the concern was with the cosmic dimension of creation, but here the attention has shifted to the earth and humanity. This shift in the text directs the reader *hier* (a word that pops up often in what follows, underscoring the narrative's grounding) to a concrete place, the earth, within which specific actions and relations take shape. Bonhoeffer's anthropocentric view arises because the text is anthropocentric.

His initial concern is slightly different though. He introduces the section with this emphasis on humanity and the earth, but he does not pick up that thread immediately. Instead, he focuses his attention theologically, that is, on God.

Auch Gott erhält hier seinen ganz bestimmten Eigennamen, Jahwe (über dessen Bedeutung man nicht einig ist). So heißt Gott wirklich, d. h. eben dieser Gott, von dem hier gesprochen wird. elohim in Gen. 1 ist nicht Eigen- sondern Gattungsname, bedeutet also etwa „Gottheit."[14]

God too here receives his quite specific personal name, Yahweh (about the meaning of which there is no agreement). That is really what God is called, that is, precisely this God, the one who is spoken of here. "Elohim" in Genesis 1 is not a personal name, but rather a generic name, meaning something roughly equivalent to "deity."

The contrast between Yahweh and Elohim is put to theological use in much the same way as the contrast between Gen. 1 and 2 was, which is fitting since a lot of the weight of the argument for seeing the two accounts as separate sources arises from the observation about what God is called, famously leading to the sources taking on the labels "J" (following the German "J" in Jahwist) and "P" (for Elohist). In the introduction to *Schöpfung und Fall*, written several months after the lecture series was concluded, Bonhoeffer uses this example as his way of fleshing out what theological exposition looks like, that is, the relationship between historical and theological concerns when interpreting the Bible. But, in addition to clarifying that relationship in that context, it also serves to expand on the somewhat clipped comments made here.[15] He says, "Wenn die Genesis „Jahve"

---

13. DBW 3:69.

14. DBW 3:69.

15. As such, this specific issue serves as another good example of the way in which the framework of relating history and theology developed in the student essay continues to serve as the grid for interpretive practice.

sagt, so „meint" sie historisch-psychologisch gesehen nichts als Jahve, so redet sie aber theologisch, d. h. von der Kirche her gesehen, von Gott. Denn daß Gott der Eine Gott ist in der ganzen heiligen Schrift, mit diesem Glauben steht und fällt die Kirche und die theologische Wissenschaft" [When Genesis says, "Yahweh," it means, from a historical and psychological point of view, nothing but Yahweh; theologically, i.e., from the viewpoint of the church, however, it is speaking of God. For in the whole of Holy Scripture God is the one and only God; with this belief the church and theological science stand or fall].[16] In Bonhoeffer's hands, the long history of critical debate grounded as it is in the text of Genesis as it has been received, which he simultaneously acknowledges and relativizes with his comment that no agreement about the meaning of the word Yahweh exists, leads to a positive theological point about divine particularity: Yahweh is God's name. This conclusion leads to a potential objection.

> Man könnte meinen, der Eigenname sei der Beweis für einen sehr primitiven Gottesgedanken und zeige, daß wir hier gerade kein Recht hätten, von dem Gott zu reden, von dessen Gewalt das 1. Kap. gesprochen hat.[17]

> One could hold that the personal name is evidence for a very primitive idea of God and show that we—precisely here—have no right to speak of the same God whose power has been discussed in chapter 1.

This is one of Bonhoeffer's signature moves when interpreting. He provides a commonsense sort of option about how something could be understood so that he can refute it and offer his own alternative. In this instance of this technique, he provides a typically modern variation, hypothetically presenting the personal name as at odds with the generic one, and on that basis disconnecting Yahweh from the creation of the cosmos, limiting the sphere of his activity to that covered in Chapter 2. He opposes this:

> Und doch ist gerade hier zu erwidern: Anthropomorphismus im Gottesgedanken, offenkundige Mythologie ist keine unsachgemäßere, unangemessenere Ausdrucksweise für das Wesen Gottes als die abstrakte Verwendung des Gattungsnamens „Gottheit". Vielmehr ist gerade in deutlichem Anthropomorphismus die Tatsache viel stärker zum Ausdruck | gebracht, daß wir „Gott an sich" eben so oder so nicht denken können,—der abstrakte Gottesbegriff ist im Grunde viel anthropomorpher, eben weil er es nicht sein will, als der kindliche Anthropomorphismus—daß wir einen Eigennamen Gottes brauchen, damit wir Gott recht denken können.[18]

> And yet it is necessary here to reply: anthropomorphism in thinking of God or even overt mythology is no more inappropriate or unreasonable as an

---

16. DBW 3:22-23; DBWE 3:23.
17. DBW 3:69.
18. DBW 3:69-70.

expression for the being of God than the abstract uses of the generic term "deity." Rather, it is precisely in a clear anthropomorphism that the fact is more strongly expressed that we cannot think of "God in himself" whether in one way or the other—the abstract concept of God is essentially more anthropomorphic than childlike anthropomorphism, precisely because it wishes not to be—that we need a personal name for God so that we can think of God rightly.

Two things are at play in his response. He wants to level the playing field by pointing out that both forms of theological language—generic and personal—are just that, forms of theological language. Determining to speak of God as "deity," an abstract concept of God, does not get any further toward describing God as he really is, even if it wants to, because precisely in desiring such, it evidences the fact that it just is human speech, anthropomorphism. The so-called "objective" position of the observer is called into question. The second, positive point is that to think of God rightly is to think of a specific, particular, nameable reality, God as he has made himself known. Bonhoeffer is here opposing a widespread tendency to think in universal terms about God rather than particular terms, and this is underwritten by a doctrine of revelation in which God communicates with us. It is this deep structure in his reflections on God as named Yahweh in Gen. 2, or what could fittingly be described as the text's *Sache* [subject matter], that leads to the following affirmation:

> Ja, der Eigenname ist Gott selbst. Wir haben Gott nicht anders als in seinem Namen, auch heute: Jesus Christus, das ist der Name Gottes, höchst anthropomorph und höchst sachlich zugleich.[19]

> Indeed, the personal name is God himself. We have God in no other way than in his name, even today: Jesus Christ, that is the name of God, highly anthropomorphic and highly objective at the same time.

His phrase *auch heute* [even today] introduces a contrast between, on the one hand, the Old Testament attribution of the personal name Yahweh to God, as in this text and perhaps also Exod. 3 with the note about the name being God himself, which presses this emphasis upon Bonhoeffer, and on the other hand, the place of the interpreter and his audience/readers "today." He is not, then, reading Jesus Christ into Gen. 2, thus obliterating the particularity of that text or its integrity. He is rather recognizing a similarity. When talking about God biblically, one is talking about divinity, not in general, but in particular. In this way, and in keeping with his desire to read Gen. 1-3 from Christ, Jesus is faintly foreshadowed in Gen. 2 rather than forced into it.[20]

19. DBW 3:70.

20. Bonhoeffer's comments in the introduction could be unhelpfully translated into being about "Christ in the Old Testament," rather than being precisely an introduction to an exposition in which the sort of subtlety of what is here being described is undertaken. One

Bonhoeffer transitions from an emphasis on "Yahweh God," the focus of his commentary thus far, to a consideration of the event of formation. As before, he restates the biblical text and then begins his exposition.

> Gott bildete den Menschen aus Staub vom Ackerboden und blies in seine Nase Lebensodem. Auch hier wieder geht alles sehr irdisch vor; die Redeweise ist überaus kindlich und für den Menschen, der wirklich etwas einsehen, „wissen" will, sehr anstößig.[21]

> God formed man out of dust from the ground and blew into his nose the breath of life. Once again, everything proceeds in a very earthy way; the style throughout is childlike and, for the person who really wants to understand something, "to know," it is very offensive.

He picks up the theme of anthropomorphism again, being led there by the interests of the text (*geht alles* [everything proceeds]), but he does so in order to draw out a potential effect it can produce in a modern, scientifically minded person, that is, a person who wants a specific kind of knowledge about origins. For this type of person the childlike anthropomorphism can serve as an insult. Here, as is often the case with Bonhoeffer's writing in the academic period, he does not feel the need to spell out what would constitute the exact nature of the offense. He is rather cryptic, but it is likely the fact that a person who wants, as he says to *wissen* [know] something, would like to bypass all this business about gods and gardens, preferring instead to engage in a more exact kind of description of origins. Genesis 1–2 is not going to provide a scientific kind of knowledge, so Bonhoeffer can imagine someone, again placing an objection in the mouth of a hypothetical opponent, protesting with the following:

> Wie kann man von Gott so reden, wie man von einem Menschen redet, der sein Gefäß aus Erde und Ton bildet? Die Anthropomorphismen werden immer unerträglicher, Gott, der Former, der Bildner des Tons und der Mensch gebildet wie ein Gefäß, aus einem Erdenkloß. Hieraus kann doch kein Wissen über den Ursprung des Menschen gewonnen werden![22]

> How can one speak of God in the same way as one speaks of a man who forms his vessel out of earth and clay? The anthropomorphisms become more and more unbearable: God, the molder, the one who creates out of clay and the man formed as a vessel out of a lump of earth. One cannot possibly gain knowledge about the origin of humanity from all this!

of the chief strengths of offering a close reading is that the detailed examples can interpret the more abstractly described "methodological" comments.

21. DBW 3:70.
22. DBW 3:70.

The final line reveals the nature of the insult. It would be offensive to the modern, scientifically confident person to say that one *can* gain knowledge about the origins of humanity from these chapters in Genesis, but this is exactly what Bonhoeffer thinks is the case. In short, the origin of humanity is creation by God. His response, culminating in this point, comes in a threefold manner, each point corresponding to a sentence in the final three sentences of the paragraph:

Gewiß, diese Geschichte ist als Erzählung zunächst ebenso belanglos und ebenso bedeutungsvoll wie manche andere Schöpfungsmythen.[23]

Without any doubt, this story, as a story in the first instance, is just as unimportant and just as meaningful as many other Creation-myths.

His first response is very strongly stated, making life really hard for himself. He admits that the text of Genesis has no precedence over other texts similar in kind. This recalls the concession he made to the historical approach to biblical interpretation profiled in the first main section of his 1925 essay. The Bible's two-part story of creation is not special over against those other creation stories, and it is not special in providing unique scientific knowledge accessible in a nonscientific idiom.[24] He grants the point, but then goes on to his second response.

Und doch ist sie nun in ihrer Qualifikation als Wort Gottes *die Quelle* des Wissens über den Ursprung des Menschen schlechthin.[25]

And yet—in its character as the word of God—it is *the source* of knowledge about the origin of humanity as such.

23. DBW 3:70.
24. The dynamic at play in these three sentences is present throughout the lectures. For example, see DBW 3:47-48; DBWE 3:50-51 where on the firmament, Bonhoeffer writes,

Here the ancient image of the world confronts us in all its scientific naïveté. To us today its ideas appear altogether absurd. In view of the rapid changes in our own knowledge of nature, a derisive attitude that is too sure of itself is not exactly advisable here; nevertheless in this passage the biblical author is exposed as one whose knowledge is bound by all the limitations of the author's own time. Heaven and the sea were in any event not formed in the way the author says, and there is no way we could escape having a very bad conscience if we let ourselves be tied to assertions of that kind. The theory of verbal inspiration will not do. The writer of the first chapter of Genesis sees things here in a very human way. This state of affairs makes it seem then that there is very little to say about this passage. Yet on this next day of creation something completely new takes place.

For a similar point, see also DBW 3:45; DBWE 3:49.
25. DBW 3:70, emphasis original.

In keeping with his major point developed in 1925 and using very similar language in this context, Bonhoeffer's second response is to affirm the text of Genesis as a witness to revelation about human origins. It is *the source* for the one who wants to know about humanity. It is the source precisely and irreducibly as an anthropomorphic narrative about a potter and his work.

> Und nun wird sich auch zeigen, daß das hier Gesagte genau zu dem vorher Gesagten gehört, mit ihm eine Einheit bildet.[26]

> And now it will also be apparent that what is said here belongs precisely with what was said previously, a unity is formed with it.

The third response is an invitation to see how this works out by treating the text in this way. It is as if Bonhoeffer is saying, "Since this is the kind of text that it is—the kind that speaks of God in both a Genesis 1 and 2 idiom—then interpreting it accordingly, with anthropomorphisms and all, will make the difference." Everything he has said up to now has been to clear the way, so that he could draw attention to the central point of Gen. 2:7. He does so in the next paragraph of his exposition, returning again, before his own comments, to a slightly expanded restatement of the text.

> Damit daß Jahwe den Menschen mit eigenen Händen bildet, ist das Doppelte gesagt: einmal die leibliche Nähe des Schöpfers zum Geschöpf, daß es wirklich Er ist, der mich—den Menschen—macht mit eigenen Händen; seine Sorge, sein Denken an mich, seine Absicht mit mir, seine Nähe zu mir—und andererseits eben doch seine Vollmacht, seine schlechthinnige Überlegenheit, in der er mich bildet und schafft, in der ich sein Geschöpf bin; seine Väterlichkeit, in | der er mich schafft und in der ich ihn verehre,—das ist Gott selbst, von dem die ganze Bibel zeugt.[27]

> To say that Yahweh forms man with his own hands is to communicate a two-fold message: on the one hand, the physical closeness of the creator to the creature, that it really is he who makes me—as a human being—with his own hands; his concern, his thinking of me, his intention with me, his closeness to me; and, on the other hand, even yet his power, his absolute superiority in that he forms and creates me, where I am his creature; his fatherliness, in which he creates me and in which I worship him—that is God himself, of whom the entire Bible bears witness.

The two creation accounts, Gen. 1 and 2, come together in the summary, "Jahwe den Menschen mit eigenen Händen bildet" [Yahweh forms man with his own hands], which is a slight expansion of what the text itself says even while sticking with the text. Bonhoeffer takes the anthropomorphism seriously, seeing here an

26. DBW 3:70.
27. DBW 3:70.

implication of the relationship between the potter (God) who forms the clay (the man). In order to form him, God must use his hands. From this physical closeness it is not hard to see the quick connection to metaphors of "concern," "thinking of me," "his intention with me," and "his fatherliness." The text's narrative has, as he says in the first line of his commentary, "directed" the reader to the earth, the place where this sort of intimacy takes shape. And yet, the other side of the two-fold message (which is still one long attempt at making theological sense of the fact of two creation accounts) is that Yahweh is the one who does the creating or forming. Translated into first-person speech, an interesting rhetorical move on Bonhoeffer's part, "I am his creature ... I worship him." This is the central dynamic of the creation story, God and humanity, creator and creature. This witness (again in language directly related to the essay from 1925) is what the Bible is for. Though he has a lot more ground to cover before he has completed his interpretation of Gen. 2:7, this paragraph is the high point because it distills what he thinks the subject matter of Gen. 1–2 is. Everything that follows flows from this way of framing the relation between God and humanity.

Stressing the links to Gen. 1 again, with its emphasis on the *imago dei*, he moves back to the Genesis text that launched the previous two paragraphs, moving from the act of formation by God's hands ("God *formed*," Gen. 2:7) to the material God used in order to form the man ("God formed man *out of dust from the ground*," Gen. 2:7).

> Der Mensch, den Gott nach seinem Ebenbilde, d. h. in Freiheit geschaffen hat, ist der Mensch, der aus Erde genommen ist. Stärker konnte selbst Darwin und Feuerbach nicht reden, als hier geredet ist. Aus einem Stück Erde stammt der Mensch. Seine Verbundenheit mit der Erde gehört zu seinem Wesen. Die „Erde ist seine Mutter", aus ihrem Schoß kommt er.[28]

> The man, the one whom God has created after his image, that is, in freedom, is the man who is taken out of the earth. Even Darwin and Feuerbach could not speak more strongly than what is said here. Out of a piece of earth the man comes. His relationship to the earth belongs to his being. The "earth is his mother;" he comes out of her womb.

It is an interesting decision to draw Darwin and Feuerbach in at this point, especially because he does nothing to help the reader understand what precise aspect of either one's work is in view. Perhaps the well-educated Berlin University student sitting in the lecture hall caught the drift, which presumably, in light of the stronger point Bonhoeffer paraphrases the Bible to be making, was that both Darwin and Feuerbach were concerned with the relationship of human beings to the earth, Darwin's view of the origins of the species and Feuerbach's emphasis on bodiliness drawing this out. The precise nature of the connection is less important than the fact that Bonhoeffer here nods to an affinity, an affinity in which the Bible

---

28. DBW 3:71.

takes the leading role, pushing the modern scientist and philosopher to a more radical form of their own recognition.

These sentences also introduce us to a feature that will characterize the rest of this section of his commentary, namely, a staccato piling up of short phrases that serve as a way of repeating a point and, in some cases, adding something to it. Here, the three short sentences, which constitute the intensification of Darwin and Feuerbach, simply repeat the point the biblical text is making, that is, until the final sentence, which introduces the metaphor of mother earth.[29] Here the metaphor continues to evoke the tenderness of the creation account, a point he will pick up further below.

> Aber freilich, noch ist der Ackerboden, von dem der Mensch genommen ist, nicht der verfluchte, sondern der gesegnete Acker. Es ist die Erde Gottes, aus der der Mensch genommen ist.[30]

> But, of course, even the ground from which the man was taken is not the cursed ground, but rather the blessed ground. It is God's earth out of which man is taken.

Nothing Bonhoeffer has said in the previous sentences really serves as the impetus for the contrast he now draws. The text has not indicated a need to clarify the state of the ground from which the man was taken, but Bonhoeffer introduces a contrast between the cursed and blessed ground, anticipating Gen. 3. It seems likely that this contrast is introduced to foreshadow the future of the ground in the narrative, a future that has implications for Bonhoeffer and his hearers/readers, as well as to prepare the way for the positive perspective on the body that he pursues in the rest of the paragraph. He wants to underscore that the ground is the blessed ground precisely because it is God's ground, his creation. If it is good, then that which is derived from it is also good (cf. Gen. 1:31).

He moves quickly from the emphasis of the text, man out of the dust of the ground, to what he thinks it means. It is interpreted to be all about "body," the word he emphasized in what follows:

> Aus ihr hat er seinen *Leib.* Sein Leib gehört zu seinem Wesen. Sein Leib ist nicht sein Kerker, seine Hülle, sein Äußeres, sondern sein Leib ist er selbst. Der Mensch „hat" nicht einen Leib und „hat" nicht eine Seele, sondern er „ist" Leib und Seele. Der Mensch am Anfang ist wirklich sein Leib, er ist einer. So wie Christus sein Leib ganz ist, wie die Kirche der Leib Christi ist. Der Mensch, der sich seines Leibes entledigt, entledigt sich seiner Existenz vor Gott, dem Schöpfer. Der Ernst des menschlichen Daseins ist seine Gebundenheit an die

---

29. See DBW 3:71, footnote 8; DBWE 3:76, in which the editors note that Bonhoeffer may be dependent here on Sir. 40:1b. Elsewhere, as in the case of Eph. 5:14, Bonhoeffer cites biblical texts to which he is explicitly referring. I think the case is good for an allusion to Sirach here, but I will limit my comments to texts he cites in the body of the lecture.

30. DBW 3:71.

mütterliche Erde, sein Sein als Leib. Er hat sein Dasein als Dasein auf Erden, nicht von oben her kommend ist er von einem grausamen Schicksal in die irdische Welt verschlagen und geknechtet, sondern aus der Erde, in der er schlummerte, tot war, ist er herausgerufen vom Worte Gottes, des Allmächtigen, selbst ein Stück Erde, aber von Gott zum Menschsein berufene Erde. „Wach auf, der du schläfst, stehe auf von den Toten, so wird dich Christus erleuchten" (Eph. 5, 14).[31]

Out of it he has his *body*. His body belongs to his being. His body is not his prison, his shell, his appearance, but rather he himself is his body. Man does not "have" a body and does not "have" a soul, but rather he "is" body and soul. Man in the beginning really is his body; he is one. In the same way that Christ is wholly his body and the church is the body of Christ. The person who denies his body denies themselves of their existence before God, the one who creates. The profound reality of human existence is its connection to the maternal earth, its being as body. He has his existence as existence on earth; he is not coming from above—of a cruel fate, cast out into the earthly world and enslaved; rather he is coming out of the earth, that in which he slept and was dead; he is called out by the Word of God, the Almighty. He is a piece of earth, but a piece of earth called by God into human existence. "Wake up, you who sleep, rise from the dead, and Christ will shine on you." (Eph. 5:14)

Bonhoeffer does quite a lot in this string of sentences, but it is important to take it all in one whole. The first two short sentences communicate the meaning of man coming out of the dust of the ground. He has a material body and that body is who he is.

This positive point is contrasted twice from different angles with the notion that the human being is imprisoned in the body, that there is something more fundamental to the person that is trapped. Both times that he draws out the contrast between the biblical view and the one he opposes to it, he grounds his point theologically, drawing resources from Christology, ecclesiology, and the doctrines of God and creation. This is subtle in that he does not draw a lot of attention to how this works. The double analogy of Christ and his body and the church and the body of Christ underscores a notion of unity but also the strange notion, developed in the sentence that follows, that one could distance oneself from the body, a notion that does not work for the human or for the member of Christ's body, the church.

In the second instance, he writes that the man "is coming out of the earth, that in which he slept and was dead; he is called out by the Word of God, the Almighty. He is a piece of earth, but a piece of earth called by God into human existence. 'Wake up, you who sleep, rise from the dead, and Christ will shine on you' (Eph. 5:14)." It is hard to tell which came first, the way of describing the scene from Genesis of the man's coming out of the ground as sleeping, as dead and then

---

31. DBW 3:71-72, emphasis original.

called, or the language and sequence from Eph. 5.[32] The point is these two sets of descriptions speak about the same thing when put next to one another. It is as if Yahweh in Gen. 2:7 said the words from Ephesians as he formed/called/created the man out of the earthly material. The persistent emphasis is on the creation, the *Sache* of Gen. 1–2.

> So hat es auch Michelangelo gemeint. Der am jungen Erdboden ruhende Adam ist so fest und innig mit dem Boden, auf dem er liegt, verbunden, daß er selbst in seinem noch träumenden Dasein ein höchst seltsames, höchst wunderbares— aber eben doch ein Stück Erde ist, ja gerade in diesem völligen Hingeschmiegt- | sein an den gesegneten Boden der Schöpfungserde wird die ganze Herrlichkeit des ersten Menschen sichtbar. Und in diesem Ruhen an der Erde, in diesem tiefen Schöpfungsschlaf erfährt nun der Mensch durch die leibliche Berührung mit dem Finger Gottes Leben—es ist dieselbe Hand, die den Menschen gemacht hat, die ihn nun wie aus der Ferne zart berührt und zum Leben erweckt. Nicht hält die Hand Gottes den Menschen mehr in sich gefaßt, sondern sie hat ihn freigegeben und ihre schöpferische Kraft wird zur verlangenden Liebe des Schöpfers zum Geschöpf. Die Hand Gottes auf diesem Bilde der Sixtina enthüllt mehr Wissen über die Schöpfung als manche tiefe Spekulation.[33]

> Michelangelo too thought in this way. Adam who rests on the young earth is so firmly and intimately joined with the ground on which he lies that he himself, in his still dreaming existence, is a very strange, very wonderful entity but yet still just a piece of earth; indeed, precisely in this state, totally nurtured on the holy ground of the created earth, the whole glory of the first man becomes visible. And in this rest on the ground, in this deep creaturely sleep, the man now experiences life through physical touch by the finger of God; the same hand, that which has made the man, delicately touches him now—as if from afar—and awakens him to life. The hand of God no longer holds the man in his grasp; rather, the hand of God has freed him and the creative power of God's hand becomes the longing love of the creator toward the creature. The hand of God in this picture in the Sistine Chapel discloses more knowledge about the creation than any amount of speculation.

The introduction of Michelangelo's painting on the ceiling of the Sistine Chapel, a painting that, among many other things, captivated the young Bonhoeffer on his trip to Rome several years earlier, serves to draw together some threads in an aesthetically, imaginatively pleasing way, but it is also not simply an illustration of the points he has made.[34] It is also doing some work for him, a point hinted at

32. The issue is an eisegesis–exegesis question, and it will show up often in this study (cf. Bonhoeffer's discussion of "conscience" below).
33. DBW 3:72-73.
34. Charles Marsh writes, "Enraptured again by the ceiling of the Sistine Chapel, he was still unable, he said, 'to move beyond Adam.' For in that immemorial icon, 'man is about to

in the concluding sentence of the quotation above. It works both to introduce the main point of the second half of Gen. 2:7, the next section of the text that he will deal with, emphasizing the fact that the man comes to life, but it also works to flesh out the character of that creaturely life. Bonhoeffer says that God's hand, his delicate touch by his finger, frees the man, making him a partner in a relationship between creator and creature.[35] The man is no robot. But there is more: Bonhoeffer sees love in the painting, and the sight of it, God's longing look and reach toward his creature, is now just there in the text of Gen. 2:7. He makes theological points from the text with Michelangelo's help.

This meditation leads directly back to the text itself:

Und Gott blies in seine Nase Lebensodem; so wurde der Mensch ein lebendiges Wesen. Leib und Leben treten hier ganz ineinander. Gott haucht dem Leib des Menschen seinen Geist ein. Und dieser Geist ist Leben, macht den Menschen lebendig.[36]

And God blew into his nose the breath of life; so the man became a living being. Body and life come entirely together here. God breathed his spirit into the body of the man. And this spirit is life, making the man alive.

Three terse statements result from Bonhoeffer's reflection on the last sentence of Gen. 2:7. Two themes, body/being and life, are present in the verse, and their coming together is the result of God breathing his spirit into the body. The man is only alive because life is spirit and spirit is life. You cannot have one without the other since these two things talk about only one thing. This interplay of spirit, life, and body, having been derived from the text, is the focus of the next large section of his exposition, progressing, again, by contrasts.

Anderes Leben schafft Gott durch sein Wort, beim Menschen gibt er von seinem Leben, von seinem Geist. Der Mensch als Mensch lebt eben nicht ohne den Geist Gottes. *Als Mensch* leben heißt als Leib im Geist leben. Die Flucht aus dem Leib ist ebenso Flucht aus dem Menschsein, wie die Flucht aus dem Geist. Leib ist die Existenzform von Geist, wie Geist die Existenzform von Leib ist. Dies alles ist nur vom Menschen gesagt, denn nur beim Menschen wissen wir um Leib und Geist. Der menschliche Leib ist von allen nicht menschlichen Körpern dadurch unterschieden, daß er die Existenzform des Geistes Gottes auf Erden ist, wie er von allem anderen Leben doch dadurch ganz ununterschieden ist, daß er wie dieses Erde ist. Der menschliche Leib lebt wirklich nur durch Gottes Geist, das

awaken to life for the first time.' ... The painting was so very lush and pure, he said. 'In short, one can't express it.'" See Marsh, *Strange Glory*, 39.

35. It is worth pointing out that though Bonhoeffer says that God's hand "delicately touches him now," the hands of God and Adam do not touch in the painting. Rather, the painting depicts the fraction of a second before the touch.

36. DBW 3:73.

eben ist sein Wesen. Gott verherrlicht sich im Leib und zwar im Leib in diesem spezifischen Sein des menschlichen Leibes.[37]

God created other life through his word, but with man he gave of his life, of his spirit. Man as man does not live at all without the spirit of God. To live *as man* means to live as a body in the spirit. Flight from the body is as much flight from human existence as is flight from the spirit. Body is the form of existence of spirit, as spirit is the form of existence of body. All this is only said of man because only with man do we know about body and spirit. The human body is distinguished therefore from all other non-human bodies in that he is the form of existence of the spirit of God on earth, even as he is entirely indistinguishable from all life in that he is of this earth. The human body really lives only through the spirit of God, that which just is his being. God glorifies himself in the body and above all in the body of this specific entity that is the human body.

Continuing to relate Gen. 1 and 2 theologically, he draws attention to the fact that in Gen. 1 God created by speaking, which is a step removed, so to speak, from what God does with the man. Having equated life and spirit, as noted above, the implication is that if God gives his spirit then God gives his very life. As a result, man cannot live at all except as a body in the spirit. The various forms of repetition circle back, by the middle of the paragraph, to the contrast with which he began, making the point that the human being, creaturely just as much as any other creature, material in form, is unique in that the human is the form of existence of the spirit of God on earth. The conclusion of this train of thought, again, following the text cited at the beginning of the paragraph, is found in the final sentence: "God glorifies himself in the body and above all in the body of this specific entity that is the human body." God is glorified in the creaturely, material reality he has made, the body or material form of created realities in general, but above all in the human body since it is the form of existence of the spirit of God on earth.

This statement about the glory of the creator and the freedom of the creature as it relates to body, life, and spirit prompts the following conclusion to his commentary on the text of Gen. 2:7:

Darum geht Gott dort, wo der ursprüngliche Leib in seinem geschaffenen Sein zerstört ist, abermals in den Leib ein, in Je- | sus Christus und dann dort, wo auch dieser Leib zerrissen ist, in die Gestalten des Sakraments des Leibes und Blutes. Leib und Blut des Abendmahles sind die neuen Schöpfungswirklichkeiten der Verheißung für den gefallenen Adam. Weil Adam geschaffen ist als Leib, darum wird er auch erlöst als Leib, [kommt Gott zu ihm als Leib] in Jesus Christus und im Sakrament.[38]

---

37. DBW 3:73, emphasis original.
38. DBW 3:73.

Therefore, God goes there, where the original body in its created being is ruined, once again in the body, in Jesus Christ, and then there, where also this body is torn in the forms of the sacraments of body and blood. The body and blood of the Lord's Supper are the new created realities promised to the fallen Adam. Because Adam is created as body, he must also be redeemed as body; God comes to him as body in Jesus Christ and in the sacraments.

The intimate relation of the creator and the bodily existence of the creature prepare for a properly Christological point. The incarnation is what you would expect from reading Gen. 2. This link is warranted and made explicit in the concluding sentence: "Because Adam is created as body, he must also be redeemed as body; God comes to him as body in Jesus Christ and in the sacraments."[39] This is, to restate a point made earlier, the kind of reading from Christ that Bonhoeffer describes in the introduction of the book. Rooted as he is in the classical, Christian tradition, he cannot help, as a Christian theologian, to make these kinds of connections, connections that arise out of a close reading of the text of Genesis.

Dieser so geschaffene Mensch ist der Mensch als Ebenbild Gottes. Ebenbild nicht trotz, sondern gerade in seiner Leiblichkeit. Denn in seiner Leiblichkeit ist er bezogen auf die Erde und auf anderen Leib, ist er für andere, ist er angewiesen auf andere. In seiner Leiblichkeit findet er den Bruder und die Erde. Als solches Geschöpf ist der Mensch aus Erde und Geist seinem Schöpfer Gott „ähnlich."[40]

Man created in this way is man as the image of God. Image, not despite, but rather precisely in this bodiliness. For in his bodiliness he is related to the earth and to the other body; he is for others, he is dependent on others. In his bodiliness, he finds the brother and the earth. As such a creature, the man is of earth and spirit, resembling his creator, God.

In the final paragraph of the chapter, Bonhoeffer draws some of the themes (*imago dei* from Gen. 1, body, man's relation to the earth) together in something of a conclusion, but he also introduces another implication of bodily, human existence. The integral and interdependent relation of all creatures (assuming that the "other body" is referring to the discussion about the distinction between types of "body," human and nonhuman), but also to human sociality specifically, is crucial for existence as a human body in the material world. In one sense, this is a new theme, one that anticipates what is to come as Adam names the animals and meets Eve. But, in another sense, this has been present in the implicit ecclesiology Bonhoeffer is operating with as he reads. In any case, the relation is grounded in the relation between creator and creature, a relation that, as Bonhoeffer has

39. These points become central to Bonhoeffer's "Christology" lectures. See DBW 12:279-348; DBWE 12:299-360, where this Christology is worked out in relation to the sacrament of the Lord's Supper (300–5; 318–23).

40. DBW 3:74.

anticipated here and there throughout, is tragically altered by the other aspect of Bonhoeffer's dual-theme and two-part title, the Fall.

2.2. Fall: Gen. 3:8-13—Die Flucht [The Flight]

2.2.1. Biblical Text In this second passage from *Schöpfung und Fall*, Bonhoeffer again slightly alters the text he has received. His German text and my translation follow:

> Und sie hörten die Tritte Jahwes Gottes, der im Garten ging, da der Tag kühl geworden war. Und Adam versteckte sich mit seinem Weibe vor dem Angesicht Jahwes Gottes unter die Bäume im Garten. Und Jahwe Gott rief Adam und sprach zu ihm: Wo bist du? Und er sprach, ich hörte Deine Tritte im Garten und fürchtete mich; denn ich bin nackt, darum versteckte ich mich. Und er sprach: Wer hat dirs gesagt, daß du nackt bist? Hast du nicht gegessen von dem Baum, davon ich dir gebot, du solltest nicht davon essen? Da sprach Adam: Das Weib, das Du mir zugesellt hast, gab mir von dem Baum, und ich aß. Da sprach Jahwe Gott zum Weibe: Warum hast du das getan? Das Weib sprach: Die Schlange betrog mich also, daß ich aß.[41]

> And they heard the steps of Yahweh God, who was walking in the garden, as the day had become cool. And Adam hid himself with his woman from the face of Yahweh God under the trees in the garden. And Yahweh God called Adam and said to him: "Where are you?" And he said, "I heard your steps in the garden and I was afraid; because I am naked, that is why I hid myself." And God said, "Who told you that you are naked? You have not eaten from the tree from which I commanded you—You shall not eat from it—have you?" Then Adam spoke: "The woman whom you made my companion gave to me from the tree, and I ate." Then Yahweh God said to the woman: "Why did you do that?" The woman said: "The serpent deceived me; that is why I ate."

Following Luther's version rather than the translation of Kautzsch this time, he changes Luther's "hörten die Stimme Gottes des HErrn" [heard the voice of God the LORD] in Gen. 3:8 to "hörten die Tritte Jahwes Gottes" [heard the steps of Yahweh God], consistently rendering "Jahwes" as "Yahweh" rather than "LORD," but also changing "die Stimme" [the voice] to "die Tritte" [the steps] (the change here forcing the same rendering in v. 10). It is possible that this is the result of consulting but eventually rejecting Kautzsch, because he has "Gehen" [walking] in both instances, but it is not clear. In any case, Bonhoeffer goes his own direction on this translation, and, as noted above, this is often the case because it serves his theological purposes. In this text, concerned as it is with flight and fleeing, he wants to draw out the movements, the movement of God toward Adam and the movement of Adam away from God. His exposition is concerned with overstepping

---

41. DBW 3:119.

limits, of running, and of being in no position to stand before God. Bonhoeffer's choice highlights the dramatic character of these various steps.

2.2.2. Bonhoeffer's Commentary "Adam kann nicht mehr vor seinem Schöpfer stehen" [Adam can no longer stand before his creator].[42] With this statement, coming in the first sentence of his commentary on Gen. 3:8-13, the narrative has moved forward significantly. In the passage on Gen. 2:7, Adam was in a state of glory, lovingly made by the hands of the creator for creaturely life by the divine spirit, made for worship and full of freedom and integrity. This is no longer the case.

Bonhoeffer begins his commentary by reintroducing a number of major themes present in earlier chapters in *Schöpfung und Fall*, major themes that will also be developed throughout the pages of the chapter dealing with Gen. 3:8-13, and these lead him, in the final sentence of the quoted material below, to his paraphrase of v. 8, the first verse in this chunk of biblical text under consideration here and so, the first bit of the text to receive his attention.

Der um tob und ra wissende, der aus der Einheit in die Entzweiung gestürzte Adam kann nicht mehr vor seinem Schöpfer stehen. Er hat die Grenze überschritten, und er haßt nun seine Grenze, ja er leugnet sie ab, er ist sicut deus—grenzenlos. Aber wie er in der Scham die Grenze des anderen widerwillig anerkennen muß, so gibt er Gott, seinem Schöpfer widerwillig darin recht, daß er vor ihm flieht, daß er sich vor ihm verbirgt. Er tritt ihm nicht frech gegenüber, sondern als er seine Stimme hört, verbirgt er sich vor ihm.[43]

As one who knows *ṭôb* and *rā'*, as one who has fallen out of unity into dividedness, Adam can no longer stand before his creator. He has over-stepped the boundary, and he now hates his limit, indeed, he denies it; he is "like God," limitless. However, as he, in shame, must unwillingly acknowledge the limit of the other, so he must unwillingly admit to God his creator that he flees from him, that he hides himself from him. He does not approach him boldly, rather when he hears his voice, he hides himself from him.

Picking up the language from Gen. 2:17 about the tree of the knowledge of good and evil, Bonhoeffer retains the transliteration of the Hebrew terms in order to keep his text linked to the biblical text.[44] He also explains what "one who knows *ṭôb* and *rā'*" means by offering a paraphrase, glossed as "one who has fallen out of unity into dividedness," a description that picks up much of his earlier exposition. It is this state of being divided within himself that causes Adam to no longer be able to stand before God. Again, in language developed earlier in the book, he has overstepped the boundary, understood by Bonhoeffer to be the actual boundary

---

42. DBW 3:119.

43. DBW 3:119.

44. See DBW 3:79; DBWE 3:85 for Bonhoeffer's exposition of the tree of the knowledge of good and evil in Gen. 2:17.

around the tree of the knowledge of good and evil, which, when extrapolated becomes that which represents Adam's limit, the reminder of his status as creature rather than creator.

These two sentences summarize a lot, but the summary is provided in order to move the exposition forward. The third sentence is the pivot point: it collects the preceding two sentences by saying, "he must unwillingly acknowledge the limit of the other," which is both God and Eve (or any other), but then moves into the subject of this chapter saying, "he must admit to God that he flees from him." The crucial imaginative link is made at the end of this third sentence. In order to flesh out what the text talks about, Adam hiding, Bonhoeffer speaks of "fleeing." Actually, he presents it the other way around. He uses the language of "fleeing" and then expands on it by noting the text's language of "hiding." All of this is brought together in his paraphrase of v. 8 in the final sentence. Bonhoeffer suggests that Adam should have approached God boldly, but instead, "when he hears his voice, he hides himself from him." This point, picked up from v. 8 and talked about in terms of flight, is the subject matter Bonhoeffer has set his targets on in his exposition.

He continues:

> Merkwürdige Täuschung des Adam damals und heute, zu meinen, sich vor Gott verbergen zu können, als ob die Welt dort, wo sie uns verhüllt, verborgen, undurchsichtig erscheint, nachdem wir mit ihr zerfallen sind, auch für Gott undurchsichtig wäre! Der Mensch, der in jähem Sturz von Gott abgefallen ist, ist nun selbst noch auf der Flucht. Ihm ist der Sturz nicht genug, er kann nicht schnell genug fliehen. Diese Flucht, dieses sich vor Gott Verbergen des Adams nennen wir das Gewissen.[45]

> What a strange delusion of Adam's, then and today, to think one could hide oneself from God, as if the world—precisely where it covers us, is hidden, appears opaque—after we have fallen out with it, would also be opaque for God. The man, who has fallen away from God in a sudden fall, is even now still on the run. The fall is not enough for him; he cannot escape fast enough. This flight—Adam's hiding himself from God—we call "conscience."

Bonhoeffer gives a lot of attention to this notion of "hiding-as-flight," to very interesting effect. In this instance, hiding can perhaps work as a strategy for Adam because the fall has made the world, his material environment, opaque. The creation was previously unified, holistically communicating the goodness of God through visible signs, but now, for Adam, as one estranged from God and the world he finds himself in, the trees in the garden become something behind which one could hide, something that God might even be prohibited from seeing through. Bonhoeffer recognizes that falling out with the creator is also falling out with the world, a point textually grounded in the exposition of Gen. 2:7, concerned

---

45. DBW 3:119-120.

as it is with the bodily link between Adam and the earth, but also Adam and other nonhuman bodies.

He also conflates himself, along with his hearers/readers, with Adam, recognizing that "then and today" humans are attempting the same sort of delusional strategy, trying to hide from God by imagining that his creation, the world and humans in it, is not transparent to his gaze. There is a subtle relationship between hiding and flight that develops throughout this paragraph. Hiding, the word used in the first sentence, is described in the third and fourth sentences as being "still on the run" and trying to escape quickly from God. In the final sentence, he develops the three links explicitly. He moves from his preferred, imaginative paraphrase of what is happening, "flight," to the text's idiom, "Adam's hiding himself from God," and finally, into the introduction of a term that will dominate what follows, *Gewissen* [conscience]. He thinks bringing in this word at this point helps to draw out the significance of the narrative's depiction.

He begins his account of *Gewissen* by saying:

> Vor dem Fall gab es kein Gewissen. Erst durch die Entzweiung mit dem Schöpfer ist der Mensch in sich selbst entzweit.[46]

> Before the fall there was no conscience. Only through dividedness with the creator is man divided within himself.

The narrative has a chronology, that is, there is a before the fall and an after the fall, and one indicator of which side is which is whether wholeness or dividedness is in view. In Gen. 2, wholeness was in view; in Gen. 3, dividedness, the starting point of Bonhoeffer's exposition of these verses, is in view. There is a corresponding inner division in Adam that matches the outer division between him and God. It is this dividedness that results in hiding, in flight, in the development of conscience. The two-fold structure of division provides the outline for Bonhoeffer's comments. He proceeds to talk of two functions of conscience, that is, conscience serves as a single word that describes the two aspects of the narrative's recounting of events.

> Und zwar ist dies die Funktion des Gewissens, den Menschen in die Flucht vor Gott zu jagen, um damit im Grund wider Willen Gott recht zu geben, und doch andererseits auf dieser Flucht den Menschen sich gesichert fühlen zu lassen im Versteck, d. h. den Menschen darüber zu täuschen, daß er sich wirklich auf der Flucht befindet, ihn vielmehr glauben zu lassen, diese Flucht sei sein Siegeszug, und alle Welt befände sich vor ihm auf der Flucht.[47]

> And to be sure, this is the function of conscience: to drive man to flight from God in order to—at bottom, against one's will—prove God right, and yet on the other side, its function is to let man, in this flight, feel himself secure in hiding, that is it serves to deceive man so that he feels himself really to be in flight, it lets

---

46. DBW 3:120.
47. DBW 3:120.

him believe that this flight is actually a triumphal procession and all the world feels itself to be in flight before it.

According to Bonhoeffer, *Gewissen*, a notion that is being developed through the narrative's depiction of the events rather than a fully formed notion imported from elsewhere, serves two functions. First, it drives man to flight from God, and second, it convinces man that this flight is a good decision. In addition to spelling out this two-part, divided function of conscience, he also points out that each function has a side effect. First, in driving man to flight from God, conscience points out that God was in the right and man was in the wrong. That is, the act of fleeing (which is the same thing as the functioning of conscience) means one *needs* to flee; the side effect of this function of conscience is that in hiding one acknowledges precisely what one does not want to acknowledge. The second side effect is that when conscience convinces man that his flight was a good decision, it deceives him into thinking this was a good and effective strategy, building up his pride and further confirming his distance from the creator.

The rather brief descriptions offered of these functions are expanded slightly in the next few sentences in reverse order, beginning with the second function of conscience:

> Das Gewissen treibt den Menschen von Gott weg, in das gesicherte Versteck. Hier in der Gottesferne spielt er dann selbst den Richter und weicht eben hierdurch dem Gericht Gottes aus. Der Mensch lebt nun wirklich aus seinem eigenen Guten und Bösen, aus seiner innersten Entzweiung mit sich selbst.[48]

> Conscience drives man away from God into a safe hiding place. Here, being far from God, he then himself plays the judge and thereby evades the judgment of God. Man really lives now out of his own good and evil, out of his inner dividedness from himself.

This expansion contributes something really significant to Bonhoeffer's analysis of these first chapters of Genesis. Rather than simply noting that the fall is the result of Adam and Eve transgressing God's command concerning the tree of the knowledge of good and evil and leaving it at that, Bonhoeffer seeks to draw out what the actual, concrete consequence is of the act of doing so. In other words, in describing the Fall it is not simply the fact that they disobeyed God that he is interested in. Instead, he is interested in how having done so they are affected. It is as if he is asking: "What is the content of the knowledge of good and evil, such that Adam and Eve are actually changed by what they did?" His answer is that the knowledge of good and evil is the inner dividedness that has its correlate in dividedness with God. In short, the content is *Gewissen*, that complicated notion that captures the dynamic of the events of Gen. 3:8.

---

48. DBW 3:120.

Bonhoeffer also devotes some space to an expansion of the other function and side effect of conscience, though in this case the only new element is the introduction of *Scham* [shame] into his account. He writes:

> Das Gewissen ist die Scham vor Gott, in der zugleich die eigene Bosheit verborgen wird, in | der der Mensch sich selbst rechtfertigt und in der doch andererseits zugleich der Hinweis auf den anderen wider Willen enthalten ist.[49]

> Conscience is shame before God, in which at the same time one's own wickedness is hidden, in which man justifies himself and in which yet, on the other side, at the same time the recognition of the other is comprised against one's will.

After spelling out the way conscience functions according to this narrative, Bonhoeffer concludes his commentary on Gen. 3:8 with these words:

> Das Gewissen ist nicht die Stimme Gottes im sündigen Menschen, sondern gerade die Abwehr gegen diese Stimme, die aber eben als Abwehr doch wiederum wider Wissen und Wollen auf die Stimme hinweist.[50]

> Conscience is not the voice of God in sinful man, but rather it is precisely the defense against that voice, which however even as a defense, yet again—against knowledge and will—points to that voice.

He moves out of the text's idiom to develop a more abstract notion of conscience. He does so by contrasting that which he has developed in conversation with the text of Genesis from a popular notion of conscience as the voice of God within sinful man. This, on the basis of his exposition, simply cannot be what conscience is. It must be, instead, a more complicated picture. It is the inner resistance against God's voice but even as it resists God's voice it points to it. This brief summary captures both functions of conscience as Bonhoeffer has tracked them in the narrative of Gen. 3. And, as a concluding remark on Gen. 3:8, it has the added benefit of serving as a great introduction to the content of Gen. 3:9.

The previous paragraph of Bonhoeffer's interpretation finished with a narrative-developed notion of *Gewissen*, a term that served to collect both aspects of being driven to hide and consoling oneself when hidden about the soundness of the strategy. This analysis left Adam exactly where the text of Genesis left Adam, hiding from God among the trees in the garden. The next scene in the narrative is the dialogue between God, Adam, and Eve. Rather than quote the entirety of Gen. 3:9, Bonhoeffer introduces the text by personalizing it with the inclusion of Adam's name, a feature not included in the biblical text, and by very directly cutting to the chase, that is, to the interest of the narrative, to God's question and the implications of it.

49. DBW 3:120.
50. DBW 3:120.

Adam, wo bist du? … mit diesem Wort des Schöpfers wird der flüchtende Adam aus seinem Gewissen herausgerufen, er muß vor seinem Schöpfer stehen. Der Mensch darf in seiner Sünde nicht allein bleiben, Gott redet zu ihm, er hält ihn auf der Flucht auf.[51]

"Adam, where are you?" … with this word of the creator, the fleeing Adam is called out of his conscience: he must stand before his creator. The man is not permitted to remain alone in his sin; God speaks to him, stopping him in his flight.

These comments are, very simply, exegetical. Bonhoeffer is drawing out or opening up what is implied in God's question to Adam. The mode of expression is more distinctly homiletical than is the kind of exegesis characteristic of academic contexts, but the goal is the same. God's speech makes Adam present. This is the dynamic Bonhoeffer wants to draw attention to in what he unfolds. In this instance, he adopts the voice of God and the inner voice of Adam, imaginatively developing a dialogue that brings to the surface the narrative's major point. He presents it in four stages. First, God speaks:

Heraus aus deinem Versteck, aus deinen Selbstvorwürfen, aus deiner Verhüllung, aus deiner Heimlichkeit, aus deiner Selbstquälerei, aus deiner eitlen Reue, bekenne dich zu dir selbst, verliere dich nicht in frommer Verzweiflung, sei du selbst, Adam, wo bist du? Steh vor deinem Schöpfer.[52]

Come out of your hiding place, out of your self-reproaches, out of your concealment, out of your secrecy, out of your self-torment, out of your vain remorse, and confess yourself to yourself; do not lose yourself in pious despair, be yourself; "Adam, where are you?" Stand before your creator.

God's question is here translated into a command: Come out and stand before your creator. In order to do so, Adam must face exactly what he conceals in his hiding, that is, his self-reproach, self-torment, and vain remorse, all of which are forms of pious despair, according to Bonhoeffer. This is the case because Adam, depending as he does on his internal dividedness and his knowledge of good and evil, that is, his *Gewissen*, seeks to justify himself, consoling himself in his position as a righteous sufferer. God's question is an invitation to honesty.

The next stage is Adam's internal response, or better, the response of conscience, which, with a subtle shift in agency, is now running the show:

Dieser Anruf geht stracks gegen das Gewissen, das Gewissen sagt: Adam, du bist nackt, verbirg dich vor dem Schöpfer, du darfst nicht vor ihm stehen.[53]

51. DBW 3:120.
52. DBW 3:120.
53. DBW 3:120-121.

This challenge goes directly against conscience. Conscience says, "Adam, you are naked, hide yourself from the creator; you must not stand before him."

Conscience convinces Adam to double down. Bonhoeffer borrows content from v. 10, importing it here to draw out the sequence that makes a narrative a narrative. Adam must first think of his response to God's question before he actually responds, and that thinking is now based in his position as one who knows good and evil. Adam is convinced, one of the functions of conscience, to refrain from coming out into honesty before God.

The penultimate stage of this imagined dialogue is a repetition of the implication of God's question, since asking, "Where are you?" is, according to Bonhoeffer, simply the act of calling him to present himself. There is no difference between the two. God's question persists beyond Adam's internal defense.

Gott sagt: Adam, steh vor mir.[54]

God says, "Adam, stand before me."

The final word is given to God, his question lingers, and as such, it leads to Bonhoeffer's brief and penetrating conclusion:

Gott tötet das Gewissen.[55]

God kills conscience.

This is a very important comment. Conscience, as developed in this chapter, is equivalent to the knowledge of good and evil, and represents Adam's dividedness in its two-fold function. For God to speak to Adam, to invite him to come out into honesty and confession is to cut through Adam's divided state, to speak to him as one knowing good and evil. God killing conscience is, as Bonhoeffer will develop it in a moment, an act of grace.

To this point the hearers/readers of Bonhoeffer's exposition have only heard the inner voice of Adam's conscience, but since God has now called Adam, an act that brought him to life in the previous chapter, the voice of conscience has been killed. Adam himself must actually stand before God and speak. Bonhoeffer moves into the dialogue in the text of Gen. 3:10-11, but he does so in a very interesting way:

Der fliehende Adam muß erkennen, daß er vor seinem Schöpfer nicht fliehen kann. Der Traum, den wir alle kennen, daß wir vor etwas Entsetzlichem fliehen wollen und doch nicht fliehen können, ist die dem Unterbewußtsein immer wieder entsteigende Erkenntnis dieser wahren Lage des abgefallenen Menschen. Derselbe Sachverhalt ist nun in der Antwort des Adam ausgedrückt: ich bin nackt, darum versteckte ich mich. Er versucht sich mit etwas zu entschuldigen,

54. DBW 3:121.
55. DBW 3:121.

das ihn anklagt, er versucht weiter zu fliehen und weiß sich doch schon ergriffen. Ich bin sündig, ich kann nicht vor dir stehen; als ob man sich mit der Sünde entschuldigen könnte, unbegreifliche Torheit des Menschen.[56]

The fleeing Adam must recognize that he cannot escape from his creator. The dream, which we all know—that we want to flee from something awful and yet we cannot flee—is the knowledge, repeatedly arising out of the subconscious, that this is the true position of fallen man. That very position is now expressed in the answer of Adam: "I am naked, so I hid myself." He seeks to excuse himself with something that indicts him; he seeks to flee again and yet he knows himself to be already held. Adam is saying, "I am sinful, so I cannot stand before you," as if one could excuse oneself with sin (the incomprehensible stupidity of humanity!).

In order to make sense of the logic here, it will help to work in the opposite order of the presentation. Adam's response to God's question, "I am naked, so I hid myself," is interpreted by Bonhoeffer as an excuse, wherein Adam claims to be hiding because of his nakedness, something he would not know about if he did not yet know about good and evil. As Bonhoeffer goes on to explain in the fifth sentence of the quoted material above, again, expanding through paraphrasing, Adam tries to excuse himself by saying he is sinful. This is, in other words, not a confession of sin, but a strategy for evading a confession at all, and this elicits the rare comment, inserted as an aside in parentheses by Bonhoeffer, that humanity is incomprehensibly stupid.

Having established this train of thought, the first part becomes understandable. Bonhoeffer is describing Adam and, by implication, "us," the "us" included in the humanity in the aside and those in the "we all know," which sets up his comment about the dream. Bonhoeffer recognizes a source of genuine knowledge concerning fallen humanity through a psychological analysis of a common dream, in which conscience, as an unwilling testimony to God, leaks into the subconscious in order to, returning to the first sentence of this material above, cause fleeing Adam to recognize that he cannot escape from his creator. We want to flee but we cannot flee. A common dream is made theologically important since it corroborates and enriches what is found in Gen. 3.

God's response in Gen. 3:11 is, according to Bonhoeffer's version of the biblical text: "Who told you that you are naked? You have not eaten from the tree from which I commanded you—You shall not eat from it—have you?" Here, in the exposition though, this entire verse is summed up in the following response to Adam:

gerade weil du Sünder bist, stehe vor mir und fliehe nicht.[57]

[God says,] "Precisely because you are a sinner, stand before me and do not flee."

---

56. DBW 3:121.
57. DBW 3:121.

God's questions, much like his initial words to Adam, are translated into commands or invitations, which now include a direct comment about "not fleeing," Bonhoeffer's preferred gloss for "hiding," and thus the theme of the passage. Being sinful is the reason to stand before God, presumably, and Bonhoeffer does not spell this out, because God is the only one who can do something about the fact of sin in Adam. Adam refuses and flees again.

Aber noch hält Adam nicht stand: das Weib, das Du mir zugesellt hast, gab mir von dem Baum, und ich aß. Er bekennt seine Sünde, | aber indem er sie bekennt, ergreift er schon wieder die Flucht. Du hast mir das Weib gegeben, nicht ich, ich habe keine Schuld, du hast Schuld. Das Zwielicht von Schöpfung und Sünde wird ausgenutzt. Das Weib war doch dein Geschöpf, es ist dein eigenes Werk, das mich zu Fall brachte, warum hast du eine unvollkommene Schöpfung hervorgebracht, was kann ich dafür? Also statt sich zu stellen, greift Adam auf jene von der Schlange erlernte Kunst zurück, die Gedanken Gottes zu korrigieren, von dem Schöpfer Gott an einen besseren, anderen Gott zu appellieren, d. h. eben, er entweicht abermals. Mit ihm ergreift das Weib die Flucht und weist auf die Schlange hin, d. h. eigentlich auf den Schöpfer der Schlange selbst.[58]

However, Adam still cannot stand: "The woman, whom you made my companion, gave to me from the tree, and I ate." He confesses his sin, but by confessing it he already again takes flight. "You gave me the woman, not I. It is not my fault; it is your fault." The twilight of creation and sin is exploited. "The woman was, after all, your creature, so it is your own work that brought about my fall; why did you produce an imperfect creation? What can I do about it?" So instead of presenting himself before God, Adam falls back on the trick learned from the serpent: to correct the thoughts of God, to appeal from the creator-God to another, better God; that is, now he escapes once again. The woman takes flight with him and she points to the serpent, that is, really to the creator of the serpent.

The exposition continues through quotation of the biblical text, this time Gen. 3:12, explanation and paraphrase. Adam has, as before, pseudo-confessed, which is no confession at all. Bonhoeffer summarizes Adam's response as a shifting of blame, away from him and onto God: "It is not my fault; it's your fault." If only God had done a better job, then the woman would not have ruined Adam. His escape this time is an attempt to think up a god who would have done a perfect job of creating, rather than the supposedly limited god who did the job. Bonhoeffer ascribes this particular strategy to the serpent, who earlier in the chapter suggested the very thing. This point is not simply a clever or interesting rhetorical strategy Bonhoeffer is employing. It is that, but it is also a way of placing Adam much closer to the scene of the crime than he is currently remembering. His comment

58. DBW 3:121.

on v. 13 concludes his close engagement with the biblical text, as he rephrases the same dynamic played out between Adam and God playing out between Eve and the serpent.

This escape attempt is described, coming directly after Adam has ascribed blame to God, by Bonhoeffer in the following words, words that served as the title to the lecture series before it become a book: "Das Zwielicht von Schöpfung und Sünde wird ausgenutzt" [The twilight of creation and sin is exploited].[59] This is a really helpful image: not wholly dark, but ambiguous. Adam is not seeing clearly and he is, as a result, disillusioned with God. This is the creation into which sin has come. The creation is changed by sin and the implications for God and humanity and humanity and creation are just barely coming into focus.

The final sentences of the chapter summarize and lead into the next chapter of the exposition:

> Adam hat sich nicht gestellt, hat nicht bekannt, er hat sich auf sein Gewissen, auf sein Wissen um Gut und Böse berufen und von diesem Wissen aus seinen Schöpfer angeklagt. Er hat die Gnade des Schöpfers nicht erkannt, die sich gerade darin erweist, daß er ihn anruft, daß er ihn nicht fliehen läßt, sondern er sieht diese Gnade nur als Haß, als Zorn, und an diesem Zorn entzündet sich sein eigener Haß, seine Empörung, sein Wille, ihm zu entgehen. Adam bleibt im Fallen. Der Fall beschleunigt sich ins Unermeßliche.[60]

> Adam has not presented himself before God, he has not really confessed; he has appealed to his conscience, to his knowledge of good and evil, and on the basis of this knowledge he has indicted his creator. He has not recognized the grace of the creator, that which shows itself precisely in that God challenged him, that he would not let him flee; rather, Adam sees this grace only as hate, as wrath, and at this wrath his own hatred kindles itself, his rebellion, his will to escape from God. Adam continues to fall. This is a free fall into an immeasurable depth.

God's challenge, his questions to Adam, are construed here as the grace of the creator. The act of judgment is at the same time an act of grace. Using vivid imagery, Bonhoeffer describes the intensity of Adam's scorn of that grace, a vicious circle of hate, wrath, rebellion, and resolve to flee from God. This vicious circle, constructed out of the narrative sequence and dialogue of Gen. 3, is the continuous free fall that concludes the exposition.

59. DBW 3:121.
60. DBW 3:121-122.

3. Synthesis

This chapter set out to trace the relation between the biblical text of Gen. 2:7 and Gen. 3:8-13 and Dietrich Bonhoeffer's comments on those texts as they are presented in *Schöpfung und Fall*. This has been done to some degree of detail. In order to pull together some of the threads of this chapter it might be helpful to summarize some of what has been shown, listing the sort of interpretive techniques that were observed as each passage was analyzed.[61] Bonhoeffer often utilizes the following practices, among others, when moving from text to comment:

1. He conflates the time of the text and the time of his hearers/readers, which has the rhetorical effect of increasing attentiveness and a sense of importance but also serves to bring the human *qua* human into view, that is, he identifies a significant moment where unity is discerned in relation to the subject matter of the biblical text.[62] He does this when he says, at the beginning of the exposition of Gen. 2:7, that "we are directed," a statement that is at once about the fact that the text has an interest that is to be followed but also that the "we" who are directed is not just any interpreter but the particular group of people in the lecture hall.

2. He deals in contrasts so that he can elucidate what he is really after by slowly bringing it out rather than simply stating it. In the discussion about the positive nature of human bodies, he contrasts the freedom of creaturely being as embodied with the imprisoned or enslaved status of some flawed perspectives on human bodies. In this instance, he accomplished more by contrast than he could be making his point positively from the outset.

3. He paraphrases, often so that he can expand a dialogue, working out some of the implications of what is explicitly communicated. For example, he draws out the implications of God's question posed to Adam, "Where are you?" by paraphrase, expanding the nature of God's invitation to come out of hiding.

4. He develops hypothetical situations or positions so that he can then develop his own response, as in the case of an interpreter thinking that the personal

---

61. It is important to recognize that there is a relationship between these small-scale techniques and the implications of them for larger-scale hermeneutical issues. The in-detail approach to the smaller-scale issues will, when properly attended to, give way to the broader hermeneutical considerations here and there in the book, as in, for example, the concluding paragraph of this chapter, and especially in the conclusion.

62. On this final element, Walter Moberly helpfully analyzes Bonhoeffer's theological interpretation in *Creation and Fall*, commenting that he is concerned with "fundamental existential issues of what it means to be human in God's world." This, rather than various other potential frames of reference, is what allows Bonhoeffer to see what he does in the text of Genesis. Presentation entitled, "*Creation and Fall* and Biblical Exegesis for the Church," delivered at a conference held at St. John's College in Durham, UK, in 2017 called Reading Bonhoeffer for the Life of the Church.

name "Yahweh" is evidence that the text derives from a primitive stage rather than his own view that God's name here is an aspect of divine particularity.

5. Bonhoeffer will build assertion on top of assertion, using a staccato form of speaking/writing. When he spoke of Darwin and Feuerbach in relation to Gen. 2 he did this, quickly developing a point in short sentences that do not really add much but serve to underscore an aspect he is interested in developing further in what follows.

6. At crucial points he will use *Sperrsatz* [letter spacing] for emphasis, a technique that is displayed in the German and English editions as an italicized word or phrase. He did this with *Leib* since it was the word that captured the implication he was then concerned to discuss in detail.

Through these kinds of interpretive acts, and these are only representative of the sorts of things on display above, Bonhoeffer delivered on the kind of biblical interpretation he envisaged as a student in 1925. *Schöpfung und Fall* does not succeed in resolving all the tensions he identified for a historically and theologically oriented biblical interpretation, because he never planned to resolve those tensions. He hoped, instead, to live with those tensions, paying careful attention to each particular issue as he encountered each specific text. He offered here an exercise in interpreting, not a static theological exposition, but rather a practice of unfolding and interpreting, done here in the form of a commentary with the text taking the lead throughout the exposition. The purpose of adopting the genre of commentary was not to produce a piece of standard biblical scholarship but to focus on the text's *Sache*. The text, then, is not an end in itself but is the means to an end, offering an interpretation that benefits others by, in this case at least, telling us something about how humans relate to God, creation, and sin. On the way, he does not feel the need to interact much with biblical scholarship, nor does he feel that it is important to offer any justifications for the decisions he makes or the conversation partners he includes—Michelangelo, the author of Ephesians, Darwin, or Feuerbach. Instead, he draws out significant theological points from the text, themes which have a basis in the text of Genesis. The linguistic register is different, that is, this is not described as a pneumatological interpretation of Scripture, but it is nonetheless a straightforward, theological interpretation of Scripture, and as such, it is precisely what he had in mind when he tackled the issues that should constitute that practice in 1925.

Chapter 3

LONDON: PRACTICING INTERPRETATION IN THE CHURCH

This chapter continues to show what Bonhoeffer's pneumatological interpretation of Scripture looks like *in particular*, this time when he moves from the academic, university context where he presented the set of lectures which became *Schöpfung und Fall* to the ecclesial, pastoral context of preaching, a context where he continued to interpret Scripture but now for the benefit of his congregations. The argument, in brief and in line with the previous chapter, is that the interpretive vision from 1925 governs Bonhoeffer's hermeneutical decisions while a pastor in London from 1933 to 1935. There is, therefore, an appropriate place for an expectation of continuity, albeit continuity expressed in and shaped by a new context.

The chapter follows the pattern laid out in the preceding chapter, in that it begins with some preliminaries that set up the shape of the argument. In this case, a brief repetition of the rationale for offering close readings of Bonhoeffer's sermons and an explanation of the criteria employed to pick the two sermons chosen out of the much larger group of sixteen surviving sermons are included (Section 1.1). Developing relevant aspects of the biographical context of the London period will serve to ground the analysis of the sermons historically, hopefully guarding against various forms of misreading (Section 1.2).

The close readings of two sermons will comprise the vast majority of the chapter (Section 2). In this section it will become clear that the genre of the sermon allows Bonhoeffer to inhabit the Scriptural world, so much so that the biblical idiom becomes his own language. What Karl Barth called "the strange new world of the Bible" is precisely the environment within which Bonhoeffer lives. In this world the biblical texts of Jeremiah and 1 Corinthians are not simply external sources he draws upon to preach. In fact, there are points in these sermons when the biblical text is spoken without drawing any attention to it, so that the uninitiated listener or reader would not know that this was not simply Bonhoeffer speaking. It is his discourse now and it is proclaimed in this preacher-to-congregation encounter. This dynamic, visible by attending to the relation of biblical text to comment in the sermon, is a form of interpreting Scripture, and as such it connects to the major theme of this book. Here we see that theological interpretation of Scripture is not simply interpreting from a perspective of faith vaguely conceived or even from a straightforward and simple doctrinal framework.[1] It is, instead, a practice in which key moves made by an interpreter ensure that the directly relevant theological content of the text strikes home with one's hearers or readers. At least one implication of this is that the genre of sermon may be the most fitting or appropriate genre for this approach to interpreting Scripture. This genre enables one to move from the text in its original setting, read within a tradition to be sure, to the text as paradigmatic for the congregation. How this is done, that is, the specific techniques that enable this kind of interpretation, is on display below. Indexing these small-scale hermeneutical decisions—for instance, paraphrastic expansion or intertextual allusion or drawing upon certain forms of Lutheran pietism to highlight a textual element's emotional potential—provides the material from which to think about broader questions concerning Bonhoeffer's hermeneutics and his practice of interpreting Scripture.

These close readings provide ample opportunity to observe this practice in action, so they will be followed by some summary reflections about what has been shown and the ways in which the analysis offered contributes to our developing understanding of Bonhoeffer's form of interpretation (Section 3).

1. Preliminaries

1.1. Close Readings and Selection of Texts

The act of preaching is an act of proclamation. It is an auditory event or encounter, and this is especially emphasized in the Protestant and Lutheran tradition of which Bonhoeffer was a part.[2] Distanced from the original auditory context, these

---

1. Having said this though, it is also a confessional form of interpretation. The word "confessional" in reference to biblical interpretation is used negatively now in certain contexts, but maybe it should be rehabilitated. Theological interpretation of Scripture has the sermon at its heart, but sermons are preached in confessional contexts. In Lutheranism the sermon will likely have a gravitational pull toward the Pauline corpus (see both sermons below, and note the way a Lutheran pastor-theologian preaches on Reformation Day). In Roman Catholic church contexts the sermon will likely take the form of a homily in reference to a Gospel text. Perhaps it would be better to think of theological interpretation of Scripture in less generic terms. These interpretive efforts are products of certain confessional and ecclesial contexts. What we are engaging throughout this book is a specifically Protestant and Lutheran form of interpretation (though one that is also ecumenically inflected).

2. I have chosen to focus exclusively on just two sermons rather than Bonhoeffer's preaching in general or the broader tradition within which it is situated. This decision is simply meant to limit the scope of my engagement, thus hopefully increasing my attention to the details of Bonhoeffer's exegesis. As a result, I have not interacted with scholarly books dealing with Bonhoeffer and preaching. For helpful resources along these lines,

sermons are received as texts to read and analyze, which underscores the fact that the interpreter of his sermons has to do everything possible to keep the genre and setting in mind so as to work to "hear" these texts as sermons.[3] Two methodological principles arise from the form of these texts as sermons. Bonhoeffer's German texts need to be central and are reproduced here nearly in full so that the force of his rhetoric, precisely as preaching rhetoric in the German language, can come to the fore, and as much as it is possible to discern it, the setting of each sermon needs to accompany its interpretation. These principles exist to serve the real purpose of the close reading strategy employed in this book, which is to trace the relation between the text of Scripture and Bonhoeffer's comments in these particular sermons. Ample time must be taken with each sermon to allow its contribution to come to light.

The following points served as guides for determining which sermons should receive attention. First, there are temporal considerations: the sermons should be representative, if possible, of the whole of his time in London, so a sermon was chosen from both the beginning and end. Second, there is the issue of which testament in the Bible; it seemed important to find sermons that used a passage from both the Old Testament and the New Testament. Third, genre: somewhat related to the previous point, the sermons should engage different genres in the Bible in order to see how, if at all, a text's genre affects Bonhoeffer's interpretive effort. Finally, length was, again, a major concern since the sermons needed to be short enough so that the whole sermon could be studied in detail but long enough to trace the relation of text to comment at the level of the text's movement or argument as a whole. These criteria yielded an Old Testament sermon on the prophetic book of Jeremiah from January 1934, a few months after Bonhoeffer arrived in London, and a New Testament sermon on the first epistle to the Corinthians from November 1934, several months from the end of his time in London.

see the following: the recent offering by Michael Pasquerello III, *Dietrich: Bonhoeffer and the Theology of a Preaching Life* (Waco, TX: Baylor University Press, 2017); Keith W. Clements, "'This Is My World' The Intentionality of Bonhoeffer's Preaching in London 1933-35," in *Dietrich Bonhoeffers Christentum: Festschrift für Christian Gremmels*, ed. Florian Schmitz and Christiane Tietz (Germany: Gütersloher Verlagshaus, 2011), 17–36. For some older works on the topic, see Edwin Robertson, *The Shame and the Sacrifice: The Life and Preaching of Dietrich Bonhoeffer* (London: Hodder and Stoughton, 1987); Ernst Georg Wendel, *Studien zur Homiletik Dietrich Bonhoeffers: Predigt—Hermeneutik—Sprache* (Heidelberg, Germany: Mohr Siebeck, 1985).

3. Bonhoeffer did intend at least some people to read the sermons as texts, since he sent them to various people in the post, and if he had not done so they probably would not have survived for future readers. For more detailed biographical context, the relevant sections of the biographies provide much illumination (see below).

1.2. The Context of the Sermons

In October 1933 Bonhoeffer moved to London to serve as a pastor.[4] Up to that point, the year had been a whirlwind for him. In early February, just after Hitler was named *Reichskanzler* [Reich Chancellor] of Germany, Bonhoeffer gave a radio lecture entitled "The Younger Generation's Altered View of the Concept of the Führer." He also continued his engagement in church ministry and teaching at Berlin University, which included lectures and seminars on "Christology" and "Hegel's Philosophy of Religion." In April, he worked on the essay "The Church and the Jewish Question," publishing it in June, and interviewed with the London congregations he would eventually pastor. In addition to all this, Bonhoeffer helped write the "Bethel Confession," partnered with several people to establish the *Pfarrernotbund* [Pastors' Emergency League], and participated in ecumenical gatherings, conferences, and a protest in Wittenberg at the "National Synod" of German Christians in September.

The invitation to serve outside of Germany in a London pastorate came from the Church Foreign Officer, Theodor Heckel. Bonhoeffer had some experience as an assistant pastor in Barcelona and, after his ordination, by serving as a chaplain in Berlin while he lectured at the university. The opportunity in London was attractive, partly because it brought focus to the developing shape of his vocation as a pastor, a role he valued but on which he had not yet focused, but also partly because it seemed like an option that would bring some relief from the struggles he had been locked up in throughout the duration of 1933. He accepted the invitation, despite intense conversations with the newly elected *Reichsbischof* [Reich Bishop], Ludwig Müller, and Heckel over Bonhoeffer's protests and published work on the so-called Aryan Paragraph.[5] He started his pastoral duties on October 17, 1933.[6]

---

4. For more of the historical and biographical context, see Bethge, *Bonhoeffer*, 325–417; Keith W. Clements, *Bonhoeffer and Britain* (Church Together in Britain and Ireland, 2006); Marsh, *Strange Glory*, 194–226; Julius Rieger, *Bonhoeffer in England* (Germany: Lettner-Verlag, 1966); Ferdinand Schlingensiepen, *Dietrich Bonhoeffer 1906–1945: Martyr, Thinker, Man of Resistance* (New York: T&T Clark: 2012), 144–76; Christiane Tietz, *Theologian of Resistance: The Life and Thought of Dietrich Bonhoeffer*, trans. Victoria J. Barnett (Minneapolis, MN: Fortress Press, 2016), 45–54.

5. The Aryan clause or paragraph, passed on April 7, 1933, appeared in the Law for the Restoration of the Professional Civil Service and pertained initially to the exclusion of all non-Aryans from jobs in the civil services. It was eventually expanded to include education, most professions, and the church. Bonhoeffer's resistance to it began in April and never abated. Comprehensive coverage of the church situation in Germany at the time, including information about the Aryan clause, can be found in Klaus Scholder, *The Churches and the Third Reich*, 2 vol., Eng. trans. John Bowden (London: SCM Press, 1987).

6. He took up his duties despite the opinions of many of his comrades in the developing church struggle, Karl Barth among them. The dramatic exchange of letters between Barth and Bonhoeffer is fascinating, but not relevant enough to warrant inclusion here. See Bethge, *Bonhoeffer*, 325–8; Marsh, *Strange Glory*, 197–8; Tietz, *Theologian of Resistance*, 45–6.

For nineteen months, from October 1933 to April 1935, the 28-year-old was the sole pastor responsible for overseeing two German congregations in London. Neither congregation, the German Reformed congregation of St. Paul's in Whitechapel in south London and the German Evangelical congregation in Sydenham-Forest Hill in the East End, was very large, each with fifty or so attending church, but Bonhoeffer found the workload more than he expected. Continuous with his prior experiences in Spain and Germany, he infused his enormous amount of energy into these churches by developing activities for the children, Sunday schools and Christmas plays, revitalized a choir and focused much of his attention on pastoral visitation and preaching twice each Sunday, delivering the same sermon for one congregation in the morning and another in the evening. His sermons were written out word for word and very direct. They called for, and still call for, careful listening and attention from their recipients.

1.2.1. Sermon on Jer. 20:7 On the third Sunday after Epiphany, January 21, 1934, Bonhoeffer preached a sermon on Jer. 20:7.[7] A number of factors are relevant for interpreting the sermon.[8] The story begins in November 1933. A group of *Reichskirche* [Reich Church] leaders held an event for German Christians that filled the large *Berlin Sportpalast* [Berlin Sports Palace] venue. There, among other things, they heard a keynote address by Reinhard Krause in which he spoke of Hitler's new Germany as affording an opportunity for the Church to liberate itself from the Old Testament, for Nazi members to occupy all Church offices, and for the Aryan paragraph to be implemented everywhere. This bold expression of the shape of German Christianity did not call forth a tempering response from any prominent leader in the movement, and as a result large numbers of people left the German Christians.[9]

This put the appointed, but not yet installed, *Reichsbischof* Müller in hot water with Hitler and caused a number of those who recently resigned from Müller's group to express an interest in joining the Pastors' Emergency League. Müller acted quickly, needing to regain Hitler's confidence, which would ensure that his appointment became an installation and bolster the ranks of the German Christians again. In a brilliant and strategic maneuver, he consolidated all of

---

7. For some brief remarks on the sermon in biographical context, see Bethge, *Bonhoeffer*, 331; Schlingensiepen, *Dietrich Bonhoeffer*, 154.

8. It is certainly possible, and probably even likely, that Bonhoeffer followed his church's lectionary while in London, but even though Charles Marsh, *Strange Glory*, 204, assumes this to be the case while citing no evidence, I cannot definitively say that he did follow the lectionary. In the case of the sermon on Jer. 20:7, it seems like Bonhoeffer simply chose this text because of its importance for him at the moment. In the case of the sermon on 1 Cor. 13:13, he explicitly says he planned for that text to fall on that specific Sunday, Reformation Sunday.

9. For a helpful introduction to the beginning stages of the church conflicts, see Victoria Barnett, *For the Soul of the People: Protestant Protest against Hitler* (Oxford: Oxford University Press, 1992), 47–73.

the German Evangelical Church Youth groups in the country into one, bringing everyone under the *Hitlerjugend* [Hitler Youth] designation. This became a kind of Christmas present for the Führer and put Müller back in his good graces. Next, he reinstated the Aryan paragraph and in early January developed a "muzzling decree," which stipulated that Protestant pastors in Germany were not allowed to publicly speak about the German Church situation.

In response, the Pastors' Emergency League scheduled a protest to this ban, resulting in a large crowd very publicly singing Luther's "Ein feste Burg ist unser Gott" [A Mighty Fortress Is Our God]. In addition, several members of the Pastors' Emergency League also sent requests to Reich President Hindenburg, requesting his involvement in the recent struggles in the church, specifically seeking his influence in removing Müller from his position. Having been petitioned by pastors in Germany, congregations in England and from George Bell, the Bishop of Chichester and a recent friend of Bonhoeffer's, Hindenburg expressed his concerns directly to Hitler. Around the same time, Hitler hosted a Chancellery reception for church leaders on January 25, 1934. At this gathering he was given a transcript of a wiretapped phone conversation in which Martin Niemöller, leader of the Pastors' Emergency League, spoke of the League's upcoming preparations for the Chancellery reception. In the conversation he alluded to Hindenburg's desire to influence events in the League's favor. Hitler, knowing in advance that he would be given the transcript at the reception, responded in dramatic fashion, calling for the church leaders present to distance themselves from Niemöller. The balance shifted back in favor of the German Christians.

It was in the middle of these circumstances that Bonhoeffer preached on Jer. 20:7. Bonhoeffer had been waiting for either a phone call or telegram to know how things would turn out with the ever-shifting situation in Germany. The sermon was delivered just four days before the Chancellery reception, and it was in the state of anticipation and anxiety that he preached. Tension and emotion are present everywhere in the sermon, even if the political context is, for the most part, not explicit.

1.2.2. Sermon on 1 Cor. 13:13 The sermon on 1 Cor. 13:13 was preached on Reformation Sunday, November 4, 1934.[10] Bonhoeffer planned for this sermon, the concluding sermon of a four-part series, to fall on this date. The church struggle continued to occupy Bonhoeffer's attention. He followed the eventual production of the Barmen Declaration, a confession something like the one he had hoped to develop the previous August when he helped to write the Bethel Confession, and he took enormous interest in the Confessing Church organizational developments that would take place in the synod at Dahlem. He also traveled often to various ecumenical gatherings, both in order to continue to develop his passion for a united church and also to utilize his ecumenical contacts to share happenings in the German church situation in the hopes that churches in other countries would

---

10. Bethge and Marsh briefly comment on this sermon in their biographies. See Bethge, *Bonhoeffer*, 331; Marsh, *Strange Glory*, 203–4.

support the newly developing Confessing Church. Bonhoeffer was effective at building relationships and convincing people to join along with him·in opposing the German Christians. Consequently, many months after his first attempts to consolidate the oppositional position of the German congregations in England, the day after he preached on 1 Cor. 13:13, they resolved at his urging to leave the Reich Church government. This was, for Bonhoeffer, no doubt an expression of faithful Christianity, Reformation Day faith, hope, and love.

2. Close Readings

2.1. Predigt zu Jeremia 20,7. London, 3 Sonntag nach
Epiphanias, 21.1.1934 [Sermon on Jeremiah 20:7. London,
Third Sunday after Epiphany, January 21, 1934]

2.1.1. Biblical Text Bonhoeffer's biblical text is a reproduction of Luther's translation of Jer. 20:7, though he does stop short of including and commenting upon the final phrase in the text, at least explicitly, for the theme of that phrase, the ridicule and mocking of Jeremiah, is included in his exposition but only insofar as he summarizes that aspect of Jeremiah's narrative. Other than this exclusion, he makes no alterations to the text he has received, but he does utilize his freedom as a preacher to exploit an ambiguity opened up by Luther's translation decisions and the text's own thematic juxtaposition. The text is as follows:

> Herr, du hast mich überredet und ich habe mich überreden lassen. Du bist mir zu stark gewesen und hast gewonnen.[11]

> Lord, you have persuaded me and I allowed myself to be persuaded. You have been too strong for me and have won.

The ambiguity concerns the verb in the first sentence, first as "überredet" and repeated as "überreden." The verb is employed to render the Hebrew Piel verb פִּתִּיתַנִי, the semantic range of which includes persuading, seducing, enticing, or deceiving. The German verb "überreden" stays much more within the realm of persuading and convincing, rather than either the sexual or overtly deceitful connotations. Though one could imagine how these English glosses relate to one another, so that a man might persuade a woman so as to seduce or entice her, they do not have to; persuasion does not *by necessity* lead to enticement or deception. The choice of Luther's milder translation affords Bonhoeffer the opportunity to draw out the Hebrew verb's ambiguity, highlighting the dialectical relationship between the first and second parts of the verse. The relation between the sentences—one speaking more neutrally of persuasion and the other speaking more strongly about having been subdued or won over by God's strength—leads Bonhoeffer to a rhetoric that moves back-and-forth, as we will see, between a more intimate and

---

11. DBW 13:347.

a more violent idiom throughout the sermon. This is not only the result of what the text gives him, however. It is also the result of the situation sketched above. Bonhoeffer draws out the juxtaposition in order to depict Jeremiah's conflicted situation, the text's language, and the troubling situation in which he and his hearers find themselves. This is a text well suited to Bonhoeffer's dialectical style of thinking. As a result, all of this is considered together and in tension for the theologically oriented biblical interpretation taking shape throughout the sermon.

2.1.2. Bonhoeffer's Sermon In the first three paragraphs of the sermon Bonhoeffer introduces the themes that he will develop throughout, and he canvases the context of Jeremiah's life, familiarizing his audience with the prophet and setting the scene for interpreting the verse he has chosen as his main sermon text. The text itself is not quoted until the very last line of the third paragraph, but the themes and the language used in the introduction anticipate the verse. In the first paragraph, we find a vivid depiction of Jeremiah's call, followed by an analysis of the divine call, more generally conceived, and finally, he moves back to Jeremiah's life, but now newly equipped with his "call analysis" to present it as paradigmatic for his hearers. He begins:

> Jeremias hat sich nicht dazu gedrängt, Prophet Gottes zu werden. Er ist zurückgeschaudert, als ihn plötzlich der Ruf traf, er hat sich gewehrt, er wollte ausweichen—nein, er wollte dieses Gottes Prophet und Zeuge nicht sein—aber auf der Flucht packt ihn, ergreift ihn das Wort, der Ruf; er kann sich nicht mehr entziehen, es ist um ihn geschehen, oder, wie es einmal heißt, der Pfeil des allmächtigen Gottes hat das gehetzte Wild erlegt. Jeremias ist sein Prophet.[12]

> Jeremiah was not pushing to become a prophet of God. He shrunk back when the call suddenly came to him; he defended himself against it, he wanted to avoid it—no, he did not want to be this God's prophet and witness—but on the run it seized him, the word grasped him, the call; he can no longer escape, it's all over for him, or, as it has once been said, the arrow of the almighty God has shot the hunted game. Jeremiah is his prophet.

The brevity of this paragraph is striking, and so are the first and last sentences, showing in quick succession the movement from not wanting to be God's prophet to the stark "Jeremias ist sein Prophet" [Jeremiah is his prophet]. This is the contrast of the verse itself, the juxtaposition noted above. The imagery is borrowed, a point indicated by the phrase "wie es einmal heißt" [as it has once been said]. It is commonplace in Old Testament biblical scholarship to note a relationship between the books of Jeremiah and Lamentations, and here Bonhoeffer relies on this well-worn path by paraphrasing with imagery from Lam. 3:12-13: "He drew his bow and made me the target for his arrows. He pierced my heart with arrows

---

12. DBW 13:347.

from his quiver." The central point of the imagery is that the word or call of God to Jeremiah to become a prophet was effective.

This theme is expanded upon in the next paragraph. He continues:

> Von außen her kommt es über den Menschen, nicht aus der Sehnsucht seines Herzens, nicht aus seinen verborgensten Wünschen und Hoffnungen steigt es herauf; das Wort, das den Menschen stellt, packt, gefangen nimmt, bindet, kommt nicht aus den Tiefen unserer Seele, sondern es ist das fremde, unbekannte, unerwartete, gewalttätige, überwältigende Wort des Herrn, der in seinen Dienst ruft, wen und wann er will.[13]

> From outside it comes over a person, not out of the longing of his heart, it does not arise out of his most hidden desires and hopes; the word—that which situates a person, seizes, captures, binds—does not come out of the depths of our soul, rather it is the foreign, unknown, unexpected, violent, overwhelming word of the Lord that calls into his service whomever and whenever he wants.

Bonhoeffer develops his notion of the call or word of the Lord, an often-repeated phrase in the tradition of prophetic literature he is expositing, in the contrasting spatial terms of "outside" and "inside." This distinction, taking shape here on the ground of Jeremiah's biography and text, has a history. As we have seen in his student essay from 1925, "Word of God" is a theological phrase of great importance for his theology of revelation and his hermeneutics, and was developed in conversation with Barth's emphasis on God's call or speech *as* God's action breaking into the human sphere from outside.[14] Barth advanced this point forcefully against the tradition rooted in Schleiermacher's focus on an inner God-consciousness as the place of revelation.[15] Bonhoeffer's developing "Word of God" theology is described in more general terms for all those listening to the sermon while maintaining his focus on the prophet Jeremiah.

The word does *not* come from the inside, from the heart or the depths of the soul, the place that contains a person's most hidden desires and hopes. Rather, and paying careful attention to the verbs he employs, the word of God situates, seizes, captures, and binds because it is a foreign (i.e., outside), unknown, unexpected, violent, and overwhelming word. It is thus an effective word that has content: it calls someone into God's service. As a result,

---

13. DBW 13:347.

14. See Karl Barth, CD I.1.1, 130–59.

15. Schleiermacher's primary notion is developed in the following constellation of German phrases: *Anschauung und Gefühl* [intuition and feeling], *Gefühlsglaube* [sentimental faith], *Gottesbewusstein* [God-consciousness], *Gefühl schlechthinniger Abhängigkeit* [feeling of absolute dependence]. See Friedrich Schleiermacher, *Christian Faith: A New Translation and Critical Edition*, 2 vols, ed. and trans. Terrence N. Tice, Catherine L. Kelsey, and Edwin Lawler (Louisville, KY: Westminster John Knox Press, 2016).

> Da hilft kein Widerstreben, sondern da heißt Gottes Antwort: Ich kannte dich, ehe ich dich im Mutterleib bereitete. Du bist mein. Fürchte nicht! Ich bin dein Gott, der dich hält.[16]

> Resistance is of no avail; rather, God's answer comes: I knew you before I formed you in the womb. You are mine. Fear not! I am your God, the one who holds you.

But, the reason resistance is futile is not because this is simply and straightforwardly a master–slave relationship, a conclusion we could certainly draw from the violent, subjecting language used in the previous paragraph. Instead, the language of forced servitude gives way to an intimate and loving idiom. Bonhoeffer accomplishes this strange transition by picking up a number of sentences from elsewhere in which God speaks intimate words in first-person form. The first of these comes from the "call narrative" at the beginning of the book of Jer. 1. God's knowledge of Jeremiah before he was born leads to Jeremiah being God's possession, which underwrites the command not to fear but instead to settle into God's secure and trustworthy hands, hands that are elsewhere described in Jeremiah as the hands of a potter (ch. 18). This is the language of relationship, language he continues to utilize in drawing out the nature of call and response between Jeremiah and God, and by implication, his hearers and God.

> Und dann ist dies fremde, ferne, unbekannte, gewalttätige Wort auf einmal das uns schon so unheimlich wohlbekannte, unheimlich nahe, überredende, betörende, verführen- | de Wort der Liebe des Herrn, den es nach seinem Geschöpf verlangt.[17]

> And yet, this foreign, distant, unknown, overwhelming word is suddenly the so strangely well-known, strangely near, persuading, enticing, seductive word of the Lord's love, which yearns after his creature.

Picking up some of the adjectives he used a few sentences previously in describing God's call, Bonhoeffer transposes this language into the idiom of his main text, Jer. 20:7, and it is at this point that his awareness of the translation's ambiguity becomes explicit. God's persuasive word is glossed as a word of love, which expressed through a Lutheran, pietistic lens, yearns after the creature. The harsher language of a call to service, master–slave-like, is explicitly put in touch here with God's love. This blending of positive and negative aspects of the word leads to a new, slightly different image.

> Dem Menschen ist ein Lasso über den Kopf geworfen und nun kommt er nicht mehr los. Versucht er zu widerstreben, so spürt [er] erst recht, wie unmöglich das ist; denn das Lasso zieht sich nur enger und schmerzhafter zusammen und

---

16. DBW 13:347.
17. DBW 13:347.

erinnert ihn daran, daß er ein Gefangener ist. Er ist Gefangener, er muß folgen. Der Weg ist vorgeschrieben.[18]

The man has a lasso tossed over his head and now he cannot get away. If he tries to resist, he feels even more how impossible that is because the lasso only tightens painfully and reminds him that he is a prisoner. He is a prisoner, he must follow. The way is predetermined.

Bonhoeffer continues to develop the language of binding and expands on the futility of resistance. By unfolding things in this way, he has brought the point back into the negative end of the spectrum. He has brought the violence of the call back into focus. But this is all done in order to make the following point:

Es ist der Weg des Menschen, den Gott nicht mehr losläßt, der Gott nicht mehr loswird. Das heißt aber auch, der Weg des Menschen, der nie mehr—im Guten oder Bösen—gott-los wird.[19]

It is the way of a man whom God will not let go anymore, one who cannot get rid of God anymore. But it is also the way of the man who will never again—in a good or bad sense—be god-less.

The negative, violent imagery is again qualified. The shape of his rhetoric is itself underscoring the ambivalence and ambiguity of the relation one has to God. On the one hand, positively, God will not let go anymore, but on the other hand, that also means that a person called by God cannot get rid of God. This is all nicely summed up in the word *gott-los* [god-less]. One can be hopeful because one can never be without God. It bears repeating that this two-fold—positive–negative, violent–loving—dynamic is developed out of the story of Jeremiah's call with his continued struggles with God as a prophet, out of the main text's linguistic ambiguity, and to give shape to the congregation's response to the situation in the German church.

The upshot of the preceding is that God and Jeremiah, as God's prophet, go together no matter what circumstances or tasks Jeremiah faces. Moving back out of the general reflections on "call," Bonhoeffer shifts to the frame of Jeremiah's life, moving from the crisis he has been describing in a relationship between a called human and God to a crisis in the relationship of that person to other people:

Und dieser Weg führt mitten in die tiefste menschliche Schwachheit hinein. Ein verlachter, verachteter, für verrückt erklärter, aber für Ruhe und Frieden der Menschen äußerst gefährlicher Narr—den man schlägt, einsperrt, foltert und am liebsten gleich umbringt—das ist dieser Jeremias eben weil er Gott nicht mehr loswerden kann. Phantast, Sturkopf, Friedensstörer, Volksfeind hat man

18. DBW 13:347-348.
19. DBW 13:348.

ihn gescholten, hat man zu allen Zeiten bis heute die gescholten, die von Gott
besessen und gefaßt waren, denen Gott zu stark geworden war.[20]

And this path leads right into the deepest human weakness. A laughingstock,
despised, declared crazy, but nevertheless an extremely dangerous fool for the
calm and peace of the people—who is beaten, imprisoned, tortured, and put
to death right away—that is Jeremiah's situation precisely because he can no
longer separate himself from God. He is accused of being a fantasist, a fanatic,
a disturber of the peace, an enemy of the people—just as at all times up to this
day people are accused—those who are seized and possessed by God, for whom
God has proved too strong.

The word of God opens up a negative social space for Jeremiah, isolating him
and causing strife in his relationships. Interestingly, Bonhoeffer returns to the
language of the text again by the end of the second sentence, and this move, when
placed in relation to his comment, "hat man zu allen Zeiten bis heute" [just as at all
times up to this day], conflates time, past, present, and future, making Jeremiah's
experience paradigmatic for his hearers. This is meant to provide a theological
context for viewing situations in the lives of his hearers, whether in London or
in the contemporary events unfolding in Germany, and a way of imagining a
response.

Bonhoeffer next turns his attention to Jeremiah's response to his suffering,
developed through a contrast of three hypothetical responses and the actual
response represented in the text of Jeremiah. He envisions Jeremiah's response
in language familiar to his congregation. Jeremiah may want to shout "Friede
und Heil" [peace and well-being], but he is not able to do so. One cannot miss
the relevance of the term "Heil" employed at this point, perhaps equating the
false prophets of Jeremiah's context with those acclaiming Hitler. The thrice
repeated "how gladly he would have kept silent" prepares the hearer for the
harsh reality:

> aber er konnte einfach nicht, es lag wie ein Zwang, wie ein Druck auf ihm, es war,
> als säße ihm einer im Nacken und triebe ihn von einer Wahrheit zur anderen,
> von einem Leiden zum anderen. Er war nicht mehr sein eigener Herr, er war
> seiner selbst nicht mehr mächtig, ein anderer war seiner mächtig geworden, ein
> anderer besaß ihn, von einem anderen war er besessen.[21]

But he simply could not, it was like a compulsion, like a pressure on him, it was
as if someone was breathing down his neck and driving him from one truth to
another, from one distress to another. He was no longer his own master, he was
no longer in control of himself, another was in control of him, another possessed
him; he was possessed by another.

---

20. DBW 13:348.
21. DBW 13:348.

Again channeling the broader context of Jer. 20, Bonhoeffer alludes to, rather than cites, v. 9: "But if I say, 'I will not mention his word or speak anymore in his name,' his word is in my heart like a fire, a fire shut up in my bones. I am weary of holding it in; indeed, I cannot." Jeremiah's inability to keep the fire in has been transposed into a quite vivid picture of Jeremiah being forced along. Bonhoeffer has returned to the master–slave relation and drives it home through double repetition: first, not in control of himself/another in control of him, and then second, another possessed/he was possessed. These four statements, each coming right on the heels of the others, create a bridge along which the analogy between Jeremiah and Bonhoeffer's congregation is linked. He then makes the link explicit:

> Und Jeremias war von unserem Fleisch und Blut, er war ein Mensch wie wir. Er leidet unter den dauernden Erniedrigungen, dem Spott, der Gewalt, der Brutalität der anderen, und so bricht er dann nach einer qualvollen Folterung, die eine ganze Nacht gewährt hatte, in | dieses Gebet aus: „Herr, du hast mich überredet und ich habe mich überreden lassen. Du bist mir zu stark geworden und hast gewonnen."[22]

> And Jeremiah was flesh and blood like us; he was a human being like we are. He suffers under the constant humiliations, the ridicule, the violence, the brutality of others, and so he breaks out in this prayer after an agonizing torture, which lasted a whole night: "Lord, you have persuaded me and I allowed myself to be persuaded. You have been too strong for me and have won."

Even though they are not prophets called by God in precisely this way, the present tense verbs *leidet* [suffers] and *ausbricht* [breaks out] are employed to make Jeremiah's past experience contemporaneous with his hearer's experience, making their common humanity—*von unserem Fleisch und Blut* [flesh and blood like us]—all the more explicit. The decisions to conflate time in this manner and to link Jeremiah with his hearers in 1934 serve to prepare Bonhoeffer's congregation to hear Jeremiah's prayer in 20:7 as their own prayer too. This is confirmed by the fact that he launches from a recitation of his main text into an imagined, expansive version of Jeremiah's prayer from Jeremiah's perspective.[23]

---

22. DBW 13:348.

23. Another expansion worth noting is that he includes a note about Jeremiah praying the words of Jer. 20:7 after a night of agonizing torture. I have yet to find anything in the text of Jeremiah that explicitly suggests he suffered in this way. The narrative frame at the beginning of the chapter (vv. 1-6) indicates that Jeremiah was placed in stocks, and this could have been the case overnight. It is also possible that Bonhoeffer is reading other biblical stories into Jeremiah's life, whether Gethsemane or Paul's suffering in 2 Cor. 1. It is also possible that, in line with his practice elsewhere, Bonhoeffer added this detail in order to raise the dramatic tension. Bonhoeffer's willingness to "fictionalize" accounts for the sake of the interest of his hearers in Barcelona is helpfully described by Robert Steiner and Helen Hacksley in "Enticing Otherness in Barcelona—Dietrich Bonhoeffer's Retelling of the Gospel like 'a fairy tale about a strange land,'" in *God Speaks to Us: Dietrich Bonhoeffer's*

Before moving on, it would be helpful to pause and note that the first three paragraphs through to the quotation of Jer. 20:7 are introductory. Bonhoeffer reads this single verse in some broader contexts: the context of Jer. 20 as a whole, the context of the book of Jeremiah (especially through intertexts to the "call narrative" in ch. 1), the canonical context which includes Lamentations, the context of Jeremiah's biography, the context of his "Word of God" theological perspective, and with reference to the lives of the members of his congregations in London in their relationship to the unfolding ecclesial and political situation in Germany. This sermon is a product of careful attention to both the biblical text and these various existential realities. The language of prayer, which will stretch on for some time in what follows, appropriately connects these various concerns.

Interestingly, he quotes the biblical text again, having done so at the end of the previous paragraph, but this time he quotes the two parts separately and does not set the text apart with quotation marks. The biblical text is inserted seamlessly into the prayer. He is expanding on the little biblical text he has found in Jer. 20:7, paraphrasing and spinning material out of the text so that he can blend the biblical text and his hearers together. The introductory section of the prayer repeats a lot of the language from the earlier part of the sermon, so it does not need to be included here, but it should be noted that the genre allows him to ramp up the personal, emotive, relational dynamic between Jeremiah and God. The interplay between divine and human action is precisely what Bonhoeffer wants to draw out. He does so by employing an image of a victory chariot that alludes to the ancient Roman practice of a general parading the spoils of victory, occupied peoples, in a parade of triumph, playing to the cheering crowds celebrating in the streets. Bonhoeffer relies on the Apostle Paul for the imagery as developed in 2 Cor. 2:14-17.[24] Also, before transitioning directly to the situation of his hearers, Bonhoeffer employs another Pauline element, this time the paradox of strength and weakness, also developed from 2 Corinthians.

The intertextuality on display here is hermeneutically significant. In a general way, the assumption that underlies this interpretive move is that Scripture is unified to such a degree that an interpreter can use Scripture to interpret Scripture. The unity assumed is not a feature of the text itself, inherent and thus objectively discoverable. Rather, the unity of Scripture becomes apparent as an interpreter

---

Biblical Hermeneutics, ed. Ralf K. Wüstenberg and Jens Zimmermann (Frankfurt am Main: Peter Lang, 2013), 55–84.

24. 2 Cor. 2:14-17:

> But thanks be to God, who always leads us as captives in Christ's triumphal procession and uses us to spread the aroma of the knowledge of him everywhere. For we are to God the pleasing aroma of Christ among those who are being saved and those who are perishing. To the one we are an aroma that brings death; to the other, an aroma that brings life. And who is equal to such a task? Unlike so many, we do not peddle the word of God for profit. On the contrary, in Christ we speak before God with sincerity, as those sent from God.

works with the assumption of a unified canon. More specifically, one relies on Luther by moving from any text of Scripture to a Pauline text because Paul stands at the center of Scripture with his clarity about justification by faith and his central focus on Christ crucified, both prominent aspects of the Lutheran theological tradition. Bonhoeffer connects Jeremiah to Paul because other texts are in the periphery in comparison to Paul's central importance. This is especially the case with Pauline paradoxes and antithesis—grace/works, strength/weakness, and, here, triumph/captive—because these forms of dialectical thinking draw out how the Christian life is understood and experienced in Bonhoeffer's tradition. At this point of the sermon, Paul is brought in to underscore how the close relationship between God and Jeremiah creates difficulties for Jeremiah. This, in a nutshell, is what Bonhoeffer wants to pick up and apply to his congregation.

The sermon now shifts. Though he has conflated time here and there in the first half of the sermon, he now turns explicitly to those gathered before him.

> Tausende von Gemeindegliedern und Pfarrern sind heute in unserer Heimatkirche in der Gefahr der Unterdrückung und Verfolgung um ihres Zeugnisses für die Wahrheit willen. Sie haben sich diesen Weg nicht aus Trotz und Willkür ausge- | sucht, sondern sie wurden diesen Weg geführt, sie mußten ihn gehen—oft gegen ihren Willen, gegen ihr Fleisch und Blut—weil Gott in ihnen zu stark geworden war, weil sie Gott nicht mehr widerstehen konnten, weil hinter ihnen ein Schloß zugefallen war, weil sie nicht mehr zurück konnten hinter Gottes Wort, Gottes Ruf, Gottes Befehl. Wie wünschten sie es oft, daß endlich Friede und Ruhe und Stille käme, wie wünschten sie oft, sie brauchten nicht immer wieder zu drohen, zu warnen, zu protestieren, die Wahrheit zu bezeugen. Aber ein Zwang liegt auf ihnen. „Weh uns, wenn wir das Evangelium nicht predigte." Gott, warum bist du uns so nah?[25]

> Thousands of church members and pastors in our home church are today in danger of oppression and persecution for the sake of their witness to the truth. They did not choose this way out of defiance and arbitrariness, rather they were led this way, they had to go in it—often against their wills, against their flesh and blood—because God had become too strong for them, because they could not resist God any longer, because a latch had fallen behind them, because they could no longer go back behind God's word, God's call, God's command. How often they wished that finally peace and calm and quiet would come, how often they wished they did not need to threaten again and again, to warn, to protest, to witness to the truth. But a compulsion lies on them. "Woe to us if we do not preach the gospel." God, why are you so near to us?

The earlier glimpses of Jeremiah as a paradigm for twentieth-century Christians are now rendered in full-orbed fashion. This paragraph concerns those living in Germany, whereas the next one is generalized to include those hearing the sermon

---

25. DBW 13:349-350.

in London. The contrast here is between, again, choice and subjection. They did not choose but God led them against their wills. Four coordinate phrases, all beginning with *weil* [because], underscore the forced nature of their situation. These are not four distinct reasons, but four phrases that, through repetition, make one point. And, again, echoing the *Wie gern hätte* [How gladly Jeremiah would have], Bonhoeffer says in two different phrases, *Wie wünschten sie es oft* [How often they wished], that those in Germany would also have hoped for a different circumstance, summed up with great emotion in the final question of the paragraph: "Gott, warum bist du uns so nah?" [God, why are you so near to us?] There is one final link between Jeremiah and those in the home church, and it is that they are all compelled. Bonhoeffer again brings Paul into the conversation, this time quoting from 1 Cor. 9:16: "For when I preach the gospel, I cannot boast, since I am compelled to preach. Woe to me if I do not preach the gospel!" This is another example of the significant role that Paul's theology is playing under the surface of Bonhoeffer's preaching. The first half of the verse is not quoted, but Bonhoeffer's comment leading to the quotation summarizes its concern with "compulsion." The second half of the verse, which he does quote, is slightly altered in order to fit the contemporary context. Paul's personal, singular reference is replaced by a corporate, plural reference. Reading these words, but not drawing attention to their source, works to ground the discourse in its influential Pauline theological world.

It is worth noting how delicate this paragraph is. Recalling the context of the sermon, Bonhoeffer is here bringing the political context into view, but he does so only in passing. He does not comment extensively and provides no specifics, whether about the group that is being oppressed or the nature of the oppression in view, but he does comment. Sermon conventions probably keep him from getting too explicit since the point of the sermon is not a commentary on public events but proclamation for encounter. But, having said that, this sermon is designed to provide a point of view for responding to the plight of those in the German church, a point of view that takes theology seriously precisely as reflection concerned with the intersection of divine and human action.

Generalizing to include his congregation's stuck-with-God state, Bonhoeffer concludes the sermon with three paragraphs, the first two again striking a dialectical note, a negative emphasis followed by a positive one, and a final paragraph serving as a closing call to action. There is a good deal of repetition found in these paragraphs, so it is not necessary to quote them in full. It is only necessary to say that Bonhoeffer creatively plays off the "god-less, without God" notion again, this time describing this reality as a constant state of disturbance for every Christian. Following God is too difficult, but that is precisely the place where God's comfort helps us.

Here are the final words of the sermon:

Daß er uns endlich an seinen Siegeswagen bände, daß wir doch, wenn auch gebunden und geschunden, an seinem Siege teilhätten! Er hat uns überredet, er ist uns zu stark geworden, er läßt uns nicht mehr los. Was kümmerten uns die Fesseln und die Bürde, was kümmerte Sünde und Leiden [und] Tod? Er hält uns fest. Er läßt uns nicht mehr. Herr, überrede uns immer neu und werde stark über uns, damit wir dir allein glauben, leben und sterben, damit wir deinen Sieg schauen.[26]

If only he would at last bind us to his victory chariot, if only we would yet partake in his victory, even as bound and oppressed! He has persuaded us, he has become too strong for us, he will not let us go. What do our fetters or our burdens matter, what do sins and sorrows and death matter? He holds us fast. He does not leave us any longer. Lord, persuade us ever anew and be stronger than us, so that we believe, live and die to you alone, so that we behold your victory.

This sermon shows just how much Bonhoeffer has been taken captive by Paul's "Thanks Be to God" in 2 Cor. 2:14. In fact, in the closing paragraphs of the sermon we again find a major clue to the interpretive frame Bonhoeffer has been using from the outset because we find even more allusions to 2 Corinthians. Beyond another reference to the triumphal procession, Bonhoeffer also draws on ch. 1 where Paul's extreme despair becomes the site for God's demonstration of greatest comfort and a place of freedom from anxiety. There is also an allusion to ch. 4 where weak vessels are used to show divine power. In a broader hermeneutical frame, it is safe to say that this sermon is an interpretation of Jer. 20:7 read through the Pauline paradox of strength and weakness as found in 2 Corinthians. Insofar as Paul sought to extend comfort and theological perspective to his hearers in Corinth, Bonhoeffer sought the same, declaring words of comfort in London, an exclamation of God's caring and comforting presence in the midst of turmoil and difficulty.

2.2. *Predigt zu I Korinther 13,13. London, Reformationsfest, 4.11.1934 [Sermon on 1 Corinthians 13:13. London, Reformation Sunday, November 4, 1934]*

2.2.1. *Biblical Text* Bonhoeffer again reproduces Luther's German biblical text. He makes no alterations to any of the wording found in the whole of ch. 13 upon which his three previous sermons were also based. The decision to simply receive Luther's text rather than alter it for his own purposes, as is the case with some texts from *Schöpfung und Fall*, is the result of his context. As a preacher, speaking within the very concrete sphere of the church, he may have wanted to affirm the biblical text that the church inherited from its tradition. This, as we saw in the previous sermon, does not mean he will not exploit ambiguities, those are just there, for Bonhoeffer, in the Hebrew and Greek and German texts as human linguistic products, but he will honor what he has been given in an effort not to undermine it. The change of context from university professor to church pastor is a factor in understanding his relation to the biblical text he preaches. Here is the biblical text:

26. DBW 13:351.

Nun aber bleibt Glaube, Hoffnung, Liebe, diese drei; aber die Liebe ist die größte unter ihnen.[27]

But now faith, hope and love remain, these three; but love is the greatest among them.

2.2.2. Bonhoeffer's Sermon On the first Sunday of the series that culminated on Reformation Sunday, the rationale for the focus on 1 Cor. 13 was offered. Three reasons were given: first, according to Bonhoeffer, the congregation in London needed to spend some time dwelling upon these words just as the congregation in Corinth needed to do so. He continues:

> Als Zweites hatte ich die besondere Lage unserer deutschen Kirchen im Auge. Ob man es sehen will oder nicht, ob man es für richtig hält oder nicht, die Kirchen stehen im Kampf um ihren Glauben, wie es seit mehreren hundert Jahren nicht mehr gewesen [ist]. Es geht um nichts anderes—ob man es für richtig hält oder nicht—als um das Bekenntnis zu Jesus Christus als dem alleinigen Herrn und Erlöser dieser Welt. Aber wer an diesem Kampf um dieses Bekenntnis innerlich und äußerlich teilnimmt, der weiß, daß solcher Glaubenskampf eine große Versuchung in sich trägt, die Versuchung der Selbstsicherheit, Selbstgerechtigkeit und Rechthaberei, d. h. aber die Versuchung der Lieblosigkeit gegen den Gegner. Und doch kann ja dieser Gegner nie wirklich überwunden werden, es sei denn durch Liebe, wie überhaupt kein Gegner überwunden wird außer durch Liebe. Vater, vergib ihnen, denn sie wissen nicht, was sie tun—wieviel Menschen sind durch dieses Wort Jesu wirklich überwunden worden! Auch über dem leidenschaftlichsten Glaubenskampf könnte ja der Satz stehen: „*... und hätte der Liebe nicht, so wäre er nichts.*"[28]

Second, I had the particular situation of our German churches in mind. Whether or not one wants to see it, whether or not one thinks it is right, the churches stand in the midst of a struggle for their faith such as we have not seen for hundreds of years. It is—whether or not one thinks it is right—about nothing else but the confession of Jesus Christ as the sole Lord and Redeemer of this world. But anyone who inwardly and outwardly joins in this struggle for this confession knows that such a struggle for faith carries a great temptation with it—the temptation of being self-assured, self-righteous and dogmatic, that is, the temptation to be unloving toward one's enemy. And yet this enemy can never truly be overcome except by love, because no enemy at all is ever overcome except through love. Father, forgive them; for they do not know what they are doing—how many people have truly been overcome by these words of Jesus! Even over the most ardent struggle for the faith could indeed stand the statement: "*... and had not love, it would be nothing.*"

This brief, though explicit, explanation grounds the sermon in the church struggle mapped in Section 1.2.2. In fact, some of the language here echoes the Barmen

27. DBW 13:399.
28. DBW 13:379, emphasis original.

Declaration's first article, and the tone and rhetoric, leading up to Reformation Day, recall the turning point represented by Luther's situation against the Roman Catholic Church of his day. One can imagine that this sermon series was definitive for Bonhoeffer and his congregation's increasing sense of ecclesial identity and, as such, an intense form of his hermeneutic. The culminating sermon, analyzed below, brings these themes together in a clear way. His third reason is that the Protestant church, though clearly proclaiming faith, needs to be reminded that speaking this word, faith in the Lord Jesus Christ alone, is really meant to be said in such a way that God is to be *loved* above all. Without this love, this church is nothing.

One additional observation about the sermons as a whole can be noted. The first three sermons are composed in slightly looser fashion, following the structure of the verses they are based on, but punctuated by greater amounts of illustrative material and, for lack of a better term, comments about "application" to the daily lives of congregants. By contrast, the final sermon is dense, finely structured, and without a lot of imaginative, illustrative material. This may be the result of Bonhoeffer's desire to draw all the threads together and thus cut out additional material. It may also arise out of the three-part nature of the text itself, leading to a clearer organizing principle for homiletical presentation. Additionally, Bonhoeffer may have felt the need for tighter argumentation on Reformation Sunday, a day with higher expectations than a typical Sunday because on this day this tradition's ecclesial identity, proclaimers of justification by faith alone, should be paramount. It was also the day, as noted above, before these congregations and other German congregations around England pledged their allegiance, not to *Reichsbischof* Müller and the German Christians, but instead to the Confessing Church. It is into this mix that Bonhoeffer planned a provocative text to be preached on Reformation Day, affirming faith alone, but emphasizing love.

This central theme is developed in the first paragraph of the sermon, which serves as both a compelling vision of Bonhoeffer's hope for his congregations and as a lead-up to the quotation of the main sermon text for the day, 1 Cor. 13:13. This is then followed by a three-part exposition of faith, hope, and love. He begins:

Mit voller Absicht haben wir unsere Predigtreihe über 1. Kor. 13 so eingerichtet, daß dieser Text auf den Reformationstag fällt.[29]

We deliberately have arranged our sermon series on 1 Corinthians 13 that this text falls on the day of the Reformation.

Two rationales provide the substantiation for this decision on Reformation Sunday. First:

Wir wollen damit sagen, daß die Kirche, die von der alleinigen Kraft und dem Heil und dem Sieg des Glaubens an Jesus Christus so geredet hat wie wohl keine

---

29. DBW 13:399.

andere, daß die Kirche, die groß ist im Glauben, noch größer sein müsse in der Liebe.[30]

We want thereby to say that the church, which has spoken unlike practically every other about the sole power and salvation and victory of faith in Jesus Christ, that the church, which is so great in faith, must yet be even greater in love.

This is a straightforward claim, but it is not stated very straightforwardly. The main point is found in the final few clauses of the sentence when "die Kirche" [the church] is repeated. The repetition is necessary because of the relative clause beginning "die von der," a clause which offers an important qualification. The second reason is also a diagnosis:

und wir wollen damit einerseits nichts anderes als zurück zur ursprünglichen Reformation, andererseits aber einer Gefahr und Entartung entgegentreten, die den Protestantismus von Anfang bedroht hat, nämlich daß die Botschaft von dem allein rettenden und erlösenden Glauben erstarrte, ein totes Wort wurde, weil sie nicht lebendig gehalten wurde durch die Liebe.[31]

And we want thereby, on the one hand nothing other than to return to the original Reformation, but on the other hand, [we want] to confront a danger and degeneration that has threatened Protestantism from the beginning, namely that the message of the faith which alone saves and redeems can become hardened, it can become a dead word, because it was not kept alive through love.

This bold and potentially controversial claim, coming right at the start of the sermon, is, Bonhoeffer claims, continuous with the Reformation. As such, he is not seeking to move away from the Reformation but back to it. Having said that though, there is a tendency identified here that also reaches back to the beginning of Protestantism, a tendency for the originating insight about faith alone to become routine or taken for granted so that new factors, like love, are not taken into account. Unearthing this tendency and transforming it is, as will become very clear throughout the sermon, the main aim for Bonhoeffer.

The general language used to this point, the language of an unspecified "faith," is given a fine point, a move that sharpens up the challenge.

Eine Kirche des Glaubens aber—und sei es | der bekenntnistreueste und orthodoxeste Glaube –, die nicht noch vielmehr Kirche der reinen und allumfassenden Liebe ist, ist nichts nütze.[32]

A church of faith—even one utterly true to its confession and the most orthodox in belief—which is not still more a church of pure and all-embracing love is worthless.

---

30. DBW 13:399.
31. DBW 13:399.
32. DBW 13:399.

Christian confessions and orthodox belief, the sort of thing one would find in the Augsburg Confession or the classical creeds of the church or, perhaps even, the Bethel Confession or Barmen Declaration, are in view here. The potential of a static or dead formulation and articulation of belief is contrasted with love, the former declared, picking up on Paul's rhetoric early on in the chapter (c.f. vv. 2-3), as worthless in light of the latter. Two rhetorical questions follow closely on the heels of this contrast, serving to point out the supposedly commonsense nature of his point.

> Was heißt es auch, an Christus glauben, der die Liebe war, und selbst noch hassen? Was heißt es, Christus seinen Herrn nennen im Glauben und seinen Willen nicht tun? Solcher Glaube ist kein Glaube, sondern er ist Heuchelei.[33]

> What does it mean to believe in Christ, who was love, and yet still hate? What does it mean to call Christ one's Lord in faith and not do his will? Such faith is not faith; it is hypocrisy.

These questions and the accusation that a faith of this sort, if it can really be called faith at all, is really just hypocrisy prepare the way for Bonhoeffer's positive vision. If a generalized faith was made specific by reference to confessions and creeds, a generalized "all-embracing love" is here made uncomfortably specific as reconciliation:

> Es nutzt keinem Menschen etwas, seinen Glauben an Christus zu beteuern, wenn er nicht zuvor hingegangen ist und sich mit seinem Bruder—auch mit dem gottlosen, rassefremden, geächteten und verstoßenen Bruder—versöhnt hat. Und die Kirche, die ein Volk zum Glauben an Christus aufruft, muß selbst in diesem Volk das brennende Feuer der Liebe sein, die Keimzelle zur Versöhnung, der Brandherd, in dem aller Haß erstickt wird und die Menschen aus Stolz und Haß zu Menschen der Liebe umgewandelt werden.[34]

> It does not profit someone to claim to have faith in Christ, unless he has first gone and reconciled with his brother—even with the godless, of another race, banned, and outcast brother. And the church which calls a people to belief in Christ must itself be, in the people, the burning fire of love, the nucleus of reconciliation, the source of the fire in which all hate is suffocated and people of pride and hate are transformed into people of love.

This language is striking. Not only is Bonhoeffer here clearly dependent on an idiom derived from the Gospels ("What does it profit a man" in Mk 8:36) and the words of Jesus in the so-called "Sermon on the Mount" concerning reconciliation with someone when presenting an offering at the altar (Mt. 5:23-24), but he specifies the kind of person one should love, "dem gottlosen, rassefremden,

33. DBW 13:399.
34. DBW 13:399-400.

geächteten und verstoßenen Bruder" [the godless, of another race, banned, and outcast brother]. Calling the church to love those of another race sits alongside the political back-and-forth of the application of the Aryan Paragraph. The intensity of the situation demanded Bonhoeffer's vivid and violent imagery. He wants to heighten the sensitivity of what this vision of radical reconciliation looks like in his congregations, but also, Luther-like, in the German Evangelical Church as a whole.

After the substantive introduction, he begins working through faith, hope, and love, following Paul's order, which incidentally begins where Reformation faith typically does and should if it claims to be in line with that tradition, but moves to the emphasis Bonhoeffer wants this sermon to have (which is, again, Paul's emphasis too, c.f. 1 Cor. 13:13b, and see below). First the text, 1 Cor. 13:13a, then his comments:

Nun aber bleibt Glaube, Hoffnung, Liebe, diese drei.[35]

But now faith, hope, and love remain, these three.

„Glaube"—das heißt ja nun freilich, daß kein Mensch und keine Kirche von der Größe ihrer eigenen Taten leben kann, sondern daß sie allein von der großen Tat leben, die Gott selbst tut und getan hat, und (das ist nun das Entscheidende) die großen Taten Gottes bleiben ungesehen, verborgen in der Welt.[36]

"Faith"—that certainly means that no person and no church can live by the greatest of their own deeds, but rather that they live only by the great deed, which God himself does and has done, and (this is the crucial thing) the great deeds of God remain unseen, hidden in the world.

The structure of 1 Cor. 13:13a constrains the shape of Bonhoeffer's comments, since he starts with *Glaube* [faith], setting it out by quotation marks and then, leaving out "hope and love" for the moment, connects *Glaube* to the word *bleibt* [remains]. Paul is saying that "faith, hope, and love remain," but to say that is also to say that faith considered by itself remains. What this faith is and how it remains is the burden of Bonhoeffer's exposition, even if he does not go out of his way to indicate this by the structure of the sermon itself. There are not breaks by which one could recognize each part being developed but rather we encounter one long paragraph. What Bonhoeffer does here is insert the phrase "das ist nun das Entscheidende" [this is the crucial thing] in parenthesis, underscoring just what aspect of divine action he is interested in developing. This sentence encapsulates both aspects of Bonhoeffer's version of faith remaining: faith means living by God's deed rather than one's own, and God's deeds are invisible.

Three sentences unfold what faith means:

Es ist eben mit der Kirche nicht so, wie es in der Welt und in der Geschichte der Völker ist, daß es letztlich darauf ankäme, auf große Taten hinweisen zu

35. DBW 13:400.
36. DBW 13:400.

können—die Kirche, die das versucht, wäre schon längst den Gesetzen und den Mächten dieser Welt verfallen, die *Kirche des Erfolges* ist wahrhaftig noch lange nicht die *Kirche des Glaubens.* Die Tat, die Gott in dieser Welt getan hat und von der seitdem alle Welt lebt—heißt das Kreuz von Golgatha. Das sind Gottes „Erfolge", und so werden die Erfolge der Kirche und des | Einzelnen aussehen, wenn sie Taten des Glaubens sind.[37]

In the world and in the history of nations, it is very important to be able to point out great deeds, but it is just not like that with the church; the church that tries to do that would have already, long ago, fallen prey to the laws and powers of this world; the *church of success* is truly in no way the *church of faith.* The action that God has done in the world and from which ever since all the world lives is called the cross of Golgatha. God's "successes" are like that, and the successes of the church and the individual will look like that, if they are acts of faith.

The Reformation church's achievement is here relativized, but this time it comes by associating boasting about great deeds with laws and powers of the world, which means that such boasting marks out a church as, employing letter spacing for emphasis, a church of success. This is a powerful statement. The contrast is sharpened up by the cross, an event which has, in a very subtle development in the paragraph, become *the* deed of God (rather than deeds, plural, as in the introductory sentence just before this), the criterion by which success is judged, and the chief event to which one can point when one wants to talk about invisible divine action.

The rest of the paragraph is concerned with this invisibility, and as such it is an attempt to explain how faith remains:

Daß der Glaube bleibt—das heißt, daß es wahr bleibt, *daß der Mensch vom Unsichtbaren leben muß,* daß er nicht von seinem sichtbaren Werk, sondern von der unsichtbaren Tat Gottes lebt.[38]

That faith remains—that means that it remains true *that a person must live by the invisible*, that one does not live by his visible work, but rather lives by the invisible act of God.

This initial statement brings his comments on "faith" and his comments on "remains," again both textual deposits, together in one sentence. "Remaining" is equated with living, a dynamic reality, textually derived by the present tense of the verb and linked to a dynamism of faith's object being God's past and present action, and invisible is equated with faith. Again, he uses *Sperrsatz* to set a specific phrase apart, and this very brief, summary expression serves to emphasize how these two points relate to one another. This concise formulation gets some texture:

37. DBW 13:400, emphasis original.
38. DBW 13:400, emphasis original.

Er sieht Irrtum und er glaubt Wahrheit, er sieht Schuld und er glaubt Vergebung, er sieht Sterben und er glaubt ewiges Leben, er sieht nichts—und er glaubt die Tat und die Gnade Gottes. „Laß dir an meiner Gnade genügen, denn meine Kraft ist in den Schwachen mächtig"[39]

He sees error and he believes in truth, he sees guilt and he believes in forgiveness, he sees death and he believes in eternal life, he sees nothing—and he believes the act and the grace of God. "Let my grace suffice for you, for my power is mighty in the weak person."

Here is repetition, but repetition with variation. Four different pairs—error/truth, guilt/forgiveness, death/eternal life, nothing/God's action—are spoken of with the same structure, sees but believes. Each element in the first half of each pair—error, guilt, death, and nothing—can be seen, they are visible to a degree (even "nothing," which stands in for all the common place occurrences observed in one's life), while every element in the second half of each pair—truth, forgiveness, eternal life, and God's action—is invisible. An additional word is brought in at this point to describe God's action, grace, and it prompts the unreferenced quotation of 2 Cor. 12:9. The verse acts like a pivot, moving, on the one hand, back to the reference to grace, but on the other hand, it also moves forward to ground the identity of the Reformation church.

Und so ist es mit der reformatorischen Kirche. Sie lebt nie und nimmer von ihrer Tat, auch nicht von ihrer Liebestat, sondern sie lebt von dem, was sie nicht sieht und doch glaubt—sie sieht Verhängnis und sie glaubt Errettung, sie sieht Irrlehre und sie glaubt Gottes Wahrheit, sie sieht Verrat am Evangelium und sie glaubt die Treue Gottes.[40]

And so it is with the Reformation church. It never lives from its own deed, not even from its act of love, but rather it lives by that which it does not see and yet believes—it sees doom and it believes in salvation, it sees false teaching and it believes God's truth, it sees betrayal of the gospel and it believes in the faithfulness of God.

God's power and grace, rather than the quantity or quality of the church's or an individual's actions (including the sermon's theme, love, and thus relativizing it slightly as well), sustain the life of believers and the life of the church. Three more pairs of "sees but believes" provide further rhetorical interest and texture to the potentially ambiguous notions of faith and invisibility.

He concludes the section devoted to "faith remains":

Die reformatorische Kirche ist niemals die sichtbare Gemeinschaft der Heiligen, sondern die Sünderkirche, die gegen allen Schein an die Gnade glaubt und von

---

39. DBW 13:400.
40. DBW 13:400-401.

ihr allein lebt. „Heraus aus der Kirche, wer ein Heiliger sein will" hat Luther einmal gerufen. Sünderkirche—Gnadenkirche—Glaubenskirche—das ist es. „Nun aber bleibet Glaube"—weil er vor Gott und von Gott allein lebt. Es gibt nur eine Sünde, und die heißt, ohne Glauben zu leben.[41]

The Reformation church is never the visible community of the saints, but rather the church of sinners, which believes, against all appearances, in grace and lives by it alone. "If you want to be a saint, get out of the church," Luther once exclaimed. A church of sinners, a church of grace, a church of faith—that is what it is all about. "But now faith remains"—because it lives before God and from God alone. There is only one sin, and that is to live without faith.

This is a fabulous summary. He pulls together the two threads with which he started, emphasizing faith as that which is grounded in God's action, divine initiative, but that action moves forward invisibly. He then connects this to his main vision. The dynamic of faith invisibility shapes the Reformation church as precisely a church of sinners, but also a church of grace and faith because it is a church that lives from and before God. All of this is then related back to the biblical text of 1 Cor. 13:13a. As a result, this, especially with a stark and controversial quote from Luther thrown in, is what one could expect from a sermon delivered by a German Evangelical Church pastor on Reformation Day. Faith is, though, not everything Bonhoeffer, or Paul for that matter, has to say.

"Hope" comes next in the text of 1 Cor. 13:13a and thus next in the sermon:

Aber ein Glaube, der sich mutig an das Unsichtbare hält und von ihm lebt, als wäre es schon da, hofft zugleich auf die Zeit der Erfüllung und des Schauens und des Habens.[42]

But a faith that courageously holds to the invisible and lives by it, as if it were already here, hopes at the same time for the time of fulfillment and of sight and possession.

Holding on to God through faith does not exclude hope, hope specifically for fulfillment, sight, and possession. Faith and hope go together in material terms, but also as given in the biblical text. Bonhoeffer uses three short illustrations to draw this out, a hungry child waiting for food, a patient listener holding on through dissonant sections of a piece of music, and an ill person waiting for medicine. The point he seeks to make with these illustrations is that hope, theologically considered and linked together to faith, is rooted in everyday life. Hope, rather than having its own solo focus, is being developed in reference to faith, the point being that a hope that is not grounded in faith is not hope at all, but conversely a faith that is not looking forward to sight is perverse.

41. DBW 13:401.
42. DBW 13:401.

Having made this point, the emphasis shifts from the relation between faith and hope to a unique implication of hope itself.

Und es ist keine Schande zu hoffen, grenzenlos zu hoffen.[43]

And it is not shameful to hope, to hope without limits.

The negatively stated point is made without indicating what exactly it is directed against, but one can imagine Bonhoeffer here envisioning an interlocutor pushing back against one who hopes for the invisible action of God to be visible one day. A potential emotional response to this challenge could be shame, since a _grenzenlos_ [boundless] hope or optimism could make one look dumb or silly. In the face of this imagined objection, Bonhoeffer asks five rhetorical questions designed to point out the absurdity of the objection:

Wer wollte auch von Gott reden, ohne zu hoffen. Wer wollte auch von Gott reden, ohne zu hoffen, ihn einmal zu schauen? Wer wollte von Frieden und von der Liebe unter den Menschen reden, ohne sie einmal in Ewigkeit erleben zu wollen? Wer wollte von einer neuen Welt und einer neuen Menschheit reden, ohne zu hoffen, daß er an ihr teilhaben werde? Und warum sollen wir uns unserer Hoffnung schämen?[44]

Who would want to talk about God without hope? Who would want to talk about God without hoping to see him someday? Who would want to talk about peace and love among humanity without wanting to experience it someday in eternity? Who would want to talk about a new world and a new humanity without hoping that he would participate in it? So, why should we be ashamed of our hope?

The supposedly obvious answer to the first four questions is, "No one." Positively stated, everyone who talks about God would want to see him and everyone who talks about a loving and peaceful humanity or a new world would want to live that kind of human life in that new world. Since this is the case, the obvious answer to the final question is negative as well. We should not be ashamed of our hope because intrinsic to this sort of speech is an expectation of it becoming reality. These questions are meant to work his congregation to this conclusion, which he then states explicitly. But, there is a twist:

Nicht unserer Hoffnungen werden wir uns einstmals zu schämen haben, sondern unsrer ärmlichen und ängstlichen Hoffnungslosigkeit, die Gott nichts zutraut, die in falscher Demut nicht zugreift, wo Gottes Verheißungen gegeben sind, die resigniert in diesem Leben und sich nicht freuen kann auf Gottes ewige Macht und Herrlichkeit.[45]

43. DBW 13:401.
44. DBW 13:401.
45. DBW 13:401-402.

We are not to be ashamed of our hopes on that day, but rather our miserable and fearful hopelessness, which trusts God for nothing, which in false humility does not take hold where God's promises are given, which resigns itself to this life alone and cannot rejoice in God's eternal power and glory.

There is reason for shame, but not in quite the way it was first presented. Moving back to the link with faith, Bonhoeffer says that hope, by itself, is actually hopelessness because it is not rooted in trusting God, believing the promises God has given and rejoicing in God's eternal power. The only hope worth the name is a theological hope. This is not ignorant or escapist optimism, but hope in God. Hope, a hope that reaches toward God and thus beyond the limit set by death, is not embarrassing in a modern world, but integral to Christian faith.

The confidence of all this leads to the conclusion of the section on hope:

"Wir heißen Euch hoffen!"—"Hoffnung läßt nicht zuschanden werden." Je mehr ein Mensch zu hoffen wagt, desto größer wird er mit seiner Hoffnung: Der Mensch wächst mit seiner Hoffnung—wenn es nur die Hoffnung auf Gott und seine alleinige Kraft ist. Die Hoffnung bleibt.[46]

"We call you to hope!" "Hope will not allow itself to be ashamed." The more a person dares to hope, the greater he will become with his hope: the person grows with his hope—if only it is hope in God and in his sole power. Hope remains.

Goethe ("Symbolum," 1815) and Paul (Rom. 5:5) ground—without any citation in the text of the sermon, which may or may not mean he said their names while preaching, but if he did not cite them then these words would have been, at least to the congregation, Bonhoeffer's own, so to speak—the foregoing and continue the exhortation to Christian hope in relation to faith.[47] Hope, as long as it is hope in God, moves from lesser to greater, actually causing a Christian to grow with his or her hope. This dynamic, changing, growing quality of hope is derived from the fact that, as the text says and he says to conclude, "Die Hoffnung bleibt" [Hope remains].

After dealing with that which is given him in the text, faith and hope, he quotes the biblical text again as a transition to the final element in the triad, love.

Nun aber bleibt Glaube, Hoffnung, Liebe, diese drei. Aber die Liebe ist die größeste unter ihnen.[48]

But now faith, hope and love remain, these three; but love is the greatest among them.

---

46. DBW 13:402.

47. Romans 5:5: "And hope does not put us to shame, because God's love has been poured out into our hearts through the Holy Spirit, who has been given to us."

48. DBW 13:402.

The last section is what Bonhoeffer has been aiming at all along in the sermon, and not in just this sermon, but the whole four-week series. This broader aim causes him to connect what he is about to say with where the congregation started. He takes them back to the beginning of 1 Cor. 13:2, but he also expands that text, drawing out what is implicit in Paul's text, to support his sermon as it develops.

Noch einmal klingt es aus den ersten Versen des Kapitels nach:

> und wenn ich allen Glauben hätte, also daß ich Berge versetzte—und wir fügen hinzu: wenn ich alle Hoffnung hätte—und hätte der Liebe nicht, so wäre ich nichts. Denn die Liebe ist die größeste unter ihnen.[49]

Once again it rings out from the first verses of the chapter:

> And if I have all faith, so that I can move mountains—and we could add: if I have all hope—"and have not love, then I am nothing." Because love is the greatest among them.

Borrowing Paul's "if x, but not y, then z" structure from 1 Cor. 13:2, but adding an additional "x" to it, Bonhoeffer connects the beginning and end of the chapter by drawing attention to the rationale for Paul's statement. One could rightly wonder why having effective faith and hope without love would make someone nothing. The reason, not spelled out by Paul in v. 2 but instead held at bay until the final line of v. 13, is that love is greater than both faith and hope. His burden in the final section of the sermon, the section finally devoted to love, but the climax only insofar as it is Paul's third point, is to flesh out precisely how this is so.

He begins developing his emphasis on love with a favorite technique, a string of rhetorical questions followed by some staccato responses (and in two cases some biblical warrants). This pattern can be seen several times in the section:

> Was kann größer sein, als sein Leben im Glauben *vor* Gott leben? Was kann größer sein, als sein Leben *zu* Gott *hin* leben? Größer ist die Liebe, die *in Gott* lebt. „Wandle *vor* mir!" „Wer in der Liebe bleibt, [bleibt] *in* ihm."[50]

> What can be greater than to live one's life in faith *before* God? What can be greater than to lives one's life *towards* God? Greater is the love that lives *in* God. "Walk before me!" "He who abides in love, abides in him."

The key word making these questions of comparison work is *größer*. In this first set of questions and answer, the distinctions are made by emphasizing prepositions. Faith *before* God, and, though the word is not present, hope *toward* God are contrasted with love living *in* God. The preposition "in" is greater. It is greater to

---

49. DBW 13:402.
50. DBW 13:402, emphasis original.

live in God since, presumably, that reality is love, is God himself.[51] The contrasting prepositions, which serve to unpack the way that love can be called "greater" by Paul, are then linked to supplemental passages of Scripture. The first, "Walk before me!," is taken from Gen. 17:1, a famous Abraham and faith passage.[52] Here the "before" is contrasted with 1 Jn 4:16, in which abiding in love is an abiding "in him."[53] Abraham's faith could only be "before" God, but the Christian's love is "in" God.

In another instance of the question–answer pattern, specific, positive elements of faith and hope are spoken about, the humility of faith paired, interestingly, with a kind of opposite, the confidence of faith, as well as the consequences that arise from them. Greater though than the distance between God and creatures (faith) or between current and future experience (hope) is the nearness of God's love. Improving on Paul's lack of description, Bonhoeffer suggests that love is greater because, rather than dividing or deferring, it produces and is produced by selflessness between humans and God.

> Was ist größer als der Glaube, der sein Heil in Christus erhofft und festhält und von ihm gerechtfertigt wird, was ist größer als die Hoffnung, die sich Stunde um Stunde auf ein seliges Sterben und Heimgehen richtet?—größer ist nur die dienende Liebe, die für die anderen alles vergißt, die sogar das eigene Heil hergibt, um es den Brüdern zu bringen—denn wer seine Liebe verliert um meinetwillen, der wird sie gewinnen.[54]

> What is greater than faith, which hopes for and holds fast to its salvation in Christ and is justified by him, what is greater than hope, which is focused hour by hour on a blessed death and a return home? Greater is only the serving-love, which forgets everything for the other, which even gives up its own salvation in order to bring it to its brothers—because he who loses his love for my sake, that one will win it.

The final instance of the pattern transitions from love for God (intimate, relational) to love for neighbor (serving), to put it in dominical terms (cf. Mk 12:30-31). Faith and hope both are concerned with one's own salvation and one's own longing for life after death, but love is greater because it serves others. The language

51. It is possible to discern a trinitarian shape to this section, linking one's stance before the Father, in the Son, and toward a future that can only take shape by the Spirit's inclusion of the believer in the life of the Triune God. Bonhoeffer does not speak in these terms explicitly, but I think his theological tradition has given him an implicit conceptually that situates him here (and not only his tradition, but the Triune God himself).

52. Genesis 17:1: "When Abram was ninety-nine years old, the LORD appeared to him and said, 'I am God Almighty; walk before me faithfully and be blameless.'"

53. 1 John 4:16: "And so we know and rely on the love God has for us. God is love. Whoever lives in love lives in God, and God in them."

54. DBW 13:402.

Bonhoeffer uses to make this point is very extreme, borrowing from the intense words of Paul in Rom. 9 where he speaks of being damned so that fellow Jews could experience salvation in Christ, but additionally he draws on Jesus' words in Mt. 10:39 ("whoever loses their life for my sake will find it") but switches out life for love, connecting it more closely to his theme. The overall effect of the three-fold pattern is to provide reasons why love is the greatest of Paul's triad.

Love simply is the greatest, but having drawn all this out, he would not want to give the impression that, contrary to what he has just been preaching about, faith and hope do not remain and are not themselves still great. As a result of this worry, he moves back to faith and hope for the next two paragraphs, but his return to consider them now happens in the light of the greater nature of love. The major point here is the fact that faith and hope are both unfulfilled, whereas love is fulfilled. The eschatological thrust of 1 Cor. 13 (especially vv. 8-12) is leavening Bonhoeffer's entire way of thinking and preaching here.

> Es bleiben Glaube und Hoffnung. Daß nicht einer meine, er könne die Liebe haben ohne den Glauben und ohne Hoffnung! Liebe ohne Glauben [ist] wie [ein] Strom ohne Quelle. Das hieße ja, er könne die Liebe haben ohne Christus. *Der Glaube allein rechtfertigt* vor Gott, die Hoffnung richtet uns aufs Ende hin, die Liebe vollendet.[55]

> Faith and hope remain. Let no one think one could have love without faith and without hope! Love without faith is like a stream without a source. Indeed, that would mean one could have love without Christ. *Faith alone justifies* before God, hope directs us towards the end, love perfects.

The point here is, again, the interconnected nature of faith, hope, and love. They must be taken together, and this is because of the central place of Christ, who in the earlier sermon on vv. 4-7 was simply called Love.[56] The sequence represented by the simile of stream and source is transposed into a chronology in the final sentence. Faith and then hope and then love; this is eschatology again.

In order to avoid the implication that good eschatology, with its final note about the perfection of love, could dislocate the importance of faith (especially on Reformation Sunday!), Bonhoeffer again seeks to emphasize the heart of Protestant belief, so that each element of the triad is taken *together*. One can feel the dialectical tensions here. On the one hand, Bonhoeffer is trying to correct a tendency to overemphasize right belief at the expense of love and to do so by careful attention to the concerns Paul sets before him in the text of 1 Cor. 13, namely the nature of love as greater, but on the other hand, he wants to stay true to his congregation's tradition as well as the interdependence of the text's triadic structure and eschatology. This is a difficult job, one that calls for the back-and-forth unfolding here.

55. DBW 13:402-403, emphasis original.
56. See DBW 13:393; DBWE 13:387.

Der Glaube allein rechtfertigt—auf diesem Satz ist unsere protestantische Kirche erbaut. Auf die Frage des Menschen: wie kann ich vor Gott bestehen? fand Luther in der Bibel als einzige Antwort: indem Du seiner Gnade und Barmherzigkeit in Jesus Christus glaubst. Auf die Frage, wie der Mensch vor Gott rechtfertig werde, heißt die Antwort: durch Gnade allein, durch Glauben allein.—Wir können daher hier am Ende mit allem Recht den Satz unseres Kapitels auch umdrehen und sagen:—*und wenn ich alle Liebe hätte, sodaß ich alle guten Werke vollbrächte* und hätte *den Glauben* nicht, so wäre ich nichts. Der Glaube allein rechtfertigt—aber die Liebe vollendet.[57]

Faith alone justifies—our Protestant church is built on this statement. On humanity's question, "How can I stand before God?" Luther found a single answer in the Bible: in that you believe in his grace and mercy in Jesus Christ. On the question, "how a person can become justified before God," the answer is: through grace alone, through faith alone. Therefore, we are entirely justified, here at the end, to reverse the sentence of our chapter and say: "*and if I have all love, so that I could do all good works* and have not *faith*, then I am nothing." Faith alone justifies—but love perfects.

At the beginning of the section of the sermon in which he turned from faith and hope to love, he referred back to 1 Cor. 13:2. He does so again here, but this time rather than stick with Paul's text as he did earlier (notwithstanding the insertion of "hope" above), he rewrites Paul's text, flipping the construction around. If a person loves, thus demonstrating actions appropriate as the outcome of faith (cf. Eph. 2:10), but does not have faith, and we are back to the stream and source analogy above, then he or she is nothing. So, again, faith and love are in a mutually interdependent relationship—"Der Glaube allein rechtfertigt—aber die Liebe vollendet" [Faith alone justifies—but love perfects]—but it is a relationship in which the unfulfilled nature of faith is only ever fulfilled or perfected in love.

The unfulfilled/fulfilled dynamic that has been developing under the surface of the previous few paragraphs is finally made explicit:

Glaube und Hoffnung gehen in die Ewigkeit ein in der verwandelten Gestalt der Liebe. Es muß am Ende alles Liebe werden. Vollendung heißt Liebe.[58]

Faith and hope are taken up into eternity in the transformed form of love. In the end, everything must become love. Perfection means love.

But this synthesis is quickly qualified:

Aber das Zeichen der Vollendung in dieser Welt heißt Kreuz. Das ist der Weg, den die vollendete Liebe in dieser Welt gehen muß und | immer wieder gehen wird.[59]

57. DBW 13:403, emphasis original.
58. DBW 13:403.
59. DBW 13:403.

However, the sign of perfection in this world is the cross. That is the way which perfect love must go in this world, and will go again and again.

This takes the hearer back to the earlier section of the sermon, where the cross of Golgotha served as the criterion for evaluating success. Two deferred implications of that earlier discussion, now refracted through the exposition of the interrelationship of faith, hope, and love, are now registered:

Das aber zeigt uns erstens, daß diese Welt reif ist zum Abbruch, überreif; daß es nur Gottes unbeschreibliche Geduld ist, die noch wartet bis zum Ende. Zweitens, daß die Kirche in dieser Welt Kirche unter dem Kreuz bleibt. Besonders die Kirche, die Kirche der sichtbaren Herrlichkeit schon hier werden will, sie hat ihren Herrn am Kreuz verleugnet.[60]

But this shows us, first, that this world is ripe for destruction, overripe; that it is only God's indescribable patience that still waits until the end. Second, that the church in this world remains the church under the cross. In particular, the church that wants to become a church already possessing—here and now—its own visible glory, has denied her Lord on the cross.

Since perfect love is marked by the way of the cross, then future expectation should be characterized by judgment rather than an assumption about simple progress toward perfection. That destruction is on the horizon, held back only by, alluding to Rom. 2 and 2 Pet. 3, God's patience. But also, a church that looks to be hugely impressive as an institution is to be a church that has denied Jesus.

The complicated, back-and-forth, nature of Bonhoeffer's preaching, relativizing, and qualifying with every other paragraph leads to the following concise and helpful formulation. "Glaube, Hoffnung, Liebe führen allesamt durchs Kreuz zur Vollendung" [Faith, hope and love together lead through cross to perfection].[61] The sermon's conclusion rightly turns to the situation of the church in their context. Bonhoeffer's vision of a theology of glory contrasted with a theology of the cross leads to a firm and uncompromising conviction about a corresponding false and true church. This is the sort of conviction that would lead, the next day, to the separation of the German congregations in England from the German Evangelical Church. The world longs for faith (because it is disillusioned), hope (because it is wounded), and love (because it is divided), and the church is in a position to demonstrate faith, hope, and love to them. As a result, the message for Reformation Day, what this congregation needs to hear on this particular Reformation Day in November 1934, is that they must, for the sake of the world, have faith, hope, and love, and following Paul's words, though interpreting rather than simply repeating them, they must love.

60. DBW 13:403.
61. DBW 13:403.

3. Synthesis

This chapter has provided evidence to support the argument that the interpretive vision from 1925 governs Bonhoeffer's hermeneutical decisions while a pastor in London from 1933 to 1935. The strategy has been to show the specific way that Bonhoeffer interprets the biblical text by tracing the relation between the specific texts, Jer. 20:7 and 1 Cor. 13:13, and Bonhoeffer's comments in sermon form. As was the case in the last chapter, the length and detail of the analysis demand a summary, which should aid in the attempt, undertaken in the conclusion, to reflect on Bonhoeffer's interpretation more holistically. In these sermons, he moved from text to comment by employing the following:

1) He exploits textual ambiguity, allowing the various possibilities opened up by Luther's translation to play off one another. The juxtaposition of intimate and violent themes in the sermon on Jer. 20:7 was so powerful, partly because a variety of nuances were able to texture the exposition rather than force a choice that would have limited the potential found *within* the Hebrew text.

2) Various theological perspectives or frameworks play a significant role in drawing out meaning: Pauline theology (Paul stands closest to the *Sache* of Scripture even though he is not identical to it), the theology of the cross *vs.* a theology of glory, the Lutheran tradition, and the "Word of God" theology that Bonhoeffer has developed by his time in London and is developing through preaching on a text like Jer. 20:7.

3) A biblical text's implications will be drawn out through expansion and paraphrase, as in the case of Jeremiah's lengthy, imagined prayer in the middle of the sermon. This process allows Bonhoeffer to engage the imagination, while driving toward his main idea. In addition, grounding these texts in specific, imagined, and expansive interchanges allows the historically grounded nature of the biblical text to arise.

4) Bonhoeffer regularly employs other biblical texts, by quoting them (the spate of 1 and 2 Corinthians references throughout both sermons) or alluding to them (as was the case with Paul's language borrowed, but not cited, from Romans 9).

5) Contrasts often serve to sharpen up the point that he is seeking to underscore in the biblical text. For Jeremiah, the word of God comes from outside, *not* from the innermost place of desire. This contrast, stated in a number of times and in slightly different ways, contours the hearers' thoughts, creating expectations for their own reception of the call or word of God.

6) Time is conflated in order to make Jeremiah paradigmatic or to relate the need of the Corinthians with the need of Bonhoeffer's German congregations in London.

7) A back-and-forth rhetoric, qualifying at one moment and relativizing the next, is derived from both the theological context within which Bonhoeffer was developed and from the biblical text itself. Again, the two aspects emphasized in Jer. 20:7a and 20:7b, as well as the interplay between faith and love in 1 Cor. 13:13, demand and thus produce the rhetoric.

8) In the case of the sermon on 1 Cor. 13:13, the biblical text provided the outline for the sermon: a section on faith, one on hope, and a final segment devoted to love in relation to the previous two.

9) Rhetorical questions and answers often serve to draw out elements that can be read, by Bonhoeffer at least, between the lines. The pattern discovered in the 1 Corinthians sermon, three sets of questions/answers, perfectly displayed this technique. In addition, the thrice repeated "How gladly" in the Jeremiah sermon served to adapt various story points, transposing them into a hypothetical scenario accessible to the hearers. Related to this, hypothetical objections or responses help to frame issues or texture them.

10) Repetition is a constant in Bonhoeffer's rhetoric. Returning to the theme of Jeremiah's stuck-with-God status, Bonhoeffer speaks of Jeremiah being controlled and possessed by God, but this is stated in a four-part structure, developed through repetition, which both drives it home, but also the phrase, when stated in reverse or with a new preposition, sheds new light on the meaning.

11) Vivid imagery, derived from the text, is employed: hunted game, lasso, pain from a prisoner's struggle against his bonds, victory chariot and triumphal procession, fire burning off hate in the transformation to love.

12) On occasion in these sermons, an illustration or simile or analogy shows up, and in most instances they serve simply to add some color, intriguing the listener and regaining attention: a hungry child, a patient music listener, an ill person, etc. These illustrations are not often doing a lot of conceptual work. They serve as a more engaging and subtle form of repetition.

13) He uses a number of ways of indicating importance, whether through *Sperrsatz* at crucial points, or the inclusion of a parenthetical statement, or by using quotation marks, which will set off either a quotation from a non-biblical source or be used to cite other biblical texts.

14) At a broader level, numbers seven through thirteen are the product of sermon conventions, that is, built in features of the genre, and Bonhoeffer's unique, skilled way of utilizing these features. If one uses a form, like the sermon, and wants listeners or readers who have experienced the form many times before to follow along, then one needs to stick to familiar structures and conventions given by the genre. The originality is to be found in sticking to the form even while it is slightly adapted. These sermons have all the marks of Bonhoeffer's time and place and style, but they are also representative of the conventions already present in the sermon form itself.

Before proceeding in the next chapter to analyze the mature hermeneutical vision expressed in 1935, it would also be helpful at this point to link in an explicit manner the concluding remarks of the 19-year-old Bonhoeffer on dogmatics and preaching, but to consider them now with the contexts and the particular interpretive exercises described in this and the previous chapter.

In the final paragraph of the essay on pneumatological interpretation of Scripture, Bonhoeffer provides legitimation for the exercise of Christian dogmatics and the act of preaching. Dogmatics (an activity Bonhoeffer undertook while at Berlin University) and preaching (one of the major tasks of his London pastorate) affirm that the historical elements cannot be eliminated but rather are oriented by the concerns of revelation. He envisaged an interpreter as one who speaks for the benefit of others, which means that the theologian and the preacher, or the theologian *as* preacher, both have God's revelation in history as the object of their reflections. This entails a proper relation of that revelation to Scripture as witness, but this dynamic is not engaged as an end in itself. Rather, it is engaged expressly for the sake of contemporary communication that should hopefully result in new ways of thinking and acting, new ways of being faithful. This is to say, in a different and more abstract idiom, the theological and hermeneutical framework developed in the paper from 1925 serves as a constant, as Bonhoeffer's form of interpretation through the first half of the 1930s.

Chapter 4

INTERLUDE: REFRAMING INTERPRETATION

This chapter serves as a pivot point, or in the language used in the introduction this is an interlude, a pause between various acts of interpretation. Taking stock at this stage will include an exposition of the content of Bonhoeffer's lecture of 1935, "Vergegenwärtigung neutestamentlicher Texte" [Contemporizing New Testament Texts], but this will be done in conversation with the offering from 1925 on Pneumatological Interpretation of Scripture (Section 2). The argument is that the *Vergegenwärtigung* lecture affords an opportunity to notice an increase of texturing in Bonhoeffer's reflections on Scripture and its interpretation, and this is the result of the biblical work in the first half of the decade and serves as a gathering point that pushes him forward into more of the same in the second half of the decade. The term "texture" here denotes tactile features in a piece of work, a metaphorical perception of raised or rough surfaces accomplished through a combination of different elements. In Bonhoeffer's biblical interpretation, this texturing happens when abstract notions are refined through consideration of particulars or when multiple facets of a whole are given their due recognition as contributors to the whole. Texturing in this way complicates the smoothness of the surface, so that the details of interpretive effort provide depth and thickness to his interpretive activity.

What we are witnessing, then, is development, the vindication of positioning the 1925 essay as the proper starting point for thinking about Bonhoeffer's relation to the Bible. But the notion of a starting point assumes a continual process of movement or development, and this is precisely what we find when we trace the relation between the more theoretical statements and their embodiment in textual interpretation and in the contingencies of history. The exposition will be preceded by a description of the historical setting of Bonhoeffer's lecture (Section 1), and a final synthetic section will complete the chapter (Section 3), pulling several threads together and serving as a transition into the analysis of *Nachfolge* in the next chapter.

1. Preliminaries

1.1. From London to Finkenwalde

The move from a pastorate in London to directing the preacher's seminary at Finkenwalde was not a straightforward one. This was partly due to Bonhoeffer's independence and partly due to the process of the Confessing Church forming its own educational systems and infrastructures for training pastors. Bonhoeffer first heard about and expressed interest in the Confessing Church's plans to offer "illegal" training for their pastors in June 1934.[1] It was an appealing prospect, since pastoral ministry in London was fulfilling and utilized some of his gifts, but he was also regularly feeling the desire to teach theology. In addition, though his post as a pastor was never disconnected from the ongoing church situation in Germany, he wanted to be in a more strategic position with respect to the Confessing Church. One month later, in July, he was appointed by the Old Prussian Council of the Confessing Church to take up the position of director for the Berlin-Brandenburg seminary planned to be held in Düsseldorf effective January 1, 1935.[2]

Bonhoeffer accepted the position, but he would come in his own way and in his own time. One condition of his acceptance was that he would not begin until the spring of 1935, rather than in January. There were two reasons for this timeline. He wanted to be sure that the congregations he had been responsible for were properly taken care of before his departure. He also wanted to visit various communities that could serve as analogues to the type of community he wanted to develop at his preacher's seminary. He and his London friend and fellow pastor, Julius Rieger, visited a number of denominational seminaries as well as some Anglican monastic communities, including the Society of St. John the Evangelist in Oxford, the Society of the Resurrection in Mirfield, and the Society of the Sacred Mission in Kelham.[3] After acquiring many insights and patterns for community life from these various expressions, Bonhoeffer moved back to Germany to begin his leadership of the seminary.

The launching of these seminaries (in the end there were five of them operating) was a new endeavor for the Confessing Church, which meant that effort was being extended by already overly taxed pastors and that this effort was to be undertaken as wisely as possible, since it was, again, an illegal effort. When Bonhoeffer and the students finally arrived to begin their work they discovered that a suitable

---

1. This was illegal from the start because the consolidation and establishment of the Confessing Church and its organizational structures, including these newly developed training institutions, happened apart from the jurisdiction of the German Evangelical Church. Practically, this meant no financial underwriting from the government, a privilege other preachers' seminaries connected to the State church would enjoy, and eventually outright legal opposition. See Klaus Scholder, *The Churches and the Third Reich*, 2 vol., Eng. trans. John Bowden (London: SCM Press, 1987).

2. Bethge, *Bonhoeffer*, 411.

3. Schlingensiepen, *Dietrich Bonhoeffer*, 175.

site was not yet established. The plans to locate the seminary in Düsseldorf were changed because proximity to such a populated region could increase contact with the *Gestapo*. A different location became available in a temporary capacity, so the seminary began meeting in Zingst on the Baltic Sea before eventually relocating a couple of months later to the more permanent Finkenwalde site (situated near the seaport of Stettin in the east in upper Pomerania).[4] The first course ran from April 26, 1935, through October 16, 1935, and it was populated by a number of young and excited seminarians, many of whom already had an acquaintance with Bonhoeffer from his time in Berlin. Settling into their new living situation and community rhythms, the experiment began for Bonhoeffer and the Finkenwalde Preacher's Seminary.

1.2. Bonhoeffer's Emotional State

In order to understand the significance of Finkenwalde for Bonhoeffer, it is important to register that Bonhoeffer himself regarded this period as the most satisfying time of his life so far. "Die Arbeit im Seminar macht mir Freude. Wissenschaftliche und praktische Arbeit sind schön miteinander verbunden" [The work at the seminary makes me happy. Scholarly and practical work are beautifully intertwined together].[5] So Bonhoeffer wrote to Barth about Finkenwalde in 1936. Finkenwalde finally allowed Bonhoeffer to blend his interests, not feeling fully at home as a theological lecturer in Berlin or fully at home in the round of weekly routines of pastoral life in London. In each of those previous settings, one aspect of his vocation was either underplayed or in constant competition, but now they came together in his position as director of the seminary at Finkenwalde. There are a number of elements contributing to the synergy of this period: he finally had the opportunity to implement his long percolating thoughts on community life, he was satisfied relationally with this brotherhood, the seminary task focused his efforts in relation to the *Kirchenkampf*, and he was able to utilize his leadership gifts to lend shape to theological education. One additional factor, relevant to this study, was the centrality of the Bible in daily life during the Finkenwalde years, 1935–7.

One can see the centrality of the Bible on display in Bonhoeffer's correspondence from the period. The previously mentioned letter to Barth not only flags Bonhoeffer's satisfaction in his role as seminary director, but in it he fleshes out how questions about the basics of Christian faith, prayer, and Bible reading consume the seminarians as they enter Finkenwalde. This serves as a defense of the somewhat unusual practices of daily Bible meditation undertaken in the seminary. In a fascinating letter to his brother-in-law, Rüdiger Schleicher, Bonhoeffer is again providing a defense with respect to the Bible. Though he is communicating with a family member, he fully presses his self-identification as a

---

4. Schlingensiepen, *Dietrich Bonhoeffer*, 177; Bethge, *Bonhoeffer*, 425.
5. DBW 14:236.

pastor, which allows him to speak forcefully and to talk of his relation to the Bible in both his personal reading and in his preaching. The letter shows some thematic similarity to the lecture delivered eight months earlier in 1935, "Contemporizing New Testament Texts," and anticipates the "Guide to Scriptural Meditation," delivered just two weeks after he wrote the letter in April 1936. After providing a representative sampling of the kinds of questions Rüdiger has put to Bonhoeffer at various points in their conversations or correspondence, Bonhoeffer recognizes a unifying factor that leads him to pose Rüdiger's main question as such: "Wie lebe ich in dieser wirklichen Welt ein christliches Leben, und wo sind die letzten Autoritäten eines solchen Lebens, das sich allein lohnt zu leben?" [How can I live a Christian life in this concrete world, and where are the ultimate authorities for such a life that alone is worth living?][6] His answer:

Ich will da zunächst ganz einfach bekennen: ich glaube, daß die Bibel allein die Antwort auf alle unsere Fragen ist, und daß wir nur anhaltend und etwas demütig zu fragen brauchen, um die Antwort von ihr zu bekommen. Die Bibel kann man nicht einfach *lesen* wie andere Bücher. Man muß bereit sein, sie wirklich zu fragen. Nur so erschließt sie sich. Nur wenn wir letzte Antwort von ihr erwarten, gibt sie sie uns. Das liegt eben daran, daß in der Bibel Gott zu uns redet. Und über Gott kann man eben nicht so einfach von sich aus nachdenken, sondern man muß ihn fragen. Nur wenn wir ihn suchen, antwortet er.[7]

First of all, I will confess quite simply: I believe that the Bible alone is the answer to all our questions, and that we only need to ask persistently and somewhat humbly in order to get the answer from it. One cannot simply *read* the Bible like other books. One must be willing genuinely to question it. Only thus does it open itself up. Only if we expect an ultimate answer from it will it give it to us. That is because God speaks to us in the Bible. And one cannot simply think on God on one's own, but rather one must ask him. Only if we seek him will he answer.

This not only provides a rationale for Rüdiger, but it is also the reason why, when writing to supporters of the seminary, Bonhoeffer could summarize the curriculum in the following way: "Die Bibel steht im Mittelpunkt unsrer Arbeit" [The Bible stands at the center of our work].[8] The centrality of the Bible and his satisfaction are closely linked. Bonhoeffer engaged the Bible more at Finkenwalde than anywhere else. His position as seminary director afforded him the time to read, meditate, study, teach, preach, counsel, and pray with and through Scripture daily. After completing the first session of seminary training at Finkenwalde, the session in which the lecture "Vergegenwärtigung neutestamentlicher Texte" was delivered, Bonhoeffer wrote, "Der Sommer 1935 ist für mich, glaube ich,

6. DBW 14:144.
7. DBW 14:144-145, emphasis original.
8. DBW 14:90-91; DBWE 14:111.

die beruflich und menschlich ausgefüllteste Zeit bisher gewesen" [The summer of 1935 was, I believe, the most fulfilling period in my entire life thus far both professionally and personally].[9]

1.3. The Setting of the Lecture

The lecture was delivered on August 23, 1935, in Hauteroda, in the province of Saxony, to the Brotherhood of Assistant Pastors and Vicars of the Saxon Provincial Confessing Church. The circumstances leading to Bonhoeffer's giving this lecture are worth noting, in part because they help to remind interpreters that Bonhoeffer was not the famous person he has come to be but also in part because of the future possibilities this connection opened up for Bonhoeffer and these members of the Confessing Church. In the seminary at Finkenwalde there were some ordinands from Saxony, and upon hearing that an invited speaker, Hans Asmussen, would be unable to speak at a conference of their fellowship, they recommended the conference organizers include their esteemed teacher and seminary director, Dietrich Bonhoeffer. The problem with securing this invitation was that the brothers in this fellowship of the Confessing Church did not know anything about this "young theologian," and this resulted in some hesitation on their part.[10] In the end, they extended the invitation for him to come address them. He did so, and to great effect. Bethge writes that his "appearance there was very successful; as a result he continued to help in Saxony as long as circumstances allowed him to do so."[11] In addition to opening up a door for future ministry possibilities, Bonhoeffer also met Wolfgang Staemmler, a man who shared a number of similar perspectives with Bonhoeffer on the training and mentoring of young pastors in the Confessing Church. The two men had a lasting friendship initiated on this occasion.

The Confessing Church relied on this kind of camaraderie to bind its members relationally together in their common cause. This relational dynamic is a major key to understanding the success of the Preacher's Seminaries and also helps to put flesh on gatherings like the one that took place that August of 1935. It is unlikely that the conference was very large; in fact, it probably was not unlike the class-sized gatherings assembled for the previous several months at Finkenwalde, a factor that contributes to a more intimate communicative context for the lecturer and hearers. In this case, the lecturer was the 29-year-old Bonhoeffer, fresh out of a couple of years of pastoral ministry, still relatively fresh out of an academic career in theology and having the time of his life praying, reading the Bible, and teaching theology in a relationally rich environment. One can imagine the scene: here, gathered before him, were like-minded pastors and assistant pastors, committed both to their congregations and committed to the Confessing Church, but also experiencing the day-in and day-out realities of pastoral ministry that

9. DBW 14:97; DBWE 14:119.
10. Bethge, *Bonhoeffer*, 440.
11. Bethge, *Bonhoeffer*, 440.

Bonhoeffer just left behind him. He is realistic and sympathetic to their challenges, while unswerving in his convictions about preaching in the context of the ongoing *Kirchenkampf*. Lecturer and hearers, even though they were slightly suspicious of this no-name theologian before them, were united in their tradition and their current confession, and they were also united against the German Christians. Bonhoeffer's target is clear from the outset. The context sharpens up the rhetoric and the sense of urgency: Bonhoeffer, possibly feeling somewhat self-important in his new leadership role, is set to galvanize his hearers such that their attention and preaching is focused solely on Jesus Christ, the one whose presence determines the present moment's reality—the genuine concerns and tasks that need focus and action—for both the German Christians and the Confessing Church.

2. Exposition

What would a conversation about Scripture and its interpretation look like between the young Dietrich Bonhoeffer of 1925 and the more mature Bonhoeffer of 1935? In what ways would staging such a conversation help to elucidate both continuity and discontinuity in this area of Bonhoeffer's theology and practice? And, maybe most importantly, would this exercise provide some help in shaping expectations for the actual biblical work that characterizes the Finkenwalde period, the subject of the next, final chapter, and the period which I argue provides us the quintessential Bonhoeffer on the Bible? An affirmative answer to this final question is the reason for structuring this chapter in terms of such a conversation. As a result, what follows is an exposition of Bonhoeffer's 1935 lecture, "Vergegenwärtigung neutestamentlicher Texte," but it will be described and unfolded through comparison with the earlier essay from 1925. At the outset some of the conclusions can be anticipated: the contingencies of the intervening decade account for the vast majority of the differences between these two offerings on Scripture and its interpretation, Bonhoeffer's developing sense of vocation and satisfaction in finding himself fulfilling it as described above, the concrete tasks of interpreting the Bible in preaching as well as other genres and training preachers, and the contested sphere of the *Kirchenkampf*. Simply put, by 1935 Bonhoeffer has just done a lot more with biblical texts, so a notion continuous with his earlier theology of what Scripture is and is for is now accompanied by the concrete reality of interpreting it.

In outline, the lecture has three main sections. Part 1: *Vergegenwärtigung neutestamentlicher Texte* is devoted to contrasting a negative example of *Vergegenwärtigung* and its accompanying method and the positive form and its method. This positive form is then developed by drawing attention to how this is done in practice in Part 2: *Vergegenwärtigung als Methode* [Contemporizing as a Method]. Finally, in Part 3: *Vergegenwärtigung der neutestamentlichen Botschaft* [Contemporizing the New Testament Message], form and method are brought into relation to the various genres that make up the New Testament and the practicalities of preaching (choosing texts, translating texts, and making them credible). The lecture is geared to meet the needs and address the concerns of pastors who have preaching responsibilities. As a result, it is mostly about method, examples, and practicalities. Though dogmatic resources are present and employed, especially as they situate human action in the positive explication of Bonhoeffer's form of *Vergegenwärtigung* in part 1, they are pretty thin on the ground when compared to the bulk of the lecture's material content (parts 2 and 3).[12]

The shape and proportions of the lecture already lend themselves to a comparison with the essay from 1925. In a broad way, the two pieces share a rhetorical strategy, since in both Bonhoeffer develops his positive vision through opposition to some well-formed alternatives. In 1925, Bonhoeffer opposed and only then related his notion of the revelation-Scripture dynamic to historical criticism and differentiated it further from alternative options for envisioning Scripture's relation to revelation and history. A major difference between the two, at this big picture level, concerns their respective purposes: the purpose of the 1925 essay is to stake out Scripture's relation to history and revelation for the theologian's task. The result is a more academically oriented approach, in which the material is formal and more detached from the concrete realities of dogmatics and preaching and church life (though he nods to these in the conclusion). It serves as a way for Bonhoeffer to stake out his position in respect to some interesting contemporary conversations being had, so to speak, between Harnack and Barth. The purpose of the 1935 lecture is to clarify a false consciousness in the German Christian's theological and practical methodology and, in so doing, stake out a space for a different approach, the hope of an interpretive effort that would enable faithful preaching of Jesus Christ. In this case, as noted above, the result is a greater emphasis on the concrete sphere. The exposition of the 1935 lecture will continue to point up these sorts of similarities and differences.

Before the exposition itself begins, it is again important and necessary to note that in what follows Bonhoeffer's German text will be partly reproduced and paraphrased. This is done intentionally, in order to capture a sense of the rhetoric, as is also the case in the other chapters, but in this instance it is also necessary to ensure that the entire shape of the lecture is discerned and each section's proportions are treated rightly. Reproducing large sections of his German text does not mean that every detail of the quoted material will receive comment, and in fact, that is not necessary. It does mean, however, that the reader will have the opportunity to engage *his text* and can discern the movement of it and what it displays, as well as what has been and has not been incorporated in the choices of the exposition. This close reading strategy, applied to hermeneutical pieces and to acts of interpretation, continues to be fruitful as a way of keeping careful attention to the details and their interrelationship.

---

12. The lecture can be found in DBW 14:399-421; DBWE 14:413-433. Bonhoeffer's manuscript does not contain the final section of the lecture, so we are reliant on some notes made by Bethge.

*2.1. Bonhoeffer's Lecture, Part 1: Vergegenwärtigung neutestamentlicher
Texte [Contemporizing New Testament Texts]*

2.1.1. Introduction Bonhoeffer was given his theme and title, leading him
to simply begin his expansion on his topic without feeling any need to define
Vergegenwärtigung in respect to any ongoing conversations happening at the time.[13]
Of course, it is possible that he did so extemporaneously. The lecture as we have it
simply begins straightforwardly with two briefly stated accounts of contemporizing
New Testament texts. This contrast pits opposites against one another. The result
is clarity in the presentation since each form has a corresponding method, and
the stakes are also clearly delineated since interpreters will find themselves siding
with the German Christians or with Bonhoeffer. What is left underdeveloped is
whether there are any other options. Is this truly an either/or? Bonhoeffer clearly
thought so, and though this is a lecture it is not strictly an academic exercise,
making distinctions for the sake of clarifying distinctions on the way to a synthesis
of some kind. Bonhoeffer is presenting alternatives as a call to action. He says,

> Entweder man meint damit, daß sich die biblische Botschaft vor der Gegenwart
> rechtfertigen müsse und sich deshalb der Vergegenwärtigung fähig erweisen
> müsse, oder man meint, daß sich die Gegenwart vor der biblischen Botschaft
> rechtfertigen müsse und deshalb die Botschaft gegenwärtig werden müsse.[14]

> Either one thinks that the biblical message must justify itself before the present
> and therefore show that it is capable of being contemporized, or one thinks
> that the present must justify itself before the biblical message and therefore the
> message must already be contemporary.

In good rhetorical form, and reminiscent of the 1925 essay, Bonhoeffer first
develops the then popular form of contemporizing before he suggests serious
problems with it and offers his own account.

2.1.2. A Negative Form of Contemporizing The first form of contemporizing traces
its genealogy back several centuries to, according to Bonhoeffer, the advent of
rationalism. There is a straight line drawn between rationalism in the seventeenth
century and German Christian interpretive practice in the twentieth century because:

> Sofern der Rationalismus nichts anderes war als das Zutagetreten des bisher
> latenten Anspruches der Menschen auf autonome Lebensgestaltung aus

---

13. For some comments on the text of the lecture and a good discussion of certain
aspects of the lecture in conversation with Bultmann, demythologizing, and New Testament
theology, see Werner Kahl, "Evangeliumsvergegenwärtigung," in *Dietrich Bonhoeffers
Christentum: Festschrift für Christian Gremmels*, ed. Florian Schmitz and Christiane Tietz
(Gütersloh: Gütersloher Verlagshaus, 2011), 134–55.

14. DBW 14:400.

den Kräften der gegebenen Welt heraus, ist die Frage allerdings eine in dem
menschlichen Anspruch auf Autonomie selbst schon gestellte Frage; das heißt
der auto- | nome Mensch, der sich zugleich als Christ bekennen will, fordert die
Rechtfertigung der christlichen Botschaft vor dem Forum seiner Autonomie.[15]

Inasmuch as rationalism was nothing other than the emergence of the formerly
latent claim of man to autonomously shape their lives from the resources given
by the world, the question is indeed a question already posed in the human
claim to autonomy itself; that is, the autonomous person, who at the same time
wants to confess him or herself as a Christian, demands the justification of the
Christian message before the forum of their own autonomy.

The claim to autonomy is the claim to define the present as the time or place of
one's own presence before which other claims must be judged. Bonhoeffer has
already begun filling out the shape of the first form of contemporizing by replacing
der Gegenwart [the present] in the first articulation of the contrast above with
Autonomie [autonomy] here. This is given further historical situating when he
identifies versions of this essential claim to autonomy, whether in reason in the
eighteenth century, culture in the nineteenth century, or nationalism [*Volkstum*]
in the twentieth century. These expressions of autonomy are united because in
each case, they (1) ask the *same question*: "Läßt sich das Christentum vor uns,
die wir einmal so sind, wie wir—Gott sei Dank!—sind, vergegenwärtigen?"
[Can Christianity contemporize itself before us, given the way we are (as—thank
God!—we are)?];[16] (2) have the *same urgent need* to attach the cultural capital of
the word "Christian" to their endeavor; (3) begin with the *same presupposition*,
namely, that the fixed point is in hand and the flexible element is the Christian
message; (4) they share the *same method* in which the biblical message is forced
to run through the sieve of one's previously determined understanding, keeping
that which will aid the construct one is after while leaving behind that which does
not fit into the framework. This final element is briefly illustrated with two images,
that of an eagle with its wings clipped so that it can be put on display as a special
but tamed household pet and that of a farmer who purchases a feeble, tamed horse
rather than a powerful stallion. Christianity is tamed and made useful for some
other end. The Christian message is fitted into the unquestioned views of these
various modulations of autonomy in the present.

What is the result of this form of contemporizing? Bonhoeffer writes:

Diese Vergegenwärtigung der christlichen Botschaft führt direkt ins Heidentum.[17]

This contemporizing of the Christian message leads directly to paganism.

---

15. DBW 14:400.
16. DBW 14:400.
17. DBW 14:401, emphasis original.

This evaluative judgment is initially a bit extreme and seems to come out of nowhere, but in point of fact Bonhoeffer has prepared the listener for a conclusion along these lines. When he set out the basic similarity between this form of contemporizing and rationalism, he suggested that the success of this type of contemporizing was identified in the ability to hold together one's claim to autonomy and Christian faith. In such a situation, internal reasoning has validated the Christian message. If one cannot succeed in justifying the Christian message before the judgment of autonomous reason, then one simply, and honestly, declares oneself, not a Christian, but a pagan. Bonhoeffer has respect for the intellectually honest pagan, but he has no respect for those who want to continue to assert dishonestly that their reconstructed form of Christianity is the genuine article.

This train of thought, that this brand of contemporizing results in paganism, if one is honest, is explicitly connected to the German Christians. One implication of the German Christians employing this form of contemporizing is that they are functionally pagans, dishonest pagans, but pagans nonetheless. Bonhoeffer says it this way:

> daß auch der unzweifelhaft teilweise mit großer Leidenschaft und subjektiver Ernsthaftigkeit erschollene Ruf nach Vergegenwärtigung der christlichen Botschaft in den Anfängen der D. C. als solcher kirchlich und theologisch nicht ernstgenommen werden *durfte*; er war bestenfalls der Schreckensschrei dessen, der den Bruch zwischen Christentum und Welt sichtbar erfährt; der sich seiner völligen Weltförmigkeit bewußt wird, der erkennt, daß es für ihn mit dem Christentum aus ist, der nun aber weder stark genug ist, ein klares „Ja" und ein ebenso klares „Nein" zu sagen, sondern der feig das Christentum in seinen Verfall an die Welt mit hineinreißen will.[18]

> the call for contemporizing the Christian message that the German Christians raised at their beginning, a call raised undoubtedly partly with great passion and subjective sincerity, *cannot*, as such, be taken seriously ecclesiastically and theologically; it was, at best, the cry of terror of one who visibly experiences the break between Christianity and the world; this person has become conscious of his complete worldliness, and recognizes that Christianity is over and done with for him, but he is not strong enough to say a clear "yes" or equally a clear "no," but instead wants, in a cowardly way, to take Christianity with him in his apostasy to the world.

Bonhoeffer is offering an interpretation here. He is not afraid, among friends sympathetic to the cause, to propose a reading that goes beneath the surface, providing "the" perspective on the German Christians' motivations. The reason he offers for the recent and urgent calls for contemporizing is the fear of having to honestly confess that the Christian message should be left behind in favor of the present moment's privileged or enlightened point of view. The proof given to

---

18. DBW 14:401-402, emphasis original.

substantiate this reading is the fact that all the talk about contemporizing is just that, talk about *the act* of contemporizing, rather than that which is contemporized. The difference between Bonhoeffer's soon-to-be-unveiled form of contemporizing and that of the German Christians is where the emphasis lies. In the case of the German Christians, according to Bonhoeffer, all the emphasis rests on *"contemporizing* the Christian message." In the case of the form promoted by Bonhoeffer, the emphasis is placed on "contemporizing *the Christian message."* He writes, "Wo aber die Frage nach der Vergegenwärtigung zum *Thema der Theologie wird*, dort können wir gewiß sein, daß die Sache bereits verraten und verkauft ist" [Wherever, however, the question of contemporizing becomes *the theme of theology*, we can then be sure that the essential content is already betrayed and sold off].[19] The introduction of the word *Sache* is crucial. It features in this first part of the lecture numerous times in various forms because it is at the heart of Bonhoeffer's positive alternative vision of the relationship of the Bible in the modern world.

But there are two steps in the argument before we get to that positive vision. Bonhoeffer is aware of how easily one could be drawn into a debate about contemporizing the Christian message according to the terms of the opposition. If one is not careful, before he or she knows it, the question of contemporizing itself, with all the assumptions about the importance of the present that it contains, will overshadow the real concern of the content of the Christian message. This is precisely what Bonhoeffer thought had recently occurred with some theologians sympathetic to the Confessing Church, namely, Paul Althaus, Karl Heim, and Adolf Schlatter. One option when responding to an opponent is to make common cause by employing similar language or even assuming the question that is being asked is worth asking rather than worth upending from the start. The danger identified in the various books Bonhoeffer mentions is that they may have already given away too much by assuming that the word "German," defined in a very specific way since 1933, had theological freight. The terms of the debate have forced a certain way of thinking and asking questions that has displaced the heart of the matter, a beginning point with the essential content of the Christian message. These comments underscore that Bonhoeffer's form of contemporizing is not only to be differentiated from the German Christians, but it is also to be differentiated from others within the Confessing Church as well.

Are there any faithful left in the land? Is there anyone left who has not sold off the *Sache* in favor of passing fads? Consistent throughout the whole of Bonhoeffer's life, if one looks around and only finds examples of unfaithful representatives, whether they are the historical critics or Roman Catholics or Lutheran scholastics in the 1925 essay or they are the German Christians or somewhat compromised members of the Confessing Church in 1935, then one can always hold out hope that Luther will stand out as a positive and faithful representative of real, genuine Christianity. Bonhoeffer says:

19. DBW 14:402, emphasis original.

Wem es wirklich um die Sache zu tun war, sc. um das Heil seiner Seele, dem hat die deutsche Luther–Bibel, die *Verdeutschung der heiligen Schrift durch Luther* die Forderung nach Vergegenwärtigung und *Verdeutschung des Evangeliums* immer noch am besten erfüllt. Hier ist vergegenwärtigtes, hier ist deutsches Christentum.[20]

For the one who is really concerned to engage with the content, to wit, with the salvation of his or her soul, the German Luther Bible, *Luther's translation of the Holy Scripture into German*, still best fulfills the call for contemporizing and *translating the gospel into German*. This is what contemporizing is; this is German Christianity.

Luther succeeded where the German Christians and some members of the Confessing Church failed because he was focused on rendering the content of the Christian gospel in the German language. He was able to hold together both aspects, contemporizing and content. It is certainly the case that Luther's German is itself now a bit awkward for the German speaker in 1935 to utilize, but it is better to work with this text because at least here one can find the essential content. Bonhoeffer is here both holding up an example of faithfulness and positioning himself in this role, channeling Luther as he expounds his own positive version of contemporizing. A final statement closes this section of part 1, bringing together critique and proposal in a succinct fashion:

Wer Durst hat, der hat von jeher in der Bibel selbst und in einer *sachlich-* biblischen Predigt, auch wenn sie sehr unzeitgemäß war—das *lebendige* Wasser gefunden—und es ist ein Eingeständnis einer gefährlichen Dekadenz des Glaubens, wenn die Frage nach der Vergegenwärtigung der Botschaft als methodische Frage zu laut wird.[21]

The one who is thirsty has always found *living* water in the Bible itself and in a *substantively* biblical sermon, even if it was really behind the times, and it is an admission of a dangerous decadence of faith when the question of contemporizing the message becomes too overwhelming as a methodological question.

Being implicitly led to desire a departure from this decadent engagement with the bare fact of contemporizing, the hearer is left wondering how exactly the alternative will be developed.

2.1.3. A Positive Form of Contemporizing

Damit soll aber des Negativen und der Abgrenzung fürs erste genug sein; und der positive Sinn der Frage nach der Vergegenwärtigung wird jetzt ins rechte Licht gerückt werden können.[22]

20. DBW 14:403, emphasis original.
21. DBW 14:403, emphasis original.
22. DBW 14:403.

For the time being, however, that should be enough negation and delimitation; and the positive meaning of the question of contemporizing can now be placed at the center.

Bonhoeffer devotes two paragraphs to his major claim that the present must be justified before the Christian message. The present is placed before Christianity, rather than the other way around, when the question about the *Sache*, what Bonhoeffer calls the *Was* of Christianity, receives singular focus. This approach to contemporizing is developed, first, by explicating the concept of the *Sache* itself, and second, by describing what the present, the *Gegenwart*, is, both as a concept and in terms of linguistic analysis. He writes the following about true contemporizing, and in so doing begins to unfold his emphasis on the *Sache*:

> Es wird der *Sache selbst* zugetraut, daß dort, wo sie wirklich zu Wort kommt, in sich selbst sie das Gegenwärtigste sei; es bedarf dann gar keines besondern Aktes der Vergegenwärtigung mehr, in der Sache selbst vollzieht sich die | Vergegenwärtigung.[23]

> It has confidence in the *content itself*, that where it really comes to expression, precisely there, we find the most contemporary element; then no special act of contemporizing is needed anymore, since the contemporizing is carried out in the content itself.

The *Sache* is given a privileged position. Up to this point in the lecture, the notion of the *Sache* is still very abstract. This abstraction makes it somewhat odd that Bonhoeffer has here very nearly given the *Sache* itself a form of agency. Contemporizing is subordinated to the *Sache* such that the latter just being itself is already the act of contemporizing. How, exactly, does this work? The crucial link is that the essential content is that of, variously expressed so far, Christianity or the Christian message or the New Testament. He says:

> Allerdings—nur weil es *diese* Sache ist, um die es im Neuen Testament geht, weil die Sache hier Christus und sein Wort ist. Wo Christus im Wort des Neuen Testaments zu Wort kommt, dort ist Vergegenwärtigung.[24]

> However, only because it is *this* subject matter, that with which the New Testament is concerned, because the subject matter here is Christ and his word. Where Christ comes to expression in the word of the New Testament, there is contemporizing.

The earlier abstraction, not only of *Sache* but also of general terms like the Christian message, gives way to particularity. The meaning and translation of *Sache* is key. In the other instances when it was set alongside concepts, Christian message,

23. DBW 14:403-404, emphasis original.
24. DBW 14:404, emphasis original.

Christianity, etc., it was appropriate to translate it as "content/essential content." The *Sache* is now identified as Christ and his word, a move that necessitates a slightly different rendering. It is not easy to capture the sense in English, but "subject matter" draws sufficient attention to the fact Christ and his word are inseparable, or, in other words, that there is an agency directly related to this content.

This is the reason that the *Sache* was given a privileged position over the bare act of contemporizing. If contemporizing is about making present, as the relation between *Gegenwart* and *Vergegenwärtigung* makes clear, then Christ himself, the *Sache*, establishes or makes the present *present*. "Wo die Gegenwart vor dem Anspruch Christi steht, *dort ist Gegenwart*" [Where the present stands before the claim of Christ, *there is the present*].[25] This formulation again displays the key transition from a way of thinking about the *Sache* as the New Testament's content, that is, the New Testament is about Christ in a general way, to the *Sache* as a Christological reality. And the implication of this way of construing it is that the present is redefined.

Turning from a concern to describe the *Sache*, Bonhoeffer now begins to define this present in explicitly theological terms. If it was assumed to be the fixed point in the relation between a reader and the biblical text, now the only fixed point is the Christological one. The present is only identifiable as the presence of the speaking Christ. In fact, the present does not really have anything to do with time at all. It is not properly understood if it is temporally determined, whether by correlating it to a specific ethos of a period or what a generation might offer as the definitive interpretation of their "moment" or the so-called *Zeitgeist*. In an interesting juxtaposition, Bonhoeffer plays off *Zeitgeist* and shifts from Christ to the Spirit: "Gegenwart ist allein der Heilige Geist" [The present is solely the Holy Spirit].[26] And this shift is immediately followed by another shift to the broadly theological: God creates or establishes the present wherever God is in his word.

At first glance, the move from Christ to Spirit to God seems to demonstrate a somewhat confused relation between the trinitarian persons. But this is not exactly the case. Bonhoeffer is not trying to provide a trinitarian specification of the present. Instead his formulations are arising in an ad hoc manner. The Christological emphasis is derived from the New Testament's focus on Christ and his word, the introduction of the Spirit is initiated by the use of *Zeitgeist*, and the final note about "God" rounds out the picture. All of this is meant to define the present in a generally theological frame, running something like this: God creates the present by the Spirit through the word of Christ as the word of God. This is not, in other words, at attempt to inflect his discussion in specific Christological or Pneumatological terms. But, even this clarification is true only up to a point. The general theological determination of the present, in which God, Christ, and Spirit are all employed at various points and for various reasons, quickly transitions into an explicit discussion of the Spirit.

25. DBW 14:404, emphasis original.
26. DBW 14:404.

Das *Subjekt der Gegenwart* ist der Heilige Geist, nicht wir, darum ist auch das Subjekt der *Vergegenwärtigung* der Heilige Geist selbst. Das *concretissimum der christlichen Botschaft* und Textauslegung ist nicht ein menschlicher Akt der Vergegenwärtigung, sondern ist immer Gott selbst, ist der Heilige Geist. Weil die „Sache" des Neuen Testaments dies ist, daß Christus durch seinen Heiligen Geist zu uns redet, und weil dies nicht außerhalb oder neben, sondern allein und exklusiv *durch das Wort* der Schrift geschieht, darum ist Sachlichkeit, das heißt Schriftgebundenheit der Verkündigung selbst Vergegenwärtigung—„Sachlichkeit"—sowohl als Methode—davon werden wir gleich reden—wie auch als Gehorsam und Vertrauen zu der Sache des Heiligen Geistes. Denn das Sachliche an dieser Sache ist eben der Heilige Geist selbst und Er ist der gegenwärtige Gott und Christus.[27]

The *agent of the present* is the Holy Spirit, not we ourselves, and for this reason also the agent of *contemporizing* is the Holy Spirit itself. The *most fundamental entity of the Christian message* and textual interpretation is not a human act of contemporizing, but rather it is always God himself, it is the Holy Spirit. Because the "subject matter" of the New Testament is that Christ speaks to us through his Holy Spirit, and because this happens not outside of nor next to but rather solely and exclusively *through the word* of Scripture, therefore *a proper relation to the content*, that is, proclamation bound by Scripture, is contemporizing—"correspondence to the content"—both as a method—we will speak about that soon—and also as obedience and trust in the essential content, that is, the Holy Spirit. For the essence of this essential content is precisely the Holy Spirit himself and he is the present God and Christ.

The extended quotation is necessary because this is the most important paragraph of the first part of the lecture, for here Bonhoeffer identifies the agent of contemporizing as the Holy Spirit and labels the relationship between the Holy Spirit, Scripture, and the interpreter "*Sachlichkeit*," that is, an orientation or proper relation or correspondence to Christ and his word in Scripture. This section also demonstrates the similarity or continuity between this lecture and the essay from 1925. The phrase "Pneumatological interpretation" is left behind, but the substance of the hermeneutic developed there is still operating here. In fact, a surface reading of this *Vergegenwärtigung* lecture could lead one to the conclusion that Bonhoeffer has shifted from a hermeneutic derived from Pneumatology in 1925 to one derived from Christological resources in 1935. This conclusion could be supported by some of what we have already seen, but also from the rest of the lecture, concerned as it is with what could be described as a Christocentric reading of the New Testament's various contents. It is important, though, not to lose sight of how indebted Bonhoeffer's hermeneutic is to Pneumatology, even after an intervening decade that included his lectures on Christology and an intense concentration on the Sermon on the Mount. The New Testament proclaims Christ,

27. DBW 14:404, emphasis original.

but that proclamation is only possible by the Holy Spirit, and it is only received, echoing the final words of the 1925 essay on praying for the Holy Spirit's advent, through obedience and trust.

One other similarity between the emphasis here and that of 1925 is that Bonhoeffer presents the agency of the Spirit in contrast to human interpretive agency construed as the act of contemporizing. Is this simply and straightforwardly a diminishing of human interpretive agency, rising out of a desire to honor the Spirit's agency? This recalls the earlier essay because there the Spirit was said to provide the organs for receiving God's word, but also that the Spirit is the one who hears God's word in the human. This formulation threatens the human's faculties and agency, potentially undermining or diminishing the integrity of the creature's agency entirely. In that context, it was argued that this is a misreading, because the rest of the essay establishes the reality of the interpreter's agency, a genuine agency. The same is the case here. Bonhoeffer's emphasis that the human is not the agent of the present or the agent of contemporizing is stated in stark contrast to the Spirit's agency, not because the human interpreter is rendered totally passive in Bonhoeffer's thinking about hermeneutics but because the negative form of contemporizing assumes that the human being is the only necessary condition for contemporizing. He is seeking to undermine this emphasis, a point made only too clearly in the remaining two parts of the lecture where the concrete realities of *Sachlichkeit*, real human interpretive acts attuned to Christ by the Spirit, take center stage.

So far Bonhoeffer has contrasted two types of contemporizing, one negative and the other positive or "true." The extended quotation above could leave the impression that rightly ordering a theologically derived present and a kind of *Sachlichkeit* tells the whole story. The positive version of contemporizing, the version that Bonhoeffer is promoting, seems to make sense and work pretty straightforwardly. This is not quite the case because of another aspect of the present. He developed the present in reference to the *Sache*, but now, in a move reminiscent again of the 1925 essay's analysis of the word "word," he determines to glean an insight from a linguistic analysis of the *Begriff der Gegenwart* [concept of the present].[28] He writes:

> Daß etwas uns „*entgegen*" ist—entgegen wartet—besagt doch, daß *Gegenwart von außen her bestimmt ist* und nicht von innen, nicht von uns bestimmbar, durch das bestimmt ist, was von außen auf uns zukommt, durch das Zukommende, durch die Zukunft.[29]

> That something is "*over-against*" us—awaits—says that *the present is determined from the outside* and not from the inside, not determined by us, but is determined through what comes to us from the outside, through that which approaches, through the future.

28. DBW 14:404, emphasis original.
29. DBW 14:404-405, emphasis original.

This is a familiar enough point by now. Bonhoeffer wants to undermine any claim to define the present on the basis of the inside, whether that of an autonomous human being or the definition of the word "present" itself. But is he simply repeating himself at this point, or is something more interesting happening? He is certainly continuing to undermine a false notion of the present, but he is more interested in destabilizing an overly confident contemporizing, whether that wielded by the German Christians or the kind he himself seeks to utilize. The fact that the real present is the theologically construed present, a Christological and Pneumatological reality, unsettles everyone because all attempts at closure or a totalizing perspective on Scripture or the present is put into question by the future, the non-possessable presence of Christ being approached by the Spirit. He writes:

> Und so wird die Sachlichkeit darin bestehen, daß das Außen, das Gegenüber, das „Zukünftige" als Gegenwart zu Gehör kommt—das fremde Evangelium, nicht das bekannte Evangelium wird das gegenwärtige Evangelium sein.[30]

> And so a proper relation to the essential content will consist of the outside element, the opposite element, the "future" element as the present comes to expression—the alien gospel, not the familiar gospel, will be the present gospel.

This is key because it chastens the confidence of Bonhoeffer's proposal. No one has a privileged position because all must wait as the alien gospel does the job of sifting. The hearer is confronted by something outside himself or herself, and that foreign presence calls to account. The picture is similar to the logos/counter-logos relation developed in the lectures on Christology. As Christ confronts the human logos, which understands itself as conditioned entirely in terms of itself, the human logos is not obliterated but rather established in a true relation of creaturely dependence. The alien presence of Christ, never able to be assimilated since he is Lord, is a gracious presence by the Spirit. This all leads to an interesting comment as Bonhoeffer concludes the first part of the essay. He writes, "Anknüpfungspunkt des Ärgernisses!"[31] This is very compressed and difficult to render in English, but

---

30. DBW 14:405.

31. DBW 14:405. Bonhoeffer's use of the word *Anknüpfungspunkt*, in addition to what I have described here, is also a nod or allusion, and perhaps a kind of grim, Barth-inspired parody, to an exchange of essays between Emil Brunner and Karl Barth in 1934. Brunner's book, *Natur und Gnade*, speaks about the gospel as some kind of common ground for all people. It is, therefore, an element in a natural theology for Brunner and, as such, an apologetic move. Barth responded in his essay, *Nein! Antwort an Emil Brunner*, arguing that there is no knowledge of God outside of Jesus Christ. Both essays can be found published together in *Natural Theology: Comprising "Nature and Grace" by Professor Dr. Emil Brunner and the Reply "No!" by Dr. Karl Barth*, trans. by Peter Fraenkel (London: Centenary Press, 1946), 65–128. From Bonhoeffer's perspective, the only point of contact is, borrowing from Paul in 1 Cor. 1:18-31, the scandal the gospel creates for all.

he is trying to express the fact that the only point of contact between the gospel and the world in general is the fact that the gospel is a scandal for everyone, whether it is a scandal the German Christians are trying to update or a scandal that calls confidence into question for the Confessing Church. Bonhoeffer still thinks the first, bad form of contemporizing is just that, bad, but everything that follows in the remainder of the lecture needs to be interpreted in the light of these final comments about the way the cross-shaped Gospel, the alien and foreign Gospel, brings each way of contemporizing into question.

2.2. Bonhoeffer's Lecture, Part 2: Vergegenwärtigung als Methode [Contemporizing as a Method]

How does Bonhoeffer's vision of the positive form of contemporizing work *in practice*? Answering this question is the burden of parts 2 and 3, and that this is a burden at all is one of the distinguishing factors between the essay from 1925 and this one in 1935. The questions that each so-called "hermeneutical" offering seeks to answer are different, which inevitably leads to different emphases; this fact must be included in the comparison. But, both are concerned to articulate a relationship between Scripture and interpretation in a theological frame for the sake of theological work, whether dogmatics or preaching. At this level of similarity, the main difference between the two is the shape or contour of the interpreter as an agent and the shape and contour of Scripture as a multifaceted witness. The earlier framing of Scripture and its interpreters was general, but now it is given greater specificity. This difference can be accounted for not only by the need to interpret Scripture as a theological lecturer and pastor, that is, by shifting contexts and the requirements of certain activities, but also by the need to solidify an identity in continuity with the Lutheran tradition but distinct from the German Christians. It is not enough, therefore, to say that the best reason to explain the change is that he was young and inexperienced in 1925. That is true, but the lack of interpretive specificity was not only to do with his lack of experience up to that point. His theology itself was underdetermined with respect to real interpretive agency. The contingent realities of the 1930s called for increased responsibilities in leadership, and by implication, a recognition that interpretation matters since it is the human action that corresponds to the Spirit's action. One of the questions that will remain unresolved is what the precise character of this interpretive agency is. Bonhoeffer's concern in part 2 is how that interpretive agency works methodologically.

    This section of the lecture unfolds very clearly. He begins by drawing attention to the need to link form and method. Both forms of contemporizing have a methodology, and that method is interpretation. What will become clear is that each form is interpreting a different thing. After detailing the method that corresponds to the bad form of contemporizing as well as some of its implications, he turns to the positive form of contemporizing, describing the method and responding to some concrete questions that arise from employing it. He begins, though, with summarizing and linking:

Haben wir erkannt, daß die rechte Vergegenwärtigung darin liegt, daß wir zur Sache kommen und die Sache zu Wort kommt, so wird dem methodisch entsprechen, daß vergegenwärtigende Verkündigung wesentlich *Auslegung sein muß*, Auslegung des Wortes, das allein über die Kraft der Vergegenwärtigung verfügt, Schriftauslegung. Der Akt der Vergegenwärtigung, sofern er von uns methodisch überhaupt vollzogen werden kann, ist die strenge und exklusive Bezugnahme auf das Schriftwort.[32]

If we have recognized that proper contemporizing lies here, that we come to the essential content and the essential content comes to expression, then the methodology will correspond, that is, a contemporizing proclamation *must essentially be interpretation*, interpretation of the word which enacts the power of contemporizing, an interpretation of Scripture. The act of contemporizing, insofar as it can be carried out methodologically by us at all, is strict and exclusive reference to the word of Scripture.

There is a tension here indicated by the aside, "sofern er von uns methodisch überhaupt vollzogen werden kann" [insofar as it can be carried out methodologically by us at all]. On the one hand, the concern of the previous section was to show that the Holy Spirit carries out the act of contemporizing, and this point was made in opposition to a way of thinking of hermeneutical realization as a strictly human possibility. On the other hand, now moving into a discussion of method, it must be said that as humans interpret Scripture the act of contemporizing is carried out. For this to be the case, some things must be in place about God, Scripture, and the interpreter. All three of these will come in and out throughout the rest of the lecture, but here Bonhoeffer, in a really compressed way, brings them all together. He writes:

Wem das unverständlich erscheint, der hat die Voraussetzung noch nicht erfaßt, daß nur dort wo Christus redet und der Heilige Geist, Gegenwart ist. Diese Rückwärtswendung zur Schrift ent- | spricht genau der Rückwärtswendung des christlichen Glaubens und der christlichen Hoffnung, nämlich auf das Kreuz Christi; es ist beidemal die Geschichtlichkeit der Offenbarung Gottes, die hier zum Ausdruck kommt.[33]

The one for whom this seem incomprehensible has not yet grasped the reality that the present is only where Christ and the Holy Spirit speak. This turn back to Scripture corresponds exactly to the turn back of Christian faith and Christian hope, namely, to the cross of Christ; for both, it is the historicity of God's revelation that comes to manifestation here.

The first sentence here returns to the conception of the present construed theologically that was mapped in the previous part of the lecture. This present,

---

32. DBW 14:405, emphasis original.
33. DBW 14:405-406.

though, is not disconnected from God's previous action. The theological present, the situation of the interpreter, means that the interpreter must *Rückwärtswendung* [turn back] to Scripture because, and this is key, God's revelation is manifest in history, in Christ's cross, Scripture, and in concrete interpretive acts. Revelation, history, Scripture, and interpretation are all held together in Bonhoeffer's hermeneutic. The interrelationship between these is the exact concern of the 1925 essay, and here they ground the positive form's method, view of Scripture's multiplicity of perspective (part 2), and the pastor's concrete witness (part 3). Before he develops all this more carefully though, the methodology that the negative form of contemporizing employs must be described and evaluated.

2.2.1. The Method for the Negative Form of Contemporizing Bonhoeffer's "negative" form of contemporizing relies on the fact that there is something in history that does not stay back there in history, but goes beyond that history into the present. There is, in other words, something timeless that must be discerned and reapplied today. Contemporizing means "*Auffindung der ewigen Lehre, beziehungsweise der allgemeinen ethischen Norm, beziehungsweise des Mythos, den die heilige Schrift enthält, und es heißt sodann Anwendung dieses Allgemeinen auf die Gegenwart, auf das individuelle Heute*" [*discovering* the eternal teaching, the universal ethical norm, or the myth which Holy Scripture contains, and it then also means applying this universal element to the present, to the individual today].[34] This is only possible, however, if the interpreter already knows what he or she is trying to discover in Scripture. As a result, interpretation for this form of contemporizing is a process of relating Scripture to an already possessed insight. "Die Wahrheit steht schon fest, ehe ich an die Auslegung der Schrift herangehe" [The truth has already been determined before I approach the interpretation of Scripture].[35]

One major implication of this interpretive procedure is that the interpreter is functionally claiming the ability to distinguish God's word and human words in Scripture. The eternal truth already present in the interpreter serves as the criterion for judging whether a specific part of the Bible should stay in the past, remain time-bound, or whether it is eternal as well and, thus, divine. Bonhoeffer furnishes his listener with some examples. Paul's theology is human, but Jesus' religion is divine. The doctrine of sin is human and should be left behind, but the struggle for the good is eternal. Jesus' ethical teaching is eternal, but the miracle-stories are bound to their time. In each of these instances, reason or conscience or nationalism or some other thing that lies within the interpreter is applied to Scripture in order to determine the eternal from the merely temporal. Succinctly put: "*Die Norm der Vergegenwärtigung liegt bei uns, die Bibel ist der Stoff, an dem diese Norm Anwendung findet*" [*The norm of contemporizing lies within us, and the Bible is the raw material to which this norm is applied*].[36]

---

34. DBW 14:406, emphasis original.
35. DBW 14:407.
36. DBW 14:408, emphasis original.

2.2.2. The Method for the Positive Form of Contemporizing Referring to the final sentence quoted in the previous paragraph, Bonhoeffer continues:

> Dieser Satz ist nun genau umzukehren, damit unser Begriff der Auslegung und der Vergegenwärtigung klar wird—die Norm für das Wort Gottes in der Schrift ist das Wort Gottes selbst und unsere Gegebenheiten, Vernunft, Gewissen, völkisches Erlebnis sind der Stoff, an dem diese Norm ihre Anwendung sucht.[37]

> This statement is now to be exactly reversed, so that our notion of interpretation and contemporizing might become clear: the norm for the word of God in Scripture is the word of God itself, and our circumstances, reason, conscience, and national experience are the material to which this norm is applied.

If the upshot of the form of contemporizing that Bonhoeffer criticizes was the ability to distinguish God's word from human words in Scripture, and if that method is reversed here, then the implication of the form he advocates is that it will not seek to determine what is simply human and what is divine in Scripture. For this method, God's word and man's word are also related in Scripture, but such that "Gott selbst sagt, wo sein Wort ist und daß er das sagt *im Menschenwort*" [God himself says where his word is and that he speaks it *in human words*].[38] Human words in Scripture are God's word precisely as historical and time-bound words. This relationship is not one, though, of simple identity or transparency, so in what way does the relation between God's word and human words work? Bonhoeffer, again in continuity with his essay from 1925, employs the metaphor of witness.[39] He writes:

37. DBW 14:408.

38. DBW 14:408, emphasis original.

39. It is almost certainly the case that Bonhoeffer derived his emphasis in the 1925 paper on Scripture as *Zeugnis* from Barth. Unlike Barth, however, Bonhoeffer was able to diversify his conception of *Zeugnis*, resulting in the formulations found in this lecture in 1935. Bonhoeffer managed this emphasis by revising the conceptuality on the basis of his engagement with various biblical texts. In other words, like his conception of Scripture's unity (a point to be developed in the next chapter), the notion of *Zeugnis* is one that develops, and it takes on contours as each text's specific witnessing activity is taken into consideration; this major point will be taken up in Section 2.3.1 "The New Testament as Witness." This construal differs from Barth because he focuses more attention on that which the *Zeugnis* attests. For instance, Barth writes,

> Witnessing means pointing in a specific direction beyond the self and on to another. Witnessing is thus service to this other in which the witness vouches for the truth of the other, the service which consists in referring to the other. This service is constitutive for the concept of the prophet and also for that of the apostle. ... Standing in this service, the biblical witnesses point beyond themselves (see CD I/1:111-112)

Für die Methode der vergegenwärtigenden Auslegung heißt das, daß sie nicht an die Schrift herantritt als an ein Buch, in dem allgemeine Wahrheiten, allgemeine ethische Normen oder Mythen aufgefunden werden könnten; die heilige Schrift ist vielmehr für sie als ganze *das Zeugnis* von Gott in Christus und es wird ihr in jeder Stelle | darum gehen, den Zeugnischarakter des Wortes hörbar zu machen ... Die einzige *Methode der* Vergegenwärtigung ist mithin die sachliche Textauslegung als des Zeugnisses von Christus und solche Auslegung hat die Verheißung der Gegenwart Christi.[40]

For the method of a contemporizing interpretive practice this means that it does not approach Scripture as a book in which universal truths, universal ethical norms, or myths might be located; Holy Scripture is rather, for this method, as a whole *the witness* of God in Christ, and in every passage the point is to make the character of this word as witness audible ... The exclusive *method* of contemporizing is therefore textual interpretation oriented to the subject matter as the witness of Christ, and such interpretation has the promise of the presence of Christ.

On this model, Scripture is not viewed as a mass of material spread out that needs a previously constructed pattern applied to it, choosing the bits that most closely fit the pattern while throwing away that which does not. Instead, Scripture is viewed as a singular, coherent entity, a witness, which as a whole converges on a single center. Whatever passage is being interpreted, one can expect to see it as a perspective on the singular object, the heart of Scripture: God in Christ. This is *sachliche Textauslegung* [textual interpretation oriented to the subject matter] because each passage, when interpreted, contributes to understanding the *Sache*. Interpretation then brings out each distinctive perspective on the same reality. How does this work out in detail, when specific genres or texts are presented for interpretation? Bonhoeffer answers this question in part 3, but before he does so, expanding on how exactly the New Testament witnesses in this way, he pauses to take up two possible questions or objections that place the practical concerns of the pastors to whom he is speaking front and center.

2.2.3. Two Questions The questions Bonhoeffer addressed while delivering the lecture were not in the text of his lecture, but rather added in the margin in pen. The material is being adapted to the setting, which in this case means getting concrete and practical with the needs and concerns of the pastors before him. This section is

---

The notional or abstract level of consideration, that is, working with this specific conception of "witnessing," precludes emphasis on diversity, since the focus is on the singular object attested rather than the unique witness of any given biblical author or text. For more on Barth and "witnessing," see Richard E. Burnett, *Karl Barth's Theological Exegesis: The Hermeneutical Principles of the* Römerbrief *Period* (Grand Rapids, MI: Eerdmans, 2004), 223–30.

40. DBW 14:408-409, emphasis original.

important because we are able to observe Bonhoeffer's progress as an experienced pastor, and as such, he is able to make what appears abstract at points very concrete. He does this, though, in a dialectical fashion, putting the concrete and the universal in relation theologically. The first question is: Should I, as a preacher, provide a concrete application for the congregation, something that goes beyond the interpretation itself? He does not think this should be done because the fundamentally important aspect of preaching is not the application that the preacher provides, but the fact that the Holy Spirit speaks through Scripture. And the implication of this is that the only way for any application to become truly concrete for the congregation or the individual hearer is if the Holy Spirit makes it so.

If the first question was about the pastor to the pew, so to speak, the second question reverses matters: Should the concrete situation of the congregation require something more than simply interpreting Scripture? Bonhoeffer does not think that the concrete situation of the congregation, their gender or political situation or ethnicity, should be taken seriously to such a degree that it becomes determinative, and this is because that could divert attention from the true situation of the congregation as a group of human beings before God, those in their pride and unbelief and selfishness before God. This true situation needs to be addressed by the witness of Scripture to Christ, the one who alone is Lord, Judge, and Savior. The sermon is meant to reveal and resolve this true situation as it interprets Scripture's witness to Christ, the one after whom the listener is really asking. For this to happen, an interpretation bound to Scripture is what is necessary. He writes,

> Was gibt es denn heute Konkreteres als eine Textauslegung gewisser Kapitel der Apokalypse oder der Propheten oder der Bergpre- | digt oder der Geschichte vom barmherzigen Samariter? Ist nicht hier die Textauslegung, sofern sie wirklich diesen Text als Zeugnis des lebendigen Christus nimmt, alles?[41]

> What can be more concrete today than an interpretation of certain chapters of Revelation or of the prophets or of the Sermon on the Mount or of the story of the good Samaritan? Is not the interpretation of the text, insofar as it truly takes this text as a witness to the living Christ, everything?

Universality and particularity are here put in relation to one another, and the underlying notion is that it is a mistake to think they must be separated from one another. This is developed in two different ways in the answer to the second question. First, the particular text chosen, a chapter in Revelation, for example, is the choice for this specific or particular perspective on the universal gospel message that Scripture proclaims, the message about Christ, the *Sache*. And, second, this particular text's relation to the universal gospel is preached in a specific context, a congregation made up of a plurality, in which only the universal status of human beings as sinners before God is taken seriously in an ultimate way. What both of

41. DBW 14:410.

these questions allow Bonhoeffer to do is to further substantiate his commitment to *sachliche Textauslegung*. This, then, gets even further defining and specifying in relation to the witness of the New Testament's genres and in the witness of the pastors who preach the New Testament in part 3 of the lecture.

2.3. Bonhoeffer's Lecture, Part 3: Vergegenwärtigung der neutestamentlichen Botschaft [Contemporizing the New Testament Message]

Contemporizing is an act of the Holy Spirit in which the genuine present is established through a human act of interpretation and proclamation oriented to the essential content of Scripture which witnesses to Christ as he is in his fullness, that is, the unique Savior and Judge who lived, died, and rose again in history and now graciously confronts the human being in his or her need before God. This is an adequate summary of the positive form of contemporizing and its corresponding method as developed in the lecture up to this point, but Bonhoeffer recognizes the need to fill the picture out a bit more. In the final part, he devotes attention to the question of unity and plurality in the New Testament, especially as it relates to the notion of *Zeugnis*, and to the need to flesh out some of the concrete realities of the ongoing witness of the Christian community and its pastors, or in other words, a further filling out of the shape of the human agency at work in interpretation oriented to the subject matter of the Christian gospel.

2.3.1. The New Testament as Witness The notion of Holy Scripture as a *Zeugnis* to God in Christ was introduced just before Bonhoeffer paused to respond to the two questions that concluded part 2. He noted that the purpose of interpreting any and every passage in Scripture is to draw out how each specific text witnesses in this way. This is a crucial point, for it is possible for talk of the *Sache* and Scripture as *Zeugnis* to float free of the particularity of the biblical text.[42] In fact, Bonhoeffer's 1925 essay falls prey to this kind of abstraction. He employs both of these terms in order to develop his notion of the relation between Scripture and history, but the result is not adequate as a description of what is actually there in Scripture. This terminological continuity, therefore, also displays

---

42. John Barclay makes this point in relation to Bultmann: "Interpretation, Not Repetition: Reflections on Bultmann as a Theological Reader of Paul," *Journal of Theological Interpretation*, 9:2 (2015), 201–9. Barclay writes,

> I am conscious that Bultmann's understanding of "interpretation" was itself influenced by his (Kantian and neo-Lutheran) philosophical heritage, which tended to abstract too easily the "subject matter" from the language in which it is couched. Thus, thinking about what we are doing will involve careful scrutiny of our presuppositions about "interpretation" itself. If Bultmann's "method" is not fully detachable from his "results," we will need to utilize his challenge to rethink the method of theological interpretation, and to do so consciously even as biblical scholars. (208)

discontinuity, since by 1935 Bonhoeffer is concerned to allow the diversity of the New Testament to stand, unified by its character as witness. On this account, the collection of diverse texts is gathered around the core, which is Christ. The single gospel has a preference over the diversity, but the plurality retains its integrity, and the result is a richer witness to Christ as the whole of Scripture is able to offer its distinctive voice.

Bonhoeffer begins with Scripture as a whole, both Old and New Testaments. The unity of Scripture is found in the relation of the New to the Old. The New Testament is a witness of how the Old Testament's promise is fulfilled in Christ. The promise-fulfillment dynamic is both a Scriptural and traditional way of relating the Old and New Testaments, one which Bonhoeffer himself employed in 1925. Here it is put to use to point out that Scripture is both united and divided by the person of Christ because he is at its center or heart. And the implication is that everything in Scripture, its whole and its parts, serves to witness to him. He writes:

> Dieser Christus wird bezeugt nicht als das Ewige in Zeitlichem, als der Sinn im Zufälligen, als das Wesen im Unwesentlichen! sondern als der schlechthin Einmalige Menschgewordene, Gestorbene, Auferstandene und *diese* Einmaligkeit Christi in der Geschichte erfüllt das ganze Neue Testament.[43]

> This Christ is attested not as the eternal in the temporal, as the meaning in the accidental, as the essence in the unessential! but rather as the absolutely unique Incarnate one, the one who died, the one who was raised, and *this* uniqueness of Christ in history is what fills the entire New Testament.

Bonhoeffer moves from the broadest relation, Old and New Testaments, to their relation in reference to the concrete historical specificity of the Incarnate Christ's life, death, and resurrection, and now he moves to the various ways the New Testament actually talks about him. This is the case because in one sense the entire New Testament is not filled with this singular Christ in the straightforward way the last sentence of the quotation above might imply. It is filled, instead, with both doctrinal texts, the teaching of Jesus and the Epistles, and historical texts, like the Gospels and Acts. So, how can all of this be subsumed under the heading of "witness"?

Bonhoeffer does not spend too much time trying to describe how a doctrinal text is a witness, presumably because it is more straightforwardly the case that, for example, Paul's writings simply are about Christ. Paul is, as an apostle, a unique witness to the unique Christ, his life, death, and resurrection. The historical texts also have this character of proclaiming Christ, though, because Christ is the one who performs the miracle or teaches the parable or gives the command, that is, it is about him and what he himself is doing when he performs these various actions. The whole of the New Testament is about Christ, and in this way it witnesses to

---

43. DBW 14:411, emphasis original.

him. Bonhoeffer writes, concluding his emphasis on the New Testament's unified character as witness:

> Das Neue Testament ist in Lehre *und* Geschichte *Zeugnis* ,es ist nicht *selbst* etwas, sondern es zeugt von etwas anderem, es hat keinen Wert in sich selbst, sondern nur als Zeugnis von Christus; es ruht nicht in sich selbst, sondern es weist über sich hinaus, seine Sätze und Worte sind nicht an sich wahr und ewig und gültig, sondern nur sofern | sie Zeugnis von Christus sind—das heißt Christus selbst allein wahr sein lassen wollen. Das ganze Neue Testament in allen seinen Teilen will als Zeugnis ausgelegt sein—nicht als Weisheitsbuch, als Lehrbuch, als Buch ewiger Wahrheit, sondern als Buch eines einmaligen Zeugnisses einer einmaligen Tatsache.[44]

> The New Testament is a *witness* in doctrine *and* history; it is not something *itself*, but rather it witnesses to something other; it has no value in itself, but rather only as a witness to Christ; it does not rest in itself, but rather it points beyond itself; its sentences and words are not true and eternal and valid in themselves, but rather only insofar as they are a witness to Christ—that is, they want Christ himself, alone to be true. The whole New Testament, in all its parts, demands to be interpreted as a witness—not as a wisdom book, as a book of doctrine, or as a book of eternal truth, but rather as a book of unique witness to a unique fact.

If every passage *witnesses* to Christ, then *every passage* must so witness to Christ. Has Bonhoeffer's emphasis on the common character of the New Testament as witness been reductionistic after all? Does this picture of unity override the recognition of plurality? It does not. Bonhoeffer moves on to talk about four distinct kinds of material found in the New Testament: doctrinal texts, miracle-stories, parables, and commandments or ethical teaching. The most important thing about Bonhoeffer's discussion at this point for the purposes of this chapter is not the specific points made, but rather the fact that Bonhoeffer is texturing his understanding of *Sache* and *Zeugnis* with specific material found in the New Testament. As a result, only a brief summary of the four types is necessary.

Bonhoeffer first discusses the fact that a Pauline doctrinal text can only be rightly interpreted if its character as a witness is kept in mind.[45] This is not the same point made earlier when he drew out the distinction between a doctrinal text and an historical one. Here the point is made in contrast to viewing Paul's texts as "pure doctrine" or genuine theology. For whatever reason Bonhoeffer did not spell out precisely what he was after here, and in fact, the text we have indicates that he only had notes at this point, but it seems as if he wanted to note that it is a misunderstanding to view Paul's theology as in any way definitive. In other words,

---

44. DBW 14:412-413, emphasis original.
45. DBW 14:413.

recognizing the witness character of Paul's texts relativizes the tradition that has a tendency to elevate Paul's theology as highly as Bonhoeffer's had.

Miracle-stories are not to be interpreted as general truths or as identical to experiences of similar phenomena observable elsewhere, but as proclaiming Christ's authority.[46] Bonhoeffer chooses the example of Christ's miraculous exorcism of demons, recognizing in these stories a potent witness to Christ's power. This should be proclaimed simply as such in Bonhoeffer's time because spiritual powers, whether societal, systemic, or corporate, must be resisted by the means Jesus has made available to his followers, namely, nonviolent forms of praying and fasting as evidences of faith in the Lord who can drive out demons.

The next type of New Testament material considered is the parable.[47] The parable is, according to Mk 4, the unique form of Jesus's speech that he uses to carry out the separation of believers and unbelievers. It is not used in order to communicate general truths through everyday means. The crucial point is not the genre of the parable but about the fact that Jesus uses it to talk about himself. It is utilized to pose a challenge: one must either decide for or against Jesus after hearing the parable. Bonhoeffer spends the most time working on misunderstandings and proper interpretation of parables because of their popularity in a preaching context, and also because they helpfully underscore his main point about Christ being both the goal of the New Testament's witness and the one who actualizes the encounter with the hearer. The parable uniquely brings together Christ as the one who speaks, the one who is spoken about, and the one who brings about the result.

The New Testament's ethical teaching is also to be understood as witness to Christ, while remaining irreducibly ethical teaching. As in the case of parables, in this instance an interpreter moves back from the speech to the speaker, tracing the command to the authority. It is crucial to note, though, that this authority, this Lord, is Jesus or, even more specifically, the crucified one. Bonhoeffer says:

> Das Gebot der Bergpredigt oder die Paränese des Paulus verstanden werden als Zeugnis von dem Herrn, dem Gekreuzigten und Auferstandenen, nicht als ob das Gebot damit bagatellisiert würde, es bleibt bestehen aber es ist Zeugnis, Verkündigung von Christus, das heißt es ist nun Gnade.[48]

> The commandments of the Sermon on the Mount or the ethical teaching of Paul must be understood as witness to the Lord, the crucified and resurrected one, which is not to suggest that the commandment would be minimized—it remains as it is—but it is a witness, proclamation of Christ, that is, it is now grace.

The key question to ask when interpreting ethical material in the New Testament is: In what sense is Christ speaking this commandment with authority? As such,

46. DBW 14:413.
47. DBW 14:414.
48. DBW 14:415.

the one who is able to hear and actually obeys is the one who is enabled to perceive the way this particular text witnesses to Christ.

In all of these discussions, Bonhoeffer makes a very important move. He disavows an interest in the general or universal truth, whether of a parable or a doctrine or an ethical principle. If one focuses attention on finding this sort of thing in the New Testament, then that person is not paying attention to the actual material he or she is reading. Instead, the interpreter is after the particular witness of this or that passage of Scripture, and it is only when that particularity is in view—this parable or this command or this miracle or this doctrinal text—that the view can open up to the truly universal and concrete reality of the Christian gospel, which is the crucified and resurrected Christ. The *Sache* is served by careful attention, interpretation, of the particular witnesses of the New Testament. This, again, but now concretely textured, is *sachliche Textauslegung*.

Scripture's particularity has resulted in Bonhoeffer sharpening up his conception of the unified nature of Scripture as witness, but the difficulties that arise in trying to demonstrate how this is so in points of detail, text after text, have also called into question his position on allegorical interpretation of Scripture. In the essay from 1925, he was opposed to allegorical interpretation. By 1935, he is no longer. He now thinks that God's word is too abundant and rich a reality to be completely exhausted by grammatical or literal forms of interpretation.[49] He wonders, as a result, why the Scriptures should not be read symbolically and typologically. He states two criteria for doing so properly. First, nothing other than Christ should be discovered, and this only makes sense because the whole of Scripture is a witness to Christ. Second, it must be acknowledged that an allegorical method does not contain any special power to unleash Scripture's witness. Allegorical interpretation still depends on Christ speaking by the Spirit. If these two criteria are met, then allegorical or symbolic or typological interpretation should be employed with obscure passages, not as a way of proving points in theological argumentation but as a way of praising God for the manifold ways in which Scripture has been designated a witness to Christ. Allegorical interpretation is now a freedom the church should utilize in interpreting its Scriptures.

2.3.2. Our Witness Bonhoeffer's discussion of his form of contemporizing still needs to fill out the nature of the interpreter who does this *sachliche Textauslegung*. The New Testament as witness has a corresponding witness in the preacher. This is not an incidental afterthought in the lecture. Scripture needs an interpreter, a person who chooses the text, translates the text, interprets the texts for the benefit of others, and seeks to live the text. Christ and the Spirit contemporize the New Testament by establishing and enabling the interpretive acts of pastors like those Bonhoeffer was addressing in Hauteroda. His keyword to describe the interpreter's agency is freedom. He writes:

49. DBW 14:416-417.

Die Grenzen sind abgesteckt, innerhalb derer rechtmäßig von Vergegenwärtigung geredet werden kann. In diesen Grenzen aber bleiben dem Prediger noch einige wesentliche Freiheiten.[50]

The limits within which one can speak legitimately about contemporizing have been staked out. In these limits, though, the preacher still retains some significant freedoms.

The first freedom is translating the biblical text from its original language.[51] As we have seen in Bonhoeffer's own interpretation of Scriptural passages in other chapters of this study, he considers himself free to translate Hebrew and Greek texts, but often does so in direct conversation with Luther's translation into German. He notes here that the Luther Bible is a precious gift, but it is also not always the best translation for the circumstance. There is an opportunity in translation, a possibility of helpfully focusing Scripture as it comes to expression in a different language. This is, again, not only a freedom but also an obligation. Bonhoeffer takes it for granted that language is in service to the congregation's needs and that church language needs to be accessible for people in terms they understand. One must be careful though that the choice of language does not lose touch with the text of Scripture.

The second freedom is choosing a text for preaching.[52] Christ, the whole Christ—the Incarnate one who was crucified and raised and living as Lord—must be preached in every sermon, and since Scripture as a whole witnesses to Christ in precisely this way the selection of the text is an important decision because each text, as we have seen, provides a unique perspective on the whole Christ. But, at least on the surface, the everyday situation of the pastor and congregation is about a lot more than this since those who gather at church each week are parenting, working in a variety of different sectors, managing money, engaging politically, developing relationships, and several other practical things. Should, then, the pastor allow the questions and concerns and issues facing the congregation and its members to determine the selection of the texts to be preached? Bonhoeffer grants the legitimacy of the question, and yet recognizes a precondition from which the concern to choose texts that address these issues arises. The pastor knows that the entirety of the witness to Christ, an entirety manifest in each particular witness found in the New Testament, is the place from which to make sense of these various practical concerns. The pastor must become convinced that the congregation really does not want him or her to address their burning questions about parenting, but what they have really come to church for is the proclamation of the whole Christ. Only when this has been proclaimed will the foreground, daily concerns of life be put into proper perspective. God gave the church the Scriptures so that it could attend to Scripture as it witnesses to Christ, and it is

50. DBW 14:417.
51. DBW 14:417.
52. DBW 14:418.

the task of preaching to make this manifest. Looking to Christ as he is proclaimed from every text of Scripture, that is, Christ in all his fullness, will untangle a good many practical knots in the process.

Before addressing the final freedom the preacher has as a witness, Bonhoeffer turns his attention to an exposition of various New Testament texts in order to make a contribution to the discussion on contemporizing.[53] He has, in other words, talked about what it is and how it should be done, but he now wants to demonstrate it through three case studies. Unfortunately, his lecture manuscript breaks off at this point, and we are left only with some notes about what he was planning to cover and some student notes from the concluding sections of the lecture. These sections are not sufficient for careful analysis, but it is possible to determine that the final freedom had to do with making the New Testament credible, and it seems like Bonhoeffer meant this in two ways, the first having to do with credibility in the modern world and the second having to do with the integrity of the preacher's life as a witness to Christ. The first of these is especially tantalizing and probably finds some parallels and expansions in the comments about the world come of age in Bonhoeffer's correspondence from prison. As for his case studies, he planned to address grace and discipleship, church and world, and the Good Samaritan. Though this material is not available as it was delivered in August 1935, it is perhaps helpful to think of this lecture manuscript ending with an ellipsis, since much of the content that would have been expressed in Bonhoeffer's form of contemporizing is to be found in *Nachfolge*. The way he engages material of this kind will be picked up in the next chapter.

3. Synthesis

In 1935 Bonhoeffer has a clear theological vision of what interpretation of Scripture is and what it is for. This theological vision *developed* from the essay he wrote in 1925. This chapter has shown aspects of continuity and discontinuity between these two pieces, and though it is not necessary to rehearse each of these aspects, it is important to recognize one development in particular that has implications for Bonhoeffer's thinking about interpretation and how he actually goes about the task of interpreting Scripture, a task we will return to again in the next chapter. We are now in a position to try to understand how Bonhoeffer's emphasis on the New Testament as *Zeugnis*, an important word for him in 1925 and 1935, influences his conceptualization of the task of interpretation. The notion of *Zeugnis* has been given texture through the analysis of various New Testament forms. Before he addressed the issue of allegorical interpretation in the lecture, he summarized the meaning of contemporizing, and this formulation is modulated at this later stage of the lecture in light of his discussion of the tangible forms actually found in the

---

53. DBW 14:419.

New Testament. His summary, better treated at this point as a conclusion, is best quoted in full in order to see how all the threads come together at this point:

> Vergegenwärtigung neutestamentlicher Texte heißt also zunächst: sie als Zeugnis von Christus als dem gekreuzigten, auferstandenen und in die Nachfolge rufenden Herrn auszulegen in der Gewißheit, daß Christus das Subjekt der Vergegenwärtigung ist. Dies Zeugnis ist als streng einmaliges Zeugnis eines einmaligen Geschehens zu verstehen. Nur wo dem Neuen Testament dieser Charakter der Einmaligkeit bleibt, kann es ernsthaft als Zeugnis von Christus verstanden werden. An der Einmaligkeit—also an der Ablehnung jeglicher Möglichkeit Ewiges und Zeitgebundenes, Gottes Wort und Menschenwort in der Schrift aufweisbar zu machen und zu unterscheiden—hängt die Möglichkeit der | Vergegenwärtigung—denn Vergegenwärtigung heißt, daß Christus selbst redet durch den Heiligen Geist als der durch die Schrift bezeugte Geschichtliche—daß Christus uns *entgegen*tritt,—nicht daß wir eine allgemeine Wahrheit im Neuen Testament bestätigt finden. An der Auslegung des Neuen Testaments als dem einmaligen Zeugnis von dem geschichtlichen und lebendigen Christus hängt die Vergegenwärtigung.[54]

Contemporizing New Testament texts thus means, first of all, that they, as a witness to Christ as the crucified, resurrected Lord who calls to discipleship, are to be interpreted in the certainty that Christ is the subject of contemporizing. This witness is to be understood as an emphatically singular witness to a singular event. Only where the New Testament retains this character of singularity can it be understood seriously as a witness to Christ. On that singularity—that is, on the rejection of any possibility of making demonstrable and distinguishing the eternal and time-bound, God's word and man's word in Scripture—the possibility of contemporizing depends, for contemporizing means that Christ himself speaks through the Holy Spirit as the historical one attested through Scripture, that Christ *confronts* us, not that we discover a universal truth confirmed by the New Testament. Contemporizing depends on the interpretation of the New Testament as the singular witness to the historical and living Christ.

Bonhoeffer's intensity of focus on the New Testament as witness to Christ makes here for the most densely Christological passage in the whole lecture. At this stage, Christ is both the object to whom the witnesses point and the subject of contemporizing. Christ and Spirit are closely coordinated, but the emphasis has shifted to Christ's agency because of the content of the New Testament, conceived as witness to the singularity of Christ. *Einmaligkeit* [singularity] is a keyword in this paragraph, showing up in various forms five times, and serves to underscore the relation of the witness of Scripture as a whole and the specificity of Jesus' life, death, and resurrection with which it is concerned. There is an irreducible historical focus in all this, time-bound texts and the historical particularity of Jesus,

---

54. DBW 14:415-416, emphasis original.

that makes the confrontation, the present as the presence of Jesus, what it is. The living Lord who calls to discipleship now, an emphasis developed extensively in *Nachfolge*, does so by the Spirit through *sachliche Textauslegung*, interpretation of the New Testament's various witnesses as they serve as a singular witness to Christ. Bonhoeffer's hermeneutic was forged initially in Berlin and is here modulated through his developing theology, the conflict with the German Christians, the practicalities of pastoral ministry, training in Finkenwalde, and the need for the Spirit's guidance in the midst of the struggle.

Chapter 5

FINKENWALDE: PRACTICING INTERPRETATION IN THE SEMINARY

Dietrich Bonhoeffer's biblical interpretation in the 1930s, taking shape in the various forms of meditations, sermons, expositions, and lectures and in the various contexts of the academic lecture hall, the church's pulpit, the prayer kneeler, and in pastoral training at Finkenwalde, is indebted to the theological hermeneutic developed as a student in 1925. His vision of theology and preaching depended on a specific form of pneumatological interpretation, or interpretation of Scripture on the basis of the Spirit (Chapter 1). This revelation-Scripture dynamic is on display in his book *Schöpfung und Fall* (Chapter 2) and in his sermons from London (Chapter 3), and these new contexts also forced further development of it. By the middle of the decade and in new circumstances again, Bonhoeffer reflected on hermeneutical questions, producing a more nuanced and mature version of his earlier Spirit-hermeneutic (Chapter 4). Just as the analysis of interpretive acts in Chapters 2 and 3 displayed how the earlier hermeneutic worked, so this chapter will return to interpretive activity in order to show what the newly inflected Spirit-hermeneutic of the Finkenwalde period looks like in practice by analyzing two sections of *Nachfolge*.

The argument of this chapter, though, is not only a repetition of the theory-practice arguments made already, or even just another example of the continuity on display from 1925 through the 1930s. It is meant to continue to drive those points home, but it is also meant to say something distinctive about *Nachfolge*. The biblical interpretation in *Nachfolge* is the clearest place to see what Bonhoeffer thinks and does with the Bible. *Nachfolge* is the crowning achievement of Bonhoeffer's work with Scripture. It is the quintessential Bonhoeffer on the Bible. To a certain degree substantiation of this claim must wait until the evidence is shown through a close reading of two texts from the book, but it is important to begin giving an account for this claim.[1] For Bonhoeffer, interpretation is dependent on the Spirit and bound to Scripture as it attests Christ in the unity of the diverse

---

1. This is especially necessary because this claim is partly in conflict with a line of interpretation in Bonhoeffer scholarship that sees *Nachfolge* as a detour into the woods of Pomerania. There is a brief note along these lines in the editors' introduction to *Discipleship*. The editors write:

witnesses found in both testaments. Additionally, for Bonhoeffer, interpretation is an act of freedom on the part of the interpreter, a person who interprets a text in a context and for a purpose. In *Nachfolge*, these two poles, Scripture and interpreter, are held in tension in precisely the way Bonhoeffer thought they should be. The interpreter is bound to Scripture, thus making it central, from the first sentence of the preface and on every page thereafter.[2] Scripture is for interpretation, thus making the interpreter's freedom, actions, theology, context, and needs essential. The centrality of Scripture, given and sustained by the Spirit insofar as Christ is seen as its subject matter, and the necessary freedom of its interpreter, a freedom given and sustained by the Spirit, fuse in *Nachfolge* so that the biblical text is constantly on display through careful, detailed interpretation tailored by its expositor so that each diverse witness is honored in its distinctive contribution to Scripture's presentation of Christ and provides direction and guidance for the needs of the community being addressed. The result of this fusion is a book that shows a distinct approach to interpretation: direct, urgent, clear, and original, a book concerned with communicating accessible conceptualities, careful thinking

> In *Discipleship* the issues of peace, nonresistance to evil, and forgiveness of enemies coalesced to such an extent that some critics saw the book as too otherworldly and impractical in how Christians had to deal with an enemy such as Nazism—so dangerous to Christian civilization and so entrenched in power militarily. Some critics see *Discipleship* as more of a detour along the way to the more realistic actions of Bonhoeffer the conspirator, the affirmer of a world come of age in the prison letters. (DBWE, 4:14-15)

In a similar vein, in a letter to Bonhoeffer in 1936 Barth responded—not to the book which had not been written yet, but to the Finkenwalde context within which the book would be written—that he was concerned about a number of groups who evidenced a "resignation over against the original christological and eschatological approach in favor of (in fact, increasingly abstract!) actualizations in a specifically human sphere … a theoretical-practical system" (DBWE 14:267-268; DBW 14:251). Barth worries this is happening at Finkenwalde. Taking each respectively, the claim for continuity put forward in this book certainly puts a question mark over any notion of a "detour," but the specific claim made in this chapter is not about the content of *Nachfolge* and its relation to other aspects of Bonhoeffer's thinking or actions, but rather is about *the way* he engages the Bible. In partial response to Barth's tentative critique it is worth pointing out that the centrality of the Bible and its interpretation to Bonhoeffer's life and ministry in Finkenwalde, construed in the ecclesial–hermeneutical terms I have put forward thus far, would, at least in principle, presuppose an openness to the kind of address that characterizes the Christological and eschatological approach he thinks should be taken more seriously. In other words, biblical interpretation in *Nachfolge* is evidence of such an approach.

   2. Bonhoeffer writes the following in the first sentence of the book: "Es stellt sich in Zeiten der kirchlichen Erneuerung von selbst ein, daß uns die Heilige Schrift reicher wird" (DBW 4:21). The translators of the English edition render this sentence: "In times of church renewal holy scripture naturally becomes richer in content for us" (DBWE 4:37).

about the relation between past and present, history and theology, and a book saturated by extended engagement with Scriptural material. All of this can be seen when it is read as a species of biblical interpretation.

This chapter offers such a reading. Since *Nachfolge* is situated in the Finkenwalde period and since the previous chapter already laid out the historical setting for Bonhoeffer's time in Finkenwalde it is not necessary to devote more time to the historical setting of the book. It is important to trace Bonhoeffer's relationship to the content, themes, and texts treated in *Nachfolge* though, because the book was the product of a long period of thought and prayer and lecturing. As a result, the first section of the chapter offers some brief, preliminary comments about how *Nachfolge* came to be throughout the course of the 1930s (Section 1.1). In this same section, the criteria utilized in selecting the two texts for close readings will also be described (Section 1.2). Next, a detailed exposition of Bonhoeffer's interpretation of Mt. 6:25-34 in Part 1 of *Nachfolge* and of various Pauline texts on Baptism in Part 2 will follow (Section 2). Finally, a synthesis will complete the chapter (Section 3).

1. Preliminaries

1.1. The Production of Nachfolge

In one sense it is entirely appropriate to say, as above, that *Nachfolge* is a product of Finkenwalde. The reason this is the case is that the process of writing the book and the steps followed in order to publish it happened at the end of the Finkenwalde period, the publication coming just after Finkenwalde was shut down in September 1937. In another sense, though, it is not a completely accurate assessment because the book had been percolating for many years before Finkenwalde existed, and the end result was a reworking of a large number of lecture manuscripts, some developed at Finkenwalde and some not, into book form. It is not necessary to repeat the work of Bonhoeffer's biographers or the effort that the editors of the critical editions of Bonhoeffer's works, in both German and English, undertook to trace the exact stages of the development of *Nachfolge*.[3] For the purposes of this chapter, it is sufficient to note that *Nachfolge* was unknowingly conceived in Bonhoeffer's first engagements with the Sermon on the Mount, dating to sometime in the early 1930s, probably to his time in the United States at Union Theological Seminary.[4] In the middle of the 1930s, the New Testament lecture

---

3. Bethge, *Bonhoeffer*, 450–60; DBW 4:8-13; DBWE 4:24-28. I am dependent in this section on these two sources, and noting that here will limit the amount of additional footnotes.

4. It is hard to pin down the precise influence, but it seems most likely to be the many lengthy conversations at Union that Bonhoeffer had with his French friend, Jean Lasserre. Lasserre's pacifist reading of the Sermon on the Mount would have stood in stark contrast with Bonhoeffer's initial foray into the material just a couple years prior in the late 1920s in Barcelona.

cycles at Finkenwalde afforded ample opportunity for Bonhoeffer to develop his thinking by working through the key biblical texts that form the structure of the book—narrative texts from the Gospels, the Sermon on the Mount, and Pauline texts. At the other end of the decade, the influence of the material content of the actual published book extended beyond Finkenwalde to Bonhoeffer's practice of training pastors in the underground, illegal settings of the Collective Pastorates, gatherings that took place right up to 1940. Thus, the themes, texts, and content of *Nachfolge* were constant companions for Bonhoeffer, ranging over the entirety of the 1930s.

The point of this brief note about the production of *Nachfolge* is to situate the exposition below, but also to further substantiate the claim that what is found in the book is representative of Bonhoeffer's biblical interpretation in the entirety of the 1930s. But two additional implications also arise from this. The interpretation of *Nachfolge*, with its long development, is not dependent on a careful reconstruction of the political context. Bonhoeffer's text should not be read exclusively with an eye to specific developments in the ongoing story of the Confessing Church's engagement with Nazism.[5] It is a piece that brings Bonhoeffer's regular work of theology, and a kind of theology deeply indebted to biblical interpretation, to a climax. It is, of course, not disconnected from the events unfolding after 1933, but it cannot be reduced to a set of reactions to those developments.[6] Finally, *Nachfolge*, coming as it does at the end of a long period of gestation, is Bonhoeffer's longest and most mature piece of writing. The reception of it, both immediately following its publication and after his death, sets it apart as a defining publication for understanding his theology and, from the perspective of this study, his biblical interpretation. Unlike his reflections in his *Ethik* and *Widerstand und Ergebung*, this work is complete and it is the most sustained attempt he made at producing a piece that blends the worlds of academic rigor and pastoral sensitivity.

1.2. Selection Criteria

Since this chapter again picks up the preferred practice of close readings of Bonhoeffer's texts, which, to repeat the primary rationale, allows one to pay detailed attention to the actual interpretive decisions he makes as he moves from the biblical texts to his comments about them, it is important to briefly mention the criteria employed in choosing passages from *Nachfolge* for the exposition below. The first criterion utilized here in deciding which text to read closely is, as in other chapters of the book, the fact that a text needs to be both long enough to

---

5. The editor's introduction to the English translation of *Nachfolge*, entitled *Discipleship*, falls into this trap. See especially DBWE 4:2-7.

6. Bethge notes the important role of the events of 1933 in focusing Bonhoeffer's questions and their answers, while also relativizing this since he recognizes that Bonhoeffer's interests in these same questions and answers were present before 1933. See Bethge, *Bonhoeffer*, 457–60.

trace and show the development of the process of interpretation and short enough to realistically deal with the entire piece.

In addition, the book is structured in two parts, the first dealing with texts from the Gospels while the second part engages Pauline texts. Each part of the book offers a different style of exposition, with long quotations of Scripture and expositions characterizing the first part and more thematic engagement with biblical texts from a variety of Pauline contexts in the second part. The first half of the book looks more like *Schöpfung und Fall*, while the second half of the book looks more like *Gemeinsames Leben*. The second criterion, therefore, was derived from this two-part structure and the different styles of exposition. A text from each part of the book was chosen. The book's structure is not the only reason why this decision is helpful in an analysis of the relationship between hermeneutical statement and actual interpretive practice, however. In this specific instance, the opportunity to analyze a text from the Sermon on the Mount, Bonhoeffer's exposition of Mt. 6:25-34, and various Pauline texts on baptism afford an opportunity to test Bonhoeffer's views as they were described in his lecture, "Vergegenwärtigung neutestamentlicher Texte." In that lecture, which the previous chapter covered in detail, the unified witness of the diverse perspectives of the New Testament's authors was constantly spoken about as the goal of Bonhoeffer's brand of interpretation. In *Nachfolge*, this becomes a material point because the notion of "discipleship" is presented as a unified concept in both its different Synoptic and Pauline frameworks. The decision to treat a text from each part of the book will help to test Bonhoeffer's consistency on this point.

2. Close Readings

2.1. Bonhoeffer's Exposition of Mt. 6:25-34

2.1.1. Matthew 6:25-34 in the Context of Nachfolge The exposition of the Sermon on the Mount follows five chapters organized by various themes connected to discipleship: the call to discipleship, grace, obedience, discipleship and the cross, and discipleship and the individual. These chapters focus on aspects of discipleship through the lens of narrative, primarily from the Gospels. Bonhoeffer maintains a narrative element in his transition to the Sermon on the Mount, primarily by drawing attention to the Matthean setting of Jesus' sermon at the top and bottom of the section. But just as Matthew's text shifts its tone, from narrative to teaching, so Bonhoeffer's text shifts significantly. Those previous chapters were brief, averaging around eleven pages. Chapter 6 in *Nachfolge* is over ninety pages in the German edition and over eighty pages in the English edition. The increased length is largely due to the reproduction of the entirety of the Matthean sermon in Luther's German. Bonhoeffer works from the beginning of Mt. 5 right through to the end of Mt. 7. More often than not, he treats each segment of Matthew's text as an independent unit and gives it a new heading in his text. On occasion, and the text considered below falls into this category, he lumps some texts together under a single heading.

In these instances, he sees these texts as related, a point that surfaces in some cross-referencing between them. For Mt. 6:19-24 (storing up treasures in heaven) and 6:25-34 (do not worry), Bonhoeffer provides the summary heading, "Die Einfalt des sorglosen Lebens" [The Simplicity of Carefree Life].[7]

2.1.2. Bonhoeffer's Biblical Text Bonhoeffer kept the biblical text front and center throughout the entire section, which is to say that he gave the biblical text priority, basing his comments on it and making sure that this decision was visible in the structure. He employs Luther's translation, but as has been the case in other expositions Bonhoeffer is clearly working with the biblical texts in its original Greek, which allows him to go in different directions from Luther.[8] With respect to the text under consideration in this section, Bonhoeffer does not amend Luther's text. He reproduces it and bases his commentary upon it.

Since the biblical text he works with is quite long it will not be quoted in its entirety below, but it is helpful to have the broad contours of it in view while observing the way Bonhoeffer engages it. According to Matthew, Jesus continued his teaching with a command to not worry, particularized in the first instance about life which consists in eating and drinking and in the second instance by the body and its clothing. The rhetorical question that concludes v. 25, "Is not life more than food, and the body more than clothes?" gives way in vv. 26-30 to an exhortation to observe the way that God takes care of the birds of the air and the flowers of the field. This section is also punctuated by rhetorical questions that call into question the validity and self-evident nature of worry. In v. 31 Jesus repeats his command and draws attention to the fact that the questions that drive a person to worry—questions like "What will we eat or drink or wear?"—are questions that occupy pagans who do not know that God cares for them. In contrast to this kind of striving, in v. 33 Jesus presents a positive object to strive after, namely,

---

7. DBW 4:167; DBWE 4:161.

8. It is interesting to note that, in contrast with his approach in *Schöpfung und Fall*, in *Nachfolge* Bonhoeffer utilizes footnotes in line with scholarly conventions, both to note textual variations and translation options but also to engage in broader conversations about issues that might be either interesting to his readers or could fend off potential criticisms. For examples of his engagement with the Greek text, see DBW 4:107-108, DBWE 4:108-109 where Bonhoeffer notes a double meaning for "peacemakers" in Mt. 5:9 and where he also notes that "righteousness" is anarthrous. One could also look at Bonhoeffer's note on August Tholuck's commentary on the Sermon on the Mount in order to see his engagement with the perspectives of other scholars on this section of Scripture (see DBW 4:139; DBWE 4:136). The use of footnotes is probably due to the fact that he had been reading and reflecting on the biblical texts and the work of other scholars on these texts for a long time, but also because the educational context of Finkenwalde afforded him the time to research and write his lectures. These were "New Testament Lectures," and preparing them as such, for the purpose of theologically educating pastors for the Confessing Church, meant an increased engagement with Bonhoeffer's academic training.

God's kingdom and his righteousness, objects that bring everything else needed in tow. The final verse of the passage, v. 34, brings the discussion back to the initial command of v. 25 and repeated in v. 31, but this time draws attention to the fact that worry is directed toward tomorrow. Jesus concludes: "Therefore do not worry about tomorrow, for tomorrow will worry about itself. Each day has enough trouble of its own."

2.1.3. Bonhoeffer's Commentary on Mt. 6:25-34 Interpreters make choices. Bonhoeffer did not want to simply quote the text from Matthew and leave it at that, a reproduction of the biblical text. Nor did he want to repeat it by walking through each element of what Jesus said making sure to comment on everything in order to draw out how this or that element could be thought about or applied in his setting. Instead, he interpreted the material in front of him, and to anticipate some of what will unfold below, one of the key choices he made was, after the quotation of the biblical text and a brief introductory paragraph, to begin his exposition from the end rather than the beginning of the passage. This choice was also accompanied by a particular hermeneutical framing that allowed him to read the command of Jesus as a promise. These two observations will be expanded and substantiated in what follows, but it is important at this junction to flag up the fact that they underscore how, on the surface, it appears that Bonhoeffer is straightforwardly working through the biblical text in front of him, but upon further reflection this section of *Nachfolge* is carefully construed and constructed and presented for a particular purpose. It is an *interpretation* of Jesus' words.

In the first paragraph, Bonhoeffer juxtaposes the central element of the passage, Jesus' command, "Sorget nicht!" [Do not worry!], with the way worry or anxiety actually works in people's lives. There is a conflict here that must be understood and brought to resolution. Bonhoeffer's task is thus set out for him. He begins:

> Sorget nicht! Die Güter spiegeln dem menschlichen Herzen vor, ihm Sicherheit und Sorglosigkeit zu geben; aber in Wahrheit verursachen sie gerade erst die Sorge. Das Herz, das sich an die Güter hängt, empfängt mit ihnen die erstickende Last der Sorge. Die Sorge schafft sich Schätze, und die Schätze schaffen wieder die Sorge. Wir wollen unser Leben durch die Güter sichern, wir wollen durch Sorge sorglos werden; aber in Wahrheit erweist sich das Gegenteil. Die | Fesseln, die uns an die Güter binden, die die Güter festhalten, sind selbst—Sorgen.[9]

> Do not worry! Earthly goods deceive the human heart into believing that they give it security and freedom from worry, but in truth, they actually produce worry. The heart that clings to earthly goods receives with them the suffocating burden of worry. Worry creates treasures, and treasures create worry all over again. We want to secure our lives through earthly goods, we want, through worry, to become worry-free, but in truth, the opposite happens. The chains that bind us to earthly goods—that hold on to earthly goods—are themselves worries.

---

9. DBW 4:171.

This paragraph is succinct, efficiently introducing a number of important elements for Bonhoeffer's interpretation. It not only flags up the primary tension to be worked out, as already noted above, but it also introduces the keyword *Sorge* [worry] (in various forms) and makes links back to vv. 19-24, the immediately preceding section of Matthew's text that Bonhoeffer sees as linked to the verses he is expositing here. The link is made in lexical terms—*Die Güter* [earthly goods], *Schätze* [treasures] (synonymous, for Bonhoeffer, with earthly goods), and *Das Herz* [the heart]—though here the point is to extend the implications of the previous text so that a potential result of not storing up treasures in heaven is that a person is consigned to a life of worry that he conceives in terms of a cycle of anxiety.

The desire he identifies is that people want to be free from worry and anxiety, and the chief strategy for achieving this goal is through the acquisition of earthly goods. Worry is strictly identified with a state of psychological anxiety at this point, and thus worry and security are opposites. In a sense then, the command that starts and finishes this section of Jesus' sermon, "Sorget nicht!," is actually conceived in parallel to the desire of the human heart. The goal of both Jesus' command and the person who desires to be free of anxiety is the same: to become worry-free. The problem, which is also the reason that these two are not exactly parallel notions after all, is that the worry-cycle is a kind of concealed slavery. Bonhoeffer clearly lays out the acquisition strategy in this paragraph, but he delays in developing the alternative strategy, holding back at this stage on the reason why Jesus' command is something entirely different.

Instead, he draws out the rationale fueling the strategy of acquisition in the next paragraph. His interpretive action is subtle. Jesus speaks about worry, but does not link worry with the future until the last verse of the passage. Bonhoeffer starts here though, creatively reflecting on the way that people worryingly acquire things to secure the future. He writes, "Sorge ist immer auf das Morgen gerichtet" [Worry is always directed toward tomorrow].[10] He derived the material in the preceding, introductory paragraph, the point about the enslaving worry-cycle, from the temporal element introduced in the final verse of the passage, v. 34. He starts from where the passage ends and reads that verse back through the whole. This is a key interpretive decision, and it could have been otherwise. So, why does he do this? What does this decision accomplish? What interpretive possibilities open up for Bonhoeffer as a result of this choice?

Reading the passage from the end allows him to privilege v. 33 as the climax of the section. Read in this way, Bonhoeffer is able to conclude the section on the positive point about seeking Christ rather than on the repetition of the negative command, "Sorget nicht!" Interestingly, there is a similar structure in Lk 12:22-31. In Luke's version of this material Jesus does not repeat the command as the treatment of worrying comes to a close, and he does not put his point about worry in a future frame at all. He concludes the passage with the positive point about the

10. DBW 4:171.

heart being where a person puts his or her treasure, presenting the passages in an opposite order than that found in Matthew. Luke's account is likely influencing Bonhoeffer's reading at this point. This interpretive decision also allows Bonhoeffer to sharpen up the contrast between tomorrow and today, and this emphasis sets up the main conflict Bonhoeffer is trying to resolve since "tomorrow" implies that the worry-cycle is operating while "today" correlates with Jesus' command and the example of the birds and flowers. Bringing the future point at the end of the passage to the beginning of the passage allows Bonhoeffer to read this section of the sermon as a promise from Jesus rather than a straightforward command.

How does he do this? After his comment about worry being directed toward tomorrow, he loosely paraphrases the final sentence in v. 34 about each day having enough trouble of its own in order to underscore that a person's focus should not be on tomorrow but on today. He writes:

> Wer das Morgen ganz in die Hand Gottes legt und heute ganz empfängt, was er zum Leben braucht, der allein ist wahrhaft gesichert. Das tägliche Empfangen macht mich frei vom Morgen. Der Gedanke an das Morgen liefert mich der unendlichen Sorge aus.[11]

> Only the person who puts tomorrow completely into God's hands and fully receives today what he or she needs for life is truly secure. Receiving daily makes me free from tomorrow. The thought of tomorrow gives me endless worry.

Receiving what is needed today is the alternative to acquiring earthly goods through worry for tomorrow. The goal, again, is the same, namely, to become worry-free, but the strategies employed and the results turn out to be rather different. The latter is depicted as a kind of slavery to anxiety, whereas the former is depicted as a kind of freedom. The conflict is at its sharpest here.

Up to this point, Bonhoeffer, without saying so, has utilized the temporal element in v. 34 to construct these alternative forms of life and he has paraphrased the final part of v. 34, but now he makes his reliance on this verse for the framing of his exposition so far explicit by quoting Jesus' words, "Sorget nicht für den anderen Morgen" [Do not worry about tomorrow]. He does so, though, to raise a pointed question about how to interpret Jesus' command. After the quotation he writes:

> Das ist entweder ein furchtbarer Hohn auf die Armen und Elenden, zu denen Jesus gerade spricht, auf alle die, die—menschlich geredet—morgen verhungern, wenn sie heute nicht sorgen. Es ist entweder ein unerträgliches Gesetz, das der Mensch mit Widerwillen von sich stößt oder aber—es ist die einzigartige Verkündigung des Evangeliums selbst von der Freiheit der Kinder Gottes, die einen Vater im Himmel haben, der ihnen seinen lieben Sohn geschenkt hat. Wie sollte er uns mit ihm nicht alles schenken?[12]

11. DBW 4:171.
12. DBW 4:171-172.

This is either an awful mockery of the poor and suffering—those precisely to whom Jesus is speaking—all those who, humanly speaking, will starve tomorrow if they do not worry today. It is either an unbearable law that a person indignantly rejects, or however, it is the unique proclamation of the gospel itself, of the freedom of the children of God who have a father in heaven who has given them his beloved son. How could he not give us everything with him?

He identifies a potential problem with the general nature of Jesus' exhortation, and he raises a question about how exactly Jesus' words should be understood. People worryingly acquire earthly resources to preserve their lives in the future. It is possible, then, that Jesus is announcing a command that cannot be accomplished in the face of the way things actually work in the world and must work for a lot of people. Bonhoeffer does not think this is the case, though, or at least that is how his alternative proposal should be taken. The notion that Jesus' command should be taken as a proclamation of the gospel is Bonhoeffer's preference, and that will become clear as he continues to work through the biblical text.

Before that is traced, though, it is important to pause to note how this positive interpretive proposal is framed. The proclamation of the gospel is conceptually expanded by an allusion to Rom. 8, specifically vv. 21, on the freedom of the children of God, and 32, which mentions the Son and provides the material for the question that finishes Bonhoeffer's paragraph. The Pauline order is important because God, spoken of as the father in heaven in the Sermon on the Mount and conflated with the God of Rom. 8, first gives the Son and then everything else with him, a thought striking in its parallel with v. 33 on seeking first the kingdom and righteousness and receiving everything else as well. This kind of interpretive linking is made possible by the assumption of the New Testament's unity but also by seeing how each New Testament witness attests Christ, both points made in the lecture, "Vergegenwärtigung neutestamentlicher Texte."

"Sorget nicht für den anderen Morgen" [Do not worry about tomorrow] is to be understood as the gospel of Jesus Christ rather than as law. Two factors are determinative for reading the text in this way. First, the grammar of the sentence, the fact that it is an imperative, is not determinative for its interpretation. Rather, the subject who utters the sentence is. Thinking back again to Bonhoeffer's hermeneutic developed in the "Vergegenwärtigung neutestamentlicher Texte" lecture, it is important to recognize that a command of Jesus is "of Jesus," given by the Lord who is gracious. The second factor is the recipient. Bonhoeffer writes, "Nur der Nachfolgende, der Jesus erkannt hat, empfängt aus diesem Wort die Zusage der Liebe des Vaters Jesu Christi und die Freiheit von allen Dingen" [Only the one following, the person who knows Jesus, can receive from this word the promise of the love of the father of Jesus Christ and freedom from all things].[13] Faith in Jesus Christ makes the disciple worry-free because Jesus takes the next day out of the hands of his disciples, thus freeing them from trying anxiously to

13. DBW 4:172.

take control of their future. Because of their faith in Christ, those following him can trust that God, who alone runs the world, will take care of them. In just a few sentences, Bonhoeffer offers an interpretation of the command as promise, links it to faith in Jesus who constitutes the promise, and to a notion of faith in Christ as a precondition for a Christian understanding of providence, an interpretive link immediately validated as Bonhoeffer moves back up the passage to Jesus' emphasis on birds and flowers.

He does not quote anything from vv. 26-30, the part concerned with the birds and lilies, and he does not say much about them at all. The birds and lilies are examples for disciples insofar as they live only with reference to today. For Bonhoeffer, this section provides some expansion on what daily receiving looks like. About these creatures, he writes:

> Sie brauchen die Güter der Welt nur zum täglichen Leben, sie sammeln sie nicht, und gerade so preisen sie den Schöpfer, nicht durch ihren Fleiß, ihre Arbeit, ihre Sorge, sondern durch das tägliche, einfältige Empfangen der Gabe, die Gott gibt.[14]

> They need worldly goods only for daily life; they do not collect them, and in precisely this way they praise the Creator, not through their industry, their work, their worry, but rather through the daily, simple reception of the gift that God gives.

In a life enslaved by the worry-cycle, a life lived in one sense without an awareness of God, work is necessary for food. But, if God is the source of a creature's daily needs, as is the case for birds, lilies, and human beings, then this connection is no longer necessary. According to Bonhoeffer, Jesus is underscoring the worry-free simplicity of those who follow in his way and recognize that everything they receive is from God.

There is an open question here though. It is certainly not the case that creatures do nothing. One could conclude from this that work is not necessary at all then. What account can be given about the kind of reception Bonhoeffer envisions? Part of the reason he does not say too much on these verses of Mt. 6 is because he allows Luther to say it for him. He includes an extended quotation from Luther in order to characterize the act of receiving but also to demonstrate that his work is explicitly within the tradition of interpretation started by Luther.[15] Alongside

---

14. DBW 4:172.

15. It is certainly not rare for Bonhoeffer to refer to or quote Luther, but it is rare for him to quote him at length like this. In *Nachfolge*, he only quotes Luther a few times (DBW 4:241; DBWE 4:225 and DBW 4:287; DBWE 4:271), but does so at length only one other time (DBW 4:84-85; DBWE 4:91). This certainly does not mean that Luther is not present throughout the book. He most certainly is present, both explicitly when Bonhoeffer speaks early on in the book about Luther's departure from the monastery, as well as in his reliance on the Luther Bible. Implicitly he is present as Bonhoeffer works from a broadly Lutheran theological framework and employs more narrowly, as we will see below, Luther's

providing some color to Bonhoeffer's exposition, the passage from Luther is vivid and interesting, it also helps him to offer a realistic interpretation of the passage. Humans have an activity that is proper to them to perform, but this activity does not produce what they need. Instead, their activity gathers what God has already produced for them. Luther makes this point by delving a bit more into what a little bird does or the activity of an ox which plows, a horse which carries a warrior into battle, and a sheep which produces milk and wool. God's providential blessing undergirds creaturely activity. God's action of providing and sustaining precedes and enables creaturely action.

Bonhoeffer does not explicitly comment on the material from Luther. After he quotes it he returns to the text of Matthew by stringing together some rhetorical questions that parallel those of Jesus in the passage. If God takes care of these creatures, then how much more will he take care of those who ask him to provide for their daily needs? This is then given a poetic recapitulation in a quotation from Matthias Claudius's poem, "Täglich zu singen" [To Be Sung Daily].[16] This quotation concludes his commentary on vv. 26-30. By linking this section as closely as he does with the emphases he has drawn out of v. 34, he has a coherent way of presenting a life lived by faith in Jesus and, thus, in receptivity to God's provision. It is a life that does not need to be characterized by worry as in the case of the alternative, worry-cycle life, a notion that is now explicitly connected, because the biblical text makes the connection, to the life of the pagan.

In a new paragraph, which is often a good indicator of a shift in topic and thus provides a helpful way of tracing his interpretive activity, Bonhoeffer picks up the reference in v. 32 to pagans, briefly returning to a life of worry so that he can continue to draw out implications of the contrast with which he has been working. He devotes three sentences to v. 32, though he does not draw explicit attention to it. As is often the case, as here and as we will see shortly as well, he will often use the biblical text as an outline for his own points. Verse 32 speaks in two clauses about the pagans running to meet their needs for food and clothing but that God knows what his children need. These two clauses form the first two sentences for Bonhoeffer, and his third sentence is a conclusion he draws from the biblical material that then sets up the next stage of the contrast. In other words, he is carefully following the flow of the biblical text at this point. Pagan running is described as reliance on their strength rather than on God. It is, for them, a matter of not believing, of not having faith. Their lack of faith is due to the fact that they do not know that God knows what they need. The immediate source for this comment is, as noted above, v. 32 itself, but Bonhoeffer is likely also reaching back to an earlier section of the Sermon on the Mount, 6:7-8, where another contrast is drawn between disciples and pagans with respect to

---

Law-Gospel hermeneutic. Luther is, in this latter sense especially, a most pervasive presence, though a mostly unseen and unspoken one.

16. DBW 4:173.

prayer.[17] The difference between the two groups in those verses is the same as here. The disciples do not need to pray with many words because they know that God already knows what they need, whereas the pagans do not. All of this leads to Bonhoeffer's concluding word on the pagans: "Darum wollen sie selbst tun, was sie von Gott nicht erwarten" [Therefore they want to do for themselves what they do not expect from God].[18] A life of autonomous action, a life lived without dependence on God, is foolish because it traps a person in worry.

Bonhoeffer switches to the other pole of the contrast by quoting v. 33:

> Für den Nachfolgenden aber gilt: „Trachtet zuerst nach dem Reich Gottes und nach seiner Gerechtigkeit, so wird euch solches alles zufallen."[19]

> For disciples, however, the following stands: "Seek first after the kingdom of God and his righteousness, and all these things will be given to you."

For Bonhoeffer, v. 33, rather than v. 34, is the climax of the passage. It allows him to conclude on a word of promise rather than on a recapitulation of a negative command. It also allows him to pull together all the threads of the exposition so far, which he does. In the remainder of a relatively long paragraph, he draws out a couple of points before offering a concluding summary.

His first point is that concern for food and clothing is not by default concern for the kingdom of God; the two are distinct and must be kept apart. This is derived from the duality in v. 33, "dem Reich Gottes" [the kingdom of God] and "solches alles" [all these things]. Bonhoeffer opposes the false view that could see anxiety as the medium for the kingdom of God, a kind of comfortable secularizing of God's kingdom that interprets the process of working and everything it enables— getting food and buying a house, etc.—as identical to the kingdom of God. He counters this:

> Das Reich Gottes und seine Gerechtigkeit ist hier etwas von dem, was uns an Gaben der Welt zufallen soll, ganz und gar Unterschiedenes. Es ist nichts anderes als die Gerechtigkeit, von der Mt. 5 und 6 gesprochen wurde, die Gerechtigkeit des Kreuzes Christi und der Nachfolge unter dem Kreuz.[20]

> The kingdom of God and his righteousness is here something utterly different from what might come our way in the gifts of the world. It is nothing other than the righteousness about which Matthew 5 and 6 have spoken, the righteousness of the cross of Christ and discipleship under the cross.

---

17. Matthew 6:7-8: "And when you pray, do not keep on babbling like pagans, for they think they will be heard because of their many words. Do not be like them, for your Father knows what you need before you ask him."

18. DBW 4:174.

19. DBW 4:174.

20. DBW 4:174.

The second point continues this line of interpretation and expands on it slightly by focusing on the word *zuerst* [first] in the biblical text. Verse 33 does not only present a duality, two things that could be put in any order or be intertwined. There is a first and second, and Bonhoeffer draws attention to this necessary order, using *Sperrsatz* to emphasize his interest. He writes:

> Die Gemeinschaft Jesu und der Gehorsam gegen sein Gebot kommt *zuerst*, alles andere folgt nach … *Vor* den Sorgen um unser Leben, um Essen und Kleidung, um Beruf und Familie steht | das Trachten nach der Gerechtigkeit Christi.[21]

> Shared life with Jesus and obedience to his command come *first*; everything else follows after … *Before* the concerns of our life—for food and clothing, for job and family—stands seeking after the righteousness of Christ.

It is important to notice that Bonhoeffer does have, as Luther also had, a proper place for "concern," a rather different English gloss than "worry" for the German *Sorge* in this context. Concern for the things he mentions here, expressed through activity appropriate for human beings as creatures dependent on God, needs though to be properly ordered to the source, that is, ordered to Christ first. Bringing these two points together, from Bonhoeffer's perspective, human concern, which is action toward a goal rather than psychological worry or anxiety, is normal, but it goes wrong when it is equated with the kingdom of God without remainder and when it tries to flip its place within a proper sequence. In the latter case, concern becomes worry. Verse 33 is the climax, therefore, because it perfectly summarizes, in a condensed way, the entire passage.

"Sorget nicht für den anderen Morgen" and "Trachtet zuerst nach dem Reich Gottes" are both, grammatically speaking, commands, and so in the concluding sentences of his exposition of this passage Bonhoeffer asks the same question of v. 33 that he did of v. 34. Is "Trachtet zuerst nach dem Reich Gottes" to be understood as an unbearable law or as gospel? The answer should be obvious by this point. He says:

> Nicht von dem, was der Mensch soll und nicht kann, spricht Jesus, sondern von dem, was Gott uns geschenkt hat und noch verheißt. Ist Christus uns geschenkt, sind wir in seine Nachfolge berufen, so ist uns mit ihm alles, wirklich alles geschenkt. Es wird uns alles andere zufallen.[22]

> Jesus speaks not of what people should do and cannot, but rather of what God has given and yet promises. If Christ is given to us, if we are called into his discipleship, then everything, really everything, is given us with him. Everything else will come to us.

---

21. DBW 4:174, emphasis original.
22. DBW 4:174.

These three sentences follow the structure of v. 33, and intentionally or not, they are inflected again by the language of Rom. 8. Jesus' command is gospel because it is about God's initiative in giving and promising the kingdom of God (v. 33a). The second sentence claims Christ as that which has been given, equating Christ with the kingdom of God and making the righteousness of v. 33b his, a point Bonhoeffer already made in connecting righteousness here with the broader context of the Sermon on the Mount. The "alles, wirklich alles" [everything, really everything] of the second sentence picks up Rom. 8:32 again and paves the way for the final sentence, which is both a repetition and also adds a new element, namely, the "everything" of 33c, the concrete, daily concerns that have been the focus of human activity. This is a carefully crafted section, and it advances a Christocentric interpretation of the Sermon on the Mount, something that is not explicit in Mt. 5–7, and an interpretation that contrasts with those that see the Sermon as only about moral action (or the negation of moral action) rather than Christology first and moral action second.[23]

There are two conclusions to Bonhoeffer's exposition. The first is given in order to wrap up his textual work in the section, while the second steps back, widening the frame, to conclude the broader heading, "The Simplicity of Carefree Life," as he transitions into Mt. 7. He concludes his commentary on Mt. 6:25-34 in this way:

> Wer in der Nachfolge Jesu allein auf Seine Gerechtigkeit blickt, der ist in der Hand und Hut Jesu Christi und seines Vaters, und wer so in der Gemeinschaft des Vaters ist, dem kann nichts geschehen, der kann auch nicht mehr zweifeln, daß der Vater seine Kinder wohl ernähren kann und nicht hungern lassen wird. Gott wird zur rechten Stunde helfen. Er weiß, was wir bedürfen.[24]

> The one who in discipleship with Jesus looks only to his righteousness is in the care and protection of Jesus Christ and his father; and the one who is in communion with the father can have nothing happen to him, nor can he doubt that the father can feed his children well and will not let them go hungry. God will help at the right time. He knows what we need.

Bonhoeffer reads Mt. 6:25-34 as gospel, and he drives the point home pastorally here. This is, though, discipleship under the cross, and, alongside the need to widen the frame for the argument and structure of the book, this kind of discipleship accounts for the additional conclusion. He could have stopped at "Er weiß, was wir bedürfen," but he turns a surprising, unexpected corner, writing:

23. For a variety of interpretations on the Sermon on the Mount, including aspects of Bonhoeffer's interpretation (mainly focused on the passages on peace and love for enemies), see *The Sermon on the Mount through the Centuries: From the Early Church to John Paul II*, ed. Jeffrey P. Greenman, Timothy Larsen and Stephen R. Spencer (Grand Rapids, MI: Brazos Press, 2007).

24. DBW 4:174-175.

Der Nachfolger Jesu wird noch nach langer Jüngerschaft auf die Frage des Herrn: „Habt ihr auch je Mangel gehabt?" antworten: „Herr, niemals!" Wie sollte der auch Mangel haben, der in Hunger und Blöße, in Verfolgung und Gefahr der Gemeinschaft Jesu Christi gewiß ist?[25]

The disciple of Jesus, even after following him for a long time, will be able to answer the question of the Lord: "Were you ever in need?" with "Lord, never!" How could one lack who in hunger and nakedness, in persecution and danger is confident of communion with Jesus Christ?

The exchange between Jesus and his disciples is found in Lk 22:35 (with additional coloring from, again, Rom. 8, this time v. 35 on nakedness and persecution). Jesus references the time when he sent them on a mission without a purse, bag, or sandals and asks if they lacked anything they needed. They affirm that they did not. Bonhoeffer reads their lack, a real lack, as relativized by their communion with Jesus. God's knowledge of and ability to care for the needs of his children, to feed them well, as the previous paragraph put it, does not mean that they will not go hungry in discipleship to Jesus (seeking after Christ, following him, sharing life with him). With the final rhetorical question, Bonhoeffer puts a question mark over the assurance of his previous formulation. There is a tension here because this is, after all, discipleship with Jesus, and thus discipleship under the cross.

Bonhoeffer's interpretation of this passage in Matthew illustrates his general way of working with biblical texts, as well as the specific way of doing so in Finkenwalde, and so it will enhance the argument at this stage to probe how what he does with this passage can shed light on his theological and hermeneutical concerns. On the one hand, Bonhoeffer comes equipped with specific interests, a way of construing Scripture and Luther's Law-Gospel hermeneutic (on which, more below), but on the other hand he has the text in front of him, the text he has received and is dependent upon for access to its own *Sache*, God as he is revealed in Jesus by the Spirit. What is on display here, then, are points in the text that provide openings for Bonhoeffer's interpretive actions. In other words, his engagement with this passage demonstrates the two-way, dialogical character of his interpretation. At some point he had to sit down to look at this particular biblical text and read it, recognizing that the text says this or that and that it is his task to figure out what he is going to do with what the text presents to him. He is not simply basing his comments on the text, but is really, actively engaging the text to understand what it contributes to generating its own interpretation, an interpretation that is really Bonhoeffer's. This chapter of *Nachfolge* shows Bonhoeffer grappling or wrestling with the distinct voice of the biblical text so that he can speak it in his voice.

25. DBW 4:175.

2.2. Bonhoeffer on Die Taufe [Baptism]

2.2.1. Die Taufe in the Context of Nachfolge With the chapter entitled *Die Taufe*, the reader of *Nachfolge* encounters a different kind of text. This has caused some, notably Hanfried Müller, to criticize the book by suggesting that rather than consisting in two unified parts *Nachfolge* falls apart in two parts.[26] The critique takes the real difference in the material seriously, and as the German editors of *Nachfolge* comment in relation to Müller's criticism, "Bonhoeffer's careful correlation of Part One and Part Two is obviously not easy to detect at first sight."[27] The terrain in part 2 leaves behind Gospel narratives and long quotations of Scripture that serve as the sources for lengthy commentaries. Instead, the focus is on the non-narrative portions of the New Testament, with an emphasis especially on Pauline texts. The unity of the parts is the product of Bonhoeffer's hermeneutic, which envisions a singular, unified witness in Scripture that consists of various, diverse witnesses. He does not merely assert this, however, he shows how it is the case by carefully relating the two parts in the introductory chapter of part 2, "Preliminary Questions," and in the first section of the chapter on Baptism, as will be shown below. The chapters in part 2 are very different, therefore, because they intentionally shift in register to account for the different material found in the Pauline texts Bonhoeffer reads in the New Testament. The six chapters that make up this section of the book are probably best understood in something like the genre of systematic theology and, more specifically, as a Christologically and Pnuematologically grounded ecclesiology.[28] The treatment, therefore, is carried out in more thematic terms, which makes the task of tracing the relation between biblical text and comment slightly more difficult. This dogmatic or doctrinal structure is intensely exegetical though, which is to say explicitly presented as the product of careful attention to Scripture. This shared aspect of the two parts of the book, namely, the fact that each part is a product of biblical interpretation, is the key way, in Bonhoeffer's own terms, to talk about the book's coherence or unity in response to the kind of criticism offered by Müller.

2.2.2. Bonhoeffer's Introductory Section to Die Taufe

> Der Begriff der Nachfolge, der bei den Synoptikern fast den gesamten Inhalt und Umfang der Beziehungen des Jüngers zu Jesus Christus auszudrücken

---

26. Hanfried Müller, *Von der Kirche zur Welt: Ein Beitrag zu der Beziehung des Wort Gottes auf die societas in Dietrich Bonhoeffers theologische Entwicklung* [*From the Church to the World: A Contribution to the Relation of the Word of God to Society in Dietrich Bonhoeffer's Theological Development*] (Reich: Leipzig and Hamburg-Bergstedt, 1966), 199.

27. DBW 4:329; DBWE 4:311.

28. For a very helpful treatment of the big picture of the second part of *Nachfolge*, see Philip G. Ziegler's presentation entitled, "Listening to *Discipleship's* 'B-Side,'" delivered at a conference held at St. John's College in Durham, UK, in 2017 called Reading Bonhoeffer for the Life of the Church.

vermochte, tritt bei Paulus stark in den Hintergrund. Paulus verkündigt uns nicht in erster Linie die Geschichte des Herrn in seinen Erdentagen, sondern die Gegenwart des Auferstandenen und Verklärten und sein Wirken an uns. Dazu bedarf er einer neuen und eigenen Begrifflichkeit.[29]

The concept of discipleship, which in the Synoptics is able to express almost the whole content and scope of the relationships of disciples to Jesus Christ, recedes completely into the background with Paul. Paul does not proclaim to us, in the first instance, the story of the Lord in his earthly life, but rather his presence as the risen and glorified one and his work for us. He requires, therefore, a new and unique conceptuality.

So Bonhoeffer formally begins unfolding the material content of the second half of his book. The coherence of his book is pushed back to a question about the unity of the New Testament. *Nachfolge* is, therefore, among many other things an argument for Scripture's unity and a product of that unity. Seeing baptism as the link between the different conceptualities will be Bonhoeffer's original contribution, but this is put off in order to sharpen up the differences between the Synoptics and Paul so that they can be seen as necessary for the full witness to the entire Christ to take shape. For Bonhoeffer, and this is a key point for understanding everything that follows and also a point that differentiates him from Barth, the full witness of Christ requires a diverse conceptuality. But for it to be a witness to Christ, this diversity must be unified. This is the hermeneutic of "Vergegenwärtigung neutestamentlicher Texte" put on display in the practice of actually interpreting biblical texts. In the terms set out in the quote above, the Synoptics and Paul clearly speak about Christ differently, but these real differences cannot be played off against each other. Opposing a mainstream dichotomy that does precisely this, pitting Paul against the Synoptics by appeal either to 2 Cor. 5:16 (no longer regarding Christ from a human point of view) or to certain brands of historical scholarship that find their basis in a Reformation reading of Pauline theology, Bonhoeffer claims that the unity of Scripture is broken up if a person could demonstrate two present Christs, with Paul proclaiming a Christ present to us now (a Christ of faith) while the Synoptics speak of a present Christ that cannot be known any longer, a Christ that is only a past reality (the Jesus of history). Bonhoeffer questions those who divide the New Testament in this way because Paul's witness is a Scriptural witness, and as a result it is of a piece with the other New Testament witnesses. You cannot, that is, privilege Paul's witness without the others, unless the claim being made is not about Scripture's witness to Christ but rather a matter of an experience of Christ's presence that is not bound to a unified Scripture.

Bonhoeffer is trying here to out-reform those who claim continuity with the Reformation by his appeal to Luther's "*sola scriptura.*" This Reformation priority is a statement not so much about Scripture but about Christ. In other words,

---

29. DBW 4:219.

sola scriptura is not a statement about Scripture as the sole authority for just anything in general, but it is instead a statement about Scripture being the sole way of knowing Christ. Christ is known *by* Scripture alone or through Scriptural mediation alone.[30] For this to be the case though, Scripture must be taken as a whole as it witnesses to Christ. As a result, both Paul and the Synoptics must be read as witnesses to Christ, and only through the inclusion of the two different emphases and conceptualities will a person gain the *Sache*, a unified witness to the whole Christ. Bonhoeffer writes:

> Gegenwärtig ist uns der Christus, den uns die ganze Schrift bezeugt. Er ist der Menschgewordene, Gekreuzigte, Auferstandene und Verklärte, er begegnet uns in seinem Wort. Die verschiedene Begrifflichkeit, in der die Synoptiker und Paulus dieses Zeugnis weitergeben, tut der Einheit des Schriftzeugnisses keinen Abbruch.[31]

> The Christ who is present to us is the one to whom the whole of Scripture attests. He is the incarnate, crucified, resurrected and glorified one, and he encounters us in his word. The different conceptualities in which the Synoptics and Paul hand on this witness does not break up the unity of the witness of Scripture.

In an interesting and lengthy footnote, rare for its length in *Nachfolge*, Bonhoeffer offers a contrast that further develops his point against those holding exclusively to Paul over against the Synoptics and a qualification about Scripture's unity. He has already interpreted his opponents' position as based on an experience of Christ's presence detached from Scripture, but he now claims that they hold to a theological principle detached from Christ himself. To say, based on a reading of Paul, that "Christ is risen and present" in an absolute way, that is, in a way that assumes the utterance is true, exclusively true and unqualified, is to make a claim about the mode of Jesus' existence that can become, and has become for his opponents, a tool to criticize what the Synoptics say. The problem is that Scriptural statements, like "Christ is risen and present," perform their function as witnesses rather than principles. The same statement in Bonhoeffer's framing of the New Testament is seen as a witness that needs to be correlated with other New Testament witnesses so that the diverse witnesses constitute a unified text that presents the entire Jesus Christ in unity and duality, a historical figure but more. Scriptural mediation is indispensable because there is no access to Christ without Scripture and there is

---

30. This reading of *sola scriptura* takes the Latin case as an ablative, thus the rendering "by" in English. This is supported by analogy with *sola fide*, which must be understood to mean "by faith alone." The ablative case here indicates and emphasizes a relation to Christ. In the case of *sola scriptura*, Scripture is an instrument in enabling access to Christ and salvation to happen, rather than an entity that stands alone with an inherent soteriological power of its own.

31. DBW 4:220.

no Scripture without Christ. Paul and the Synoptics have legitimately different perspectives, but they cohere insofar as they contribute to the whole of Scripture.

This leads to a qualification as well. One could very well interpret Bonhoeffer's response to the Paul *vs.* Synoptics problem as a dogmatic claim about Scripture's unity. He recognizes at the end of the footnote that he has opened himself up to this possibility. In response to the potential objection, he qualifies his earlier claim by stating that the unity of Scripture that he is working with is a methodological assumption proved only in the actual act of interpretation. Unity is tested in practice, not imposed because of an a priori dogmatic claim. The reader is invited to consider whether "discipleship" in the Synoptics and "baptism" in Paul really cohere in the way Bonhoeffer claims they do in what follows.

2.2.3. Bonhoeffer's Commentary on Die Taufe The opening sentence of Bonhoeffer's treatment of baptism makes good on the claims he made in the first two pages of the chapter, claims about the unity of the Synoptics and Paul, and he also introduces the reader into his organizing strategy for the material in the chapter. He writes:

> Ruf und Eintritt in die Nachfolge haben bei Paulus ihre Entsprechung in der *Taufe*.[32]

> Call and entrance into discipleship have their equivalent in Paul in *baptism*.

His burden in the chapter is to demonstrate how this is the case, and his approach to presenting the material is to use *Sperrsatz* to emphasize the keyword or phrase that contributes to his argument. A quick scan of the chapter reveals that eight of the ten paragraphs that constitute the chapter contain an emphasized word or phrase near the beginning of the paragraph.[33] The eight emphasized words or phrases are derived from various Pauline contexts (though we will observe below that much of the material is based on Rom. 6) and thus utilize the terminology and concepts from those contexts, but they are described so that a comparison with the terminology and conceptuality of the Gospels can arise. This is, therefore, a carefully argued and structured presentation.

His first point is that baptism is grounded in the will of Jesus. Therefore, it is a gracious call, an offer made by Jesus rather than an act initiated by a person. In the same way that Jesus called the twelve, baptism is also Christ's call and it is experienced in a passive way as a being baptized. Bonhoeffer writes:

> Der Name Jesu Christi wird über dem Täufling genannt, der Mensch wird damit dieses Namens teilhaftig, er wird „in Jesum Christum" hineingetauft (εἰς R. 6,3, Gal. 3,27, Mt. 28,19).[34]

---

32. DBW 4:221, emphasis original.

33. The final two paragraphs do not follow this procedure because the second to last paragraph is a qualification of the whole argument of the chapter with respect to infant baptism and the final paragraph of the chapter is a conclusion.

34. DBW 4:221.

The name of Jesus Christ is spoken over the baptized person, such that he participates in that name; the person is baptized "into Jesus Christ." (εἰς Rom. 6:3; Gal. 3:27; Mt. 28:19)

The three biblical texts in the parentheses all use the cited Greek preposition in reference to Jesus (with the final text from Matthew also including the Father and the Holy Spirit, and spoken by the resurrected Christ himself). Bonhoeffer lists these biblical texts in shorthand because he is assuming his readers are familiar with them.[35] Paul's texts and a text from the Synoptics are included in order to demonstrate the similarity of the notion, which in this case is explicitly linked to Jesus in the text of Matthew. The citation of Rom. 6 is also important at this stage, because this text is the main Pauline source for Bonhoeffer in the chapter. Arising out of reflection on these texts, the upshot of this act of Jesus is that the person who is baptized participates in Jesus and belongs to him.

Bonhoeffer now moves on to his second point of emphasis, which follows directly on from the first (signaled by *So* [Therefore]). "So bedeutet die Taufe einen *Bruch*" [Baptism, therefore, signifies a *breach*].[36] In order to belong to Christ, to be his possession, to be baptized, he must snatch a person from the rule of the world. Alluding to Mk 3:23-27 (entering the strong man's house to bind him) and Col. 1:13-14 (delivered from the dominion of darkness and transferred to the Son's kingdom), Bonhoeffer unapologetically uses the language of Christ entering Satan's domain in order to take hold of his own and put them in his newly created church-community.[37] This is a breach that can only be described in the new creation terms given by Paul in 2 Cor. 5:17, a text quoted but not flagged as such.[38] The breach happened in Christ's past action, his life, death, and resurrection, but is implemented or actualized for people today in the act of baptism, an event that is, Bonhoeffer is at pains to make plain, not the result of human decision or willing.

35. I also assume the readers of this book will be familiar with them, but it is important in a study that seeks to trace the relation between biblical text and comment to allow the biblical text prominence. In this section of the chapter I will either summarize the biblical text's content, as in the case of 2 Cor. 5:16 above, or provide a quotation in the main text or a footnote. Here are the three passage Bonhoeffer's refers to in this case:

Rom. 6:3: "Or don't you know that all of us who were baptized into Christ Jesus were baptized into his death?"
Gal. 3:27: "For all of you who were baptized into Christ have clothed yourselves with Christ."
Mt. 28:19: "Therefore go and make disciples of all nations, baptizing them in the name of the Father and of the Son and of the Holy Spirit."

36. DBW 4:221, emphasis original.

37. This usage recalls Bonhoeffer's comments in "Vergegenwärtigung neutestamentlicher Texte" about how to interpret passages about demons and Satan in the New Testament. See DBW 14:413; DBWE 14:425-426, and the treatment of this theme in the previous chapter.

38. 2 Cor. 5:17: "Therefore, if anyone is in Christ, the new creation has come: The old has gone, the new is here!"

The space opened up by the breach between the baptized person who is now firmly in the church-community and the world is filled by Christ, a mediator who makes it possible for the baptized person to relate to the world only through him.

Blending 2 Cor. 5:17 and the major theme of Rom. 6 (the new creation made possible by Christ's past action and present action through being baptized), baptism as the breach with the old is spoken about, third, as a death. "Der Bruch mit der Welt ist ein vollkommener. Er fordert | und bewirkt den *Tod* des Menschen" [The breach with the world is total. It requires and effects a person's *death*].[39] In a footnote Bonhoeffer again seeks explicitly to bring Paul and the Synoptics together by noting that Jesus anticipated this Pauline point himself because he described his own death as a baptism and promises his disciples a baptism of death as well. He references Lk 12:50, in which Jesus refers to his future baptism, clearly referring to his death, and Mk 10:39, where in response to the request of James and John to sit on his right and left in the kingdom Jesus asks if they are able to be baptized with the baptism he himself will endure. They respond that they are able to do so, and Jesus says they will indeed undergo such a baptism, a baptism Bonhoeffer interprets as death (a good conclusion in light of Lk 12:50). The death brought about in baptism is, again, not something that a person can initiate on their own terms. "Der Mensch stirbt allein an Christus, durch Christus, mit Christus" [The person dies to Christ alone, through Christ, with Christ].[40] This death is a real judgment carried out on the old person and on sin, so that the new person is really dead to the world (echoing Gal. 6:14) and to sin (Rom. 6:6-7).[41] The result, though, is fellowship with Christ and the community of Christ. In this way, this death is actually grace. With Paul's emphasis on adoption in Rom. 8:12-17 lurking in the background, Bonhoeffer says:

> So ist dieser Tod nicht die letzte zornige Verwerfung des Geschöpfes durch den Schöpfer, sondern er ist gnädige Annahme des Geschöpfes durch den Schöpfer.[42]

> Thus, this death is not the final, angry condemnation of the creature by the Creator, but rather it is the gracious adoption of the creature by the Creator.

Through the gracious adoption of death, experienced as one is baptized, Jesus places his follower under the cross and what it achieved (a further connection is alluded to here between the similar language of daily picking up your cross to

---

39. DBW 4:222, emphasis original.

40. DBW 4:222.

41. Gal. 6:14: "May I never boast except in the cross of our Lord Jesus Christ, through which the world has been crucified to me, and I to the world."

Rom. 6:6-7: "For we know that our old self was crucified with him so that the body ruled by sin might be done away with, that we should no longer be slaves to sin—because anyone who has died has been set free from sin."

42. DBW 4:222.

follow Christ in Mt. 16:24-28, Mk 8:34–9:1, Lk 9:23-27, and 1 Cor. 15:31 where Paul speaks of his "daily dying"). For Christ, the cross and death were hard, but for those who follow after him the cross is, borrowing from Mt. 11:28-30 and thus continuing to draw together the Synoptic-to-Pauline links, gentle and easy through fellowship with Christ. "So wird die Taufe zum Empfang der Kreuzesgemeinschaft Jesu Christi (R. 6,3 ff., Kol. 2,12). Der Glaubende kommt unter Christi Kreuz" [Thus baptism becomes the reception of the fellowship of the cross of Jesus Christ (Rom. 6:3; Col. 2:12). The believer comes under Christ's cross].[43]

Drawing together the links Bonhoeffer has developed so far, we can say the following: baptism is a call initiated by Christ that introduced a total breach between the old person and the new, between the old world and the new creation; this breach is a death with Christ. Continuing to progress through Rom. 6 by using paraphrase, Bonhoeffer provides the next, fifth link in his developing picture of baptism as discipleship: "Der Tod in der Taufe ist die *Rechtfertigung von der Sünde*" [Death in baptism is *justification from sin*].[44] Death with Christ is necessary in order to free a person from sin.

> Wer gestorben ist, der ist gerechtfertigt von der Sünde (R. 6,7, Kol. 2,20). An den Toten hat die Sünde kein Recht mehr, ihre Forderung ist mit dem Tode beglichen und erloschen. So geschieht Rechtfertigung von (ἀπό) der Sünde allein durch den Tod.[45]

> The one who has died is justified from sin (Rom. 6:7; Col. 2:20). Sin no longer has a right to the one who is dead; its claim has been settled and expired with death. Thus, justification from (ἀπό) sin can only happen through death.

Citing the Greek preposition, ἀπό, grounds the exposition in the biblical text of Rom. 6, this time v. 7, which says, "anyone who has died has been set free from sin." Such an aggressive strategy, death, is necessary if the baptized person is going to be separated from sin. Real forgiveness can only come about through putting the sinner to death, and it is this that leads to fellowship with Christ. There is, importantly for Bonhoeffer's argument here, no difference between past (the frame of the Synoptics) and the present (the frame of Paul's texts), that is, whether the gift of justification, death with Christ, or the forgiveness of sins given by Christ is extended to a disciple in Christ's earthly life or to a follower of Christ who is baptized today. Both receive the same gift.

That gift, though, is not to be construed in passive terms, an implication that might arise from the emphasis Bonhoeffer has placed, following Paul in Rom. 6,

---

43. DBW 4:222-223. Col. 2:11-12: " In him you were also circumcised with a circumcision not performed by human hands. Your whole self ruled by the flesh was put off when you were circumcised by Christ, having been buried with him in baptism, in which you were also raised with him through your faith in the working of God, who raised him from the dead."

44. DBW 4:223, emphasis original.

45. DBW 4:223.

on baptism as a passive experience. Justification from sin, death with Christ, and the forgiveness of sins do not just happen automatically. They are gifts that only come in baptism because of the main gift that accompanies baptism and actualizes all the gifts believers receive from Christ, the Holy Spirit. The connection between baptism and Spirit, Bonhoeffer's sixth point, is linked in non-Pauline texts to the descent of the Spirit at Jesus' baptism (Mt. 3:13), the gift of the Spirit in baptism to Cornelius and his family in Acts 10:47, and Jesus' comments to Nicodemus about being born of water and Spirit (Jn 3:5), and is further linked to the Pauline texts, 1 Cor. 6:11 (you were washed by the Spirit) and 12:13 (in one Spirit we were all baptized). From this initial point, and drawing on a number of additional biblical texts, 2 Cor. 3:17, Rom. 8:9-11, 14, and Eph. 3:16, Bonhoeffer speaks of the Spirit as Christ himself living in believers, and thus bestowing on them the abiding presence of Christ and his fellowship with them.[46] The Holy Spirit does this by giving true knowledge of his nature (1 Cor. 2:10) and his will, teaching and reminding believers of Christ's words (Jn 14:26) and leading into truth (Jn 16:13). The Spirit does all this so that believers will know Christ better (1 Cor. 2:12; Eph. 1:9), so they can walk in the Spirit, taking confident steps (Gal. 5:16, 18, 25; Rom. 8:1, 4). The Pauline idiom of "walking in the Spirit" leads Bonhoeffer right back to the walking of Jesus' disciples as they followed after him. This connection leads on to another comparison:

> Das Maß der Gewißheit, das die Jünger Jesu in seiner irdischen Gemeinschaft hatten, hat Jesus den Seinen nach seinem Hingang nicht genommen. Durch die Sendung des Heiligen Geistes in die Herzen der Getauften wird die Gewißheit der Erkenntnis Jesu nicht nur erhalten, sondern durch die Nähe der Gemeinschaft noch gestärkt und gefestigt. (R. 8,16; Joh. 16,12 f.)[47]

> The measure of certainty that Jesus' disciples had in his earthly fellowship, Jesus did not take away from his own after his death. Through the sending of the Holy Spirit into the hearts of the baptized, the certainly of knowledge of Jesus is not only preserved, but through the closeness of the community it is strengthened and solidified. (Rom. 8:16; Jn 16:12)

It is important to pause at this stage to note that Bonhoeffer's text is saturated with biblical references and paraphrase from the Gospels and Paul's texts, and this

---

46. 2 Cor. 3:17: "Now the Lord is the Spirit, and where the Spirit of the Lord is, there is freedom."

> Rom. 8:9-11, 14: "And if the Spirit of him who raised Jesus from the dead is living in you, he who raised Christ from the dead will also give life to your mortal bodies because of his Spirit who lives in you."
> Eph. 3:16: "I pray that out of his glorious riches he may strengthen you with power through his Spirit in your inner being, so that Christ may dwell in your hearts through faith."

47. DBW 4:224.

is done in order to speak about baptism and its similarity to discipleship and also to draw out the fact that the New Testament is a unified witness to Christ through the diverse perspectives of its witnesses. The paragraph on the Spirit quickly becomes a sort of Pneumatology, and one that, when coordinated with Christology, as here, moves a long way toward a renewed Lutheran synthesis of Word and Spirit.

In the previous six paragraphs of the chapter, Bonhoeffer has started with Paul and moved toward the conceptuality of the Gospels toward the end of the paragraph. Here, registering his seventh element, that practice is reversed. "Rief Jesus in die Nachfolge, so forderte er einen *sichtbaren Gehorsamsakt*" [When Jesus called to discipleship, he demanded a *visible act of obedience*].[48] In another variation of his very original contribution, Bonhoeffer recognizes that just as following Jesus was a public matter, so baptism for Paul is the public event through which a person enters "die sichtbare Gemeinde" [the visible church-community].[49] In Gal. 3:27-28 and 1 Cor. 12:13, Paul explicitly connects baptism with inclusion in the life of the church.[50] Harkening back to the theme of a breach between the believer and the world, Bonhoeffer argues that the breach, where Christ is standing, must become visible through participation in the worshipping life of an actual, concrete church-community. Here, echoing the Gospels (specifically Mt. 19:29), the one who leaves everything behind, entering the church-community alone, will receive brothers, sisters, houses, and fields because the baptized person lives now exclusively within the fellowship of Jesus and his community.

The final element of eight is that "Die Taufe und ihre Gabe ist etwas *Einmaliges*" [Baptism and its gift is something *once-and-for-all*].[51] Baptism is unrepeatable, a point Bonhoeffer finds supported by the difficult passage, Heb. 6:4, which denies the possibility of a second repentance to a baptized person. He also notes an exception to the once-for-all nature of baptism, and that is noted in a footnote on Acts 19:5 where the baptism of John must be renewed through the baptism into Christ. These texts, outside of the Gospels and Paul, are kind of out of the way, but demonstrate a commitment on Bonhoeffer's part to reflect carefully on the whole biblical witness with respect to baptism. He picks up his main text, Rom. 6, again by noting that in v. 10 Paul says Christ died once-and-for-all. There can be no

---

48. DBW 4:224, emphasis original.

49. This phrase "die sichtbare Gemeinde" is the same one Bonhoeffer used to summarize his exposition of Mt. 5:13-16, the passage in the Sermon on the Mount where Jesus speaks of salt losing its saltiness and the city set on a hill. It is also the same phrase for a chapter in part 2 of *Nachfolge* devoted to an exposition of the church-community.

50. Gal. 3:27-28: "For all of you who were baptized into Christ have clothed yourselves with Christ. There is neither Jew nor Gentile, neither slave nor free, nor is there male and female, for you are all one in Christ Jesus."

1 Cor. 12:13: "For we were all baptized by one Spirit so as to form one body—whether Jews or Gentiles, slave or free—and we were all given the one Spirit to drink."

51. DBW 4:224, emphasis original.

repetition of his sacrifice, which means the baptized person, having experienced death with Christ, cannot be baptized again. That person's death with Christ is complete, and it is for this reason that Paul, in v. 11 of Rom. 6, tells the believers in Rome to consider themselves dead to sin.

There is a distinction being worked out here. On the one hand, Bonhoeffer wants to underscore how death in baptism only happens once, but on the other hand, he wants to continue to impress on followers of Christ the need that they have to die daily, to, in the language of the Gospels, pick up the cross and die each day. Paul's definitive "you have died with Christ" (v. 10) and his ongoing "consider yourselves dead" (v. 11) are transposed by Bonhoeffer into the image of a tree that is dead once its roots have been cut, but still dies, in an ongoing way, each day as the consequence of the cut roots works its way up to the tree branches. Believers are dead in principle when they are baptized into Christ, but they die in practice daily as they follow Christ in discipleship under the cross. The ongoing reality of daily death does not undermine the unique, unrepeatability of a person's baptism.

The nature of baptism as once-and-for-all leads to an implication about infant baptism, and it ends up being a pastoral coda. This is an interesting excursus, partly because Bonhoeffer puts forward both an exegetical and historical argument for his thought. The exegetical argument takes place in a footnote. Assuming that infant baptism is justified by several biblical texts, a necessary element for Protestants who want biblical justification for church practices, Bonhoeffer suggests a new text should be added to the list, namely, 1 Jn 2:12.[52] He offers a reading of the author's use of order and repetition, the twice stated "children, fathers and young men," to suggest that τεκνία (children) is not a general designation for the church-community but that it is actually referring to children. This is another example of how seriously he is taking the task of thinking carefully through the biblical material—the Synoptics, Pauline, and elsewhere. The historical argument is a negative one. He briefly refers to the ancient view that baptism and forgiveness were, rightly in his view, so closely linked that post-baptismal sin was taken seriously. Based on everything he has said in the chapter up to this point, it is not surprising that Bonhoeffer thinks this connection is a good one, though he is happy to reject the implication that a person waits for baptism until they are very old or even on their deathbeds. This discussion is not only interesting because of the decisions he makes to engage in these kinds of arguments though. It is also interesting because having assumed infant baptism throughout his treatment in this chapter, he has here pulled together some threads that would have immediate bearing on the church contexts

---

52. 1 Jn 2:12-14: "I am writing to you, dear children, because your sins have been forgiven on account of his name. I am writing to you, fathers, because you know him who is from the beginning. I am writing to you, young men, because you have overcome the evil one. I write to you, dear children, because you know the Father. I write to you, fathers, because you know him who is from the beginning. I write to you, young men, because you are strong, and the word of God lives in you, and you have overcome the evil one."

for whom he was writing and for whom he was training pastors in Finkenwalde. Bonhoeffer wants to limit infant baptism to the church's visible, liturgical setting, probably the main worship service, precisely so that it is public and incorporates the child into a church context that can provide a stable community as the child matures.[53] In other words, he envisions baptism, and infant baptism in particular, as the equivalent to the call to discipleship.

The concluding paragraph of the chapter reverts back to the Synoptic frame. The call of Jesus was unique and unrepeatable. The disciples who followed Jesus died in their past lives as Jesus demanded they leave everything to follow him. The once-and-for-all nature of that response was paralleled though with the completeness of the gift received from Jesus himself. He concludes:

> Er nahm ihnen ihr Leben, aber nun wollte Er ihnen ein Leben bereiten, ein ganzes, volles Leben, und er schenkte ihnen sein Kreuz. Das war die Gabe der Taufe an die ersten Jünger.[54]

> He took their lives from them, but now he wants to give a life to them, a complete, full life, and he gave them his cross. That was the gift of baptism to the first disciples.

Pauline baptism is here read back into the Synoptic Gospels, not in order to impose an alien structure on them but in order to demonstrate just how fully equivalent the two notions, baptism and discipleship, are. Jesus did not baptize his disciples, but their participation in his death, which put them in Gethsemane and in the vicinity of his cross on Golgotha, is taken by Bonhoeffer to be the equivalent of baptism for them. Baptism and crucifixion are so close, a point already made above in reference to the request of James and John in Mk 10:35-40, that Jesus' death is a baptism for his disciples. For Bonhoeffer, the conclusion that baptism in the Pauline context is identical with discipleship in the Synoptic context is an implication of interpretation bound to the witness of Scripture as a whole.

3. Synthesis

When Bonhoeffer and his students were furnishing the main room at Finkenwalde in which seminary activities would take place, the room which served as a dining hall, lecture hall, and chapel, they were pleased to find a large reproduction of Albrecht Dürer's *Four Apostles* to hang on the wall. Originally given by Dürer himself as a gift to the city of Nuremberg in 1526, the enormous, two-part painting depicts John (with an open book) and Peter (with a key) on the left and

53. Bonhoeffer applies these reflections interestingly and personally in a baptism meditation written from prison for his great-nephew's baptism. See DBW 8:428-436; DBWE 8:383-390.

54. DBW 4:226.

Mark (holding a scroll) and Paul (with a sword and a closed book) on the right. Attending the pictures is an inscription with four references to biblical texts about false teachers, each of which is connected to one of the Apostles. On the left side of the painting, Dürer cites 2 Pet. 2:1-2 for Peter, while John is linked to 1 Jn 4:1-3.[55] On the right side of the painting, Mark goes with his Gospel text, Mk 12:38-40, and Paul is cited in connection with 2 Tim. 3:1-7.[56] Following the biblical references are these words by Dürer himself:

> In these dangerous times all worldly rulers should take care that they do not mistake human seduction for the word of God. For God wants nothing to be taken from or added to it. Therefore, hear these four excellent men, Peter, John, Paul and Mark.[57]

55. 2 Pet. 2:1-2: "But there were also false prophets among the people, just as there will be false teachers among you. They will secretly introduce destructive heresies, even denying the sovereign Lord who bought them—bringing swift destruction on themselves. Many will follow their depraved conduct and will bring the way of truth into disrepute."

> 1 Jn 4:1-3: "Dear friends, do not believe every spirit, but test the spirits to see whether they are from God, because many false prophets have gone out into the world. This is how you can recognize the Spirit of God: Every spirit that acknowledges that Jesus Christ has come in the flesh is from God, but every spirit that does not acknowledge Jesus is not from God. This is the spirit of the antichrist, which you have heard is coming and even now is already in the world."

56. Mk 12:38-40: "As he taught, Jesus said, 'Watch out for the teachers of the law. They like to walk around in flowing robes and be greeted with respect in the marketplaces, and have the most important seats in the synagogues and the places of honor at banquets. They devour widows' houses and for a show make lengthy prayers. These men will be punished most severely.' "

> 2 Tim. 3:1-7: "But mark this: There will be terrible times in the last days. People will be lovers of themselves, lovers of money, boastful, proud, abusive, disobedient to their parents, ungrateful, unholy, without love, unforgiving, slanderous, without self-control, brutal, not lovers of the good, treacherous, rash, conceited, lovers of pleasure rather than lovers of God—having a form of godliness but denying its power. Have nothing to do with such people. They are the kind who worm their way into homes and gain control over gullible women, who are loaded down with sins and are swayed by all kinds of evil desires, always learning but never able to come to a knowledge of the truth. Just as Jannes and Jambres opposed Moses, so also these teachers oppose the truth. They are men of depraved minds, who, as far as the faith is concerned, are rejected. But they will not get very far because, as in the case of those men, their folly will be clear to everyone."

57. Cited in Philip G. Ziegler, "Dietrich Bonhoeffer: A Theologian of the Word of God," in *Bonhoeffer, Christ and Culture*, ed. Keith L. Johnson and Timothy Larsen (Downers Grove, IL: IVP Academic, 2013), 26.

The relevance of this, especially when connected to the biblical texts Dürer cites, is obvious. The Confessing Church established seminaries like Finkenwalde in order to combat the false teaching of a false church. But there is more. Philip Ziegler expands on the significance of the painting at Finkenwalde, and what he says is so well articulated that it is worth quoting in full. Ziegler writes:

> As the depiction of the crucifixion from Grünwald's Isenheim altarpiece is taken to express something of the essence of Karl Barth's theological endeavors, so Dürer's *Four Apostles* together with its inscription may be taken to epitomize both "visually and verbally" Bonhoeffer's theological program during the years of the church struggle. His writing and teaching, especially after 1933, is a single sustained effort to "hear these four excellent men;" that is, to suffer the full force of the promise and claim of the gospel attested in Scripture, and as a corollary, to summon the Christian church to "take care … not [to] mistake human seduction for the word of God." In the same letter in which he mentions Dürer's painting, Bonhoeffer makes this clear, explaining to his correspondent that "the Bible stands at the focal point of our labor. For us, it has become once more the starting point and the center of our theological endeavor and all our Christian action. Here, we have learned to read the Bible prayerfully once again."[58]

In concert with Ziegler's emphasis on the centrality of the Bible for the identity of Finkenwalde, this chapter began by claiming that the biblical interpretation of the Finkenwalde period is the quintessential Bonhoeffer on the Bible, and this claim was further focused on the particular work, *Nachfolge*. Some initial pieces of evidence were offered to substantiate this claim, but now, after a close reading of a text from each part of the book, the key question can be asked: What makes the biblical interpretation of *Nachfolge* so characteristic of Bonhoeffer's interpretation of Scripture in the 1930s?

Recalling some of what was said earlier, reasons can be given that are primarily related to the historical moment and the context of Finkenwalde. Bonhoeffer was experiencing high degrees of synergy vocationally. He was in a position to coordinate his theological and pastoral instincts and to direct them toward a contribution he felt would make a real difference in the *Kirchenkampf*. This accounts for his academic self-awareness at Finkenwalde, evidenced in his increased use of scholarly conventions in *Nachfolge*, footnotes, and engagement in mainstream scholarly conversations. This was acceptable because here, for the first time, he was able to put academic questions and methods and conversations to what he considered their proper telos of equipping pastors to faithfully witness to Christ through careful theological work that is bound to Scripture in personal devotion and through proclamation. In addition, *Nachfolge* was the culmination of his

---

58. Ziegler, "Dietrich Bonhoeffer: A Theologian of the Word of God," 27. The letter to which Ziegler refers includes Bonhoeffer's mention of the Dürer painting and also where it hangs (see DBW 14:88; DBWE 14:109).

regular, theological work, the task for which he received two advanced degrees. He spent years and years meditating on the biblical texts that constitute each section of the book, and this was increased exponentially with his move to Finkenwalde where he was given time to prayerfully and thoughtfully work through the texts and his presentation of them. These reasons for seeing *Nachfolge* as characteristic of Bonhoeffer's interpretation of Scripture are significant, but they only set the stage for the two most important considerations. These are: (1) *Nachfolge* demonstrates Bonhoeffer's interpretive approach, shown through a consistent correlation of his big-picture hermeneutical framework and many small-scale interpretive decisions, and (2) *Nachfolge* shows Bonhoeffer at his most self-conscious as an interpreter, an agent making decisions about how to think about and speak about the biblical text he has received. Each of these will be taken in turn.

The hermeneutical framework conceived in Berlin in 1925, a framework which sought to hold Scripture and revelation, theology and history, and the Holy Spirit and the interpreter in proper tension, underwent development through various contexts and interpretive endeavors before settling into a modulated form in 1935 in Bonhoeffer's Finkenwalde hermeneutic, a Spirit-based and Christ-focused interpretive approach, *Sachlichkeit*, that assumed unity, but a unity that consists of the various perspectives of diverse Scriptural witnesses, a unity-in-diversity that the interpreter must bring out in dependence on the Spirit as he or she attends to Scripture's purpose of witnessing to Christ in these texts as they are read and preached for the benefit of others. Insofar as each text analyzed in this book is a good example of Bonhoeffer's close wedding of a hermeneutical framework and a consequent practice, a formal coherence that should be evaluated positively and irrespective of the material, theological conclusions, the strong continuity also gives way to a note of discontinuity. *Nachfolge* puts this relationship between a theological hermeneutic and a concrete interpretive practice on display in a way that is more focused on the diversity of Scripture's witness because it is that very diversity that contributes to understanding Scripture's holistic, unique witness to Christ, its unity. *Nachfolge* is, in essence, the clearest expression of Bonhoeffer's hermeneutic, with all the interpretive implications to the fore.

Nachfolge is a text that shows its own production, that is, it shows its author as a fully responsible interpreter, involved in the process of making choices, ordering, structuring, and construing material for specific purposes. Observing these processes as they unfold is the chief benefit of offering close readings of texts. So, with respect to *Nachfolge*, what does Bonhoeffer do as he moves from biblical texts to his own reflections on them? How can the small-scale interpretive decisions visible in the texts examined above best be described? In *Nachfolge*, Bonhoeffer does the following:

1) He employed a Lutheran hermeneutic when he made the distinction between understanding the text as "law" or as "gospel." This framework significantly influenced the way that Jesus' commands in the Sermon on the Mount were interpreted. The way this hermeneutic is expressed is through negation, so that "Sorget nicht!" does not mean what one might think on

a surface reading of the grammar and context, but rather it must be taken a different way entirely. The negation of the law and the affirmation of the gospel go together and give his interpretation a quality of struggle and effort as he attempts to clarify the true, evangelical meaning of the text as opposed to potentially false misreadings of the text. This functions rhetorically as well because it allows Bonhoeffer to propose radical opposites or contrasts in order to sharpen up the stakes of whatever he is speaking about, while also putting his conclusion in the place of superiority. In Mt. 6, the radical contrast presented was the "either–or" of how to read Jesus' command. For Bonhoeffer, it is a command that is *either* something that is unbearable *or* something that is received with joy.

2) Key to his exposition of Mt. 6:25-34 was the choice of how to order the material in front of him. Focusing initial attention on v. 34 framed the commentary by orienting the definition of worry as a future reality. This was, no doubt, present in Matthew's text, but whereas Matthew presented this as Jesus' final word on the subject, Bonhoeffer moved v. 33 into the climactic position. This supported his Christ-centered reading strategy in the Sermon on the Mount as a whole.

3) Especially important for his comments on Rom. 6, Bonhoeffer used paraphrase to move through the biblical text. Though this was a primary technique in the chapter on Baptism, it was also present in the material on the Sermon on the Mount, leaving the reader to notice when multiple verses were slightly reworked so as to become part of Bonhoeffer's text rather than explicitly cited parts of Jesus' speech.

4) He chooses other sources to quote at important points in his exposition. Relying on others can, as was the case with his long quotation of Luther, provide additional insight into the biblical text as well as signal a desire to be firmly placed in a specific tradition of interpretation. The Claudius quote, however, functions differently, since it does not add anything new, but rather reinforces the main point in a slightly different idiom or register. Bonhoeffer's close assimilation of Jesus' (Mt. 6) and Paul's (Rom. 8) rhetorical questions is mirrored differently in Claudius.

5) The chief tactic employed in the chapter on Baptism was comparison, the use of which was signaled several times with a "Just as … so also" structure.

6) He refers to the wider context in order to interpret the section he is working on. In Mt. 6, he treated two sections under one heading, already determining to some degree that these units had some coherence. This was then shown in the way thematic connections and linguistic parallels were drawn out. In addition, he moved back up to the top of the chapter to coordinate Jesus' comments on pagans. Careful attention to Matthew's shaping of the material allows for subtlety in interpreting each subsection, a subtlety shown primarily through the process of cross-referencing.

7) He alludes to or echoes biblical texts in other contexts, which further layer his own exposition and substantiate his claim about Scripture's widespread

unity. This was especially clear in the creative fusion of Mt. 6 and Rom. 8, texts that Bonhoeffer links allusively but nowhere explicitly.

8) He employs examples or illustrations that help him draw out some aspect of the biblical text. In his attempt to coordinate two emphases from the biblical text—daily dying as a disciple picks up the cross and the once-and-for-all nature of death with Christ on the cross—he utilized the image of a tree that continues to die each day after its roots have been cut off at a specific point. Death can describe both states. The illustration is briefly employed, but it creatively and effectively works for his purposes.

9) In both chapters of *Nachfolge*, Bonhoeffer employed *Sperrsatz* to direct attention to specific aspects of the biblical text that he wanted to highlight. In his work on Mt. 6:25-34, this strategy helped him to visibly demonstrate his reliance on the ordering of Kingdom of God *first* and everything else as subsequent. In the chapter on Baptism, the use of letter spacing structured the entire exposition, doing more to demonstrate his reliance on Rom. 6 than even his explicit citation of Paul's texts in parentheses.

10) Unlike the previous examples of Bonhoeffer's biblical interpretation that have been the focus in other chapters of this book, here, in the second part of his book, he used the convention of stringing together biblical texts in parentheses to streamline his exposition, not only assuming familiarity on the part of the reader but also to demonstrate widespread attestation for the point he was making.

11) Whether in the body of the text, a footnote, or a parenthesis, he makes comments on textual details. In previous chapters, this has most often been in reference to his translation differences from Luther's text. Here, especially in the chapter on Baptism, he included some key Greek prepositions, which signals an awareness of just how many important points of interpretation of Pauline texts turn on how a preposition is understood. In addition, he included a discussion of "children" in 1 John, suggesting that this small detail could provide biblical support, and thus contribute to bigger arguments about infant baptism.

Each of these ways of moving from text to comment, and more could be added to this list, together constitutes *Sachlichkeit* for Bonhoeffer. For interpretation to be bound to Scripture, focused on Christ and dependent on the Spirit then it will be derivative or dependent on the biblical text in the way these aspects of the interpretive process are. In the 1930s, and especially with *Nachfolge* at Finkenwalde, Bonhoeffer practices his hermeneutic in dependence on Scripture's unified witness to Christ in all its diversity.

CONCLUSION

Dietrich Bonhoeffer was a biblical interpreter. This is the main argument of this book, which means that the other arguments contained in the preceding chapters—arguments about continuity in Bonhoeffer's corpus (starting from 1925) or about his theology being biblical in character or about how the social location of his acts of interpretation shift his work with Scripture or about his relationships with Luther and Barth (influenced but retaining his originality) or about how exactly to draw conclusions about Bonhoeffer's views on Scripture and its interpretation (doctrine of Scripture and the practices connected to reading Scripture are linked and mutually interpretive, and thus best pursued by watching what he does with Scripture through close readings of key texts) or about the central place Finkenwalde holds in considering Bonhoeffer on the Bible—have come into play in order to support this primary contention. In one sense, as stated in the introduction, that Bonhoeffer was a biblical interpreter is obvious because of his Lutheran tradition and the fact that much of his output is concerned with engaging biblical material. In another sense, though, this claim has become more complex as the material of each chapter has been studied. In fact, it raises an important question to be addressed here: what does the word "interpretation" mean when thought about in relation to Bonhoeffer?

One proposal for sharpening up how one should take "interpretation" with reference to Bonhoeffer is provided by John Webster in an essay called "Reading the Bible: The Example of Barth and Bonhoeffer."[1] Webster's essay is an appropriate one with which to conclude for two reasons. It was his essay that launched my interest in Bonhoeffer's relation to the Bible, leading to the initial stages of research for the PhD thesis that served as the basis for this book. It is, as a result, a bit like a "coming of age" to be able to engage it at this stage of the process, enabled by it, among other things of course, to now recognize the strengths and weaknesses of his account (there seemed to only be strengths in my first encounter with it). The other reason to conclude with it is because this essay serves as a helpful representative of the kinds of engagement I catalogued in the footnotes of the introduction; it is a clear and concise exemplar of one approach to reflecting on

---

1. John Webster, "Reading the Bible: The Example of Barth and Bonhoeffer," in *Word and Church: Essays in Church Dogmatics* (Edinburgh: T&T Clark, 2001), 87–110.

Bonhoeffer's relationship to Scripture, and as such it offers a helpful test of my claim to supplement and complement other offerings by scholars on the theme. In fact, I submit that if Webster's account and mine can be put into right relation with one another, then we would not only have an example of Bonhoeffer's cherished "polyphony," but we would also be on our way to a kind of dogmatic vision between Christ and the Spirit, indicating that perhaps, as I hinted in a footnote in another chapter, that there might be more Triune elements in Bonhoeffer's corpus from which new and creative theological work could come.

There is much with which one can agree in Webster's thought-provoking essay. For instance, Webster's claim about Bonhoeffer is that he is essentially a biblical theologian, that the majority of his work is constituted by writings on the Bible, and that the material produced in the 1930s is where one should go in order to see this on display.[2] In addition, he seeks to consider Bonhoeffer in relation to Barth and to interpret the work of both theologians with the Bible in the context of the ecclesial and political events of the time.[3] These points, correct in my view, are made, though, less to clarify specific aspects of Bonhoeffer's interpretation of the Bible and more to support Webster's own thesis as he develops it in this essay.

He is engaging Barth and Bonhoeffer in order to correct what he perceives to be an overemphasis on theory in the interpretation of Scripture. What he finds in Barth and Bonhoeffer is an attempt to offer a "theological, and therefore spiritual, portrayal of interpretive acts and agents," an account that subverts "heavy-duty hermeneutical theory" because it is seen as a "hindrance."[4] The first of three concluding implications of his study of Barth and Bonhoeffer drives this point home. Webster writes:

> Hermeneutical and methodological questions are at best of secondary importance in the interpretation of Scripture. The real business is elsewhere, and it is spiritual, and therefore dogmatic. Correct interpretation cannot be detached from correct depiction of the situation in which we as readers go to Scripture and encounter God. The task of such a depiction is a dogmatic task, calling for the deployment of the concepts and language through which the church has sought to map out as best it can the astonishing reality of God's saving self-communication. If sophisticated hermeneutical theory fails to persuade, it is largely because, in the end, it addresses the wrong problems, and leaves untouched the real difficulty with reading Scripture. That difficulty—as Bonhoeffer and Barth diagnose it—is spiritual and therefore moral; it is our refusal as sinners to be spoken to, our wicked repudiation of the divine address,

2. Webster, *Reading the Bible*, 90, 99. The final point is made not simply as an index of where to go to find material but in order to destabilize the tendency to read the 1930s as "'staging-posts' on the way to Bonhoeffer's last writings" (99). I am in full agreement with this point.

3. Webster, *Reading the Bible*, 107.

4. Webster, *Reading the Bible*, 108, 103, 90, respectively.

our desire to speak the final word to ourselves. From those sicknesses of soul, no amount of sophistication can heal us.[5]

In order to bring Bonhoeffer along in making this diagnosis, Webster describes Bonhoeffer as having two main convictions, both of which are developed primarily through a reading of Bonhoeffer's lecture, "Vergegenwärtigung neutestamentlicher Texte."[6] According to Webster, Bonhoeffer holds that Scripture is the living voice of God and the proper reader of Scripture accepts what God says in Scripture.[7] The latter conviction, since it contributes the most to Webster's aim in the essay, is modulated in a number of places, providing a handful of synonyms for Webster's characterization of what biblical interpretation means in reference to Bonhoeffer. A person's encounter with Scripture is spoken of as "reading" more often than interpreting, and it is an act of "attentiveness" and "self-relinquishment," a form of "listening" and "hearing," marked by an "attitude of ready submission and active compliance."[8] "Accept is the keyword."[9] On Webster's account, the interpreter for Bonhoeffer is in a passive position, which is, again, a helpful stance when seeking to combat the heavy-duty lifting hermeneutical theory can do in other accounts.

That Webster has an interest and is employing material for such a purpose is not objectionable in itself. But he is offering a reading of Bonhoeffer's interpretation, and if his interests cause him to overemphasize particular features of Bonhoeffer's interpretation, then aspects of his reading can be called into question. From my perspective, there is one major weakness with his account.

Webster has not allowed specific acts of Bonhoeffer's interpretation of biblical texts to factor into his account. He emphasizes the first main section of "Vergegenwärtigung neutestamentlicher Texte," but he does not discuss the sections where Bonhoeffer explicitly engages conversations about method, speaks of interpreting the diverse witnesses in Scripture, and talks extensively about the concrete freedoms of interpreters in engaging Scripture. In addition, he does not describe Bonhoeffer's practice of interpreting any actual texts in his analysis. Webster's account of Bonhoeffer's interpretation, therefore, has a tendency to undermine the interpreter and the act of interpretation because it is so easily subsumed under Christ's eloquence in his Prophetic office (inflected in a Barthian way).[10] The result is a picture of interpretation in which a person's passive

5. Webster, *Reading the Bible*, 109.

6. This primary source is coordinated with a few quotations from *Creation and Fall*, *Discipleship*, *Life Together*, "Introduction to Daily Meditation" and Bonhoeffer's letter to his brother-in-law, Rüdiger Schleicher.

7. Webster, *Reading the Bible*, 101.

8. Webster, *Reading the Bible*, 88, 89, 90, 101.

9. Webster, *Reading the Bible*, 106.

10. Webster, *Reading the Bible*, 103. There is, in fact, another minor weakness worth noting. Webster too closely assimilates Bonhoeffer to Barth. He is certainly correct to see the two theologians as closely related with respect to their work with the Bible, but for all their similarities, they are different theologians and interpreters of Scripture. As has already

acceptance is deemed more companionable to God's action than is a person's active interpretive engagement.[11]

What is needed is a description of "interpretation" that does not fall into the trap of positing this kind of "either–or" contrast, that is, a way of thinking about interpretation that does not assume the interpreter is either passive or entirely in control of a stable process. Words like "acceptance," "listening," "receiving," and "attentiveness,"—words that are good in themselves and appropriate for describing one pole of Bonhoeffer's interpretive vision—need to be correlated with the evidence that emerged in the chapters concerned with Bonhoeffer's interpretive action, the pole of interpretive activity that can be described by words like "choosing," "arranging," "emphasizing," and "adapting." Every act of interpretation is one in which an interpreter makes choices, the choice to emphasize one thing and therefore to underplay something else. To choose one thing is, therefore, not to choose something else. In fact, as we have seen, choice is at work all the way through the entire process of Bonhoeffer's interpretation, made up as it is of a bunch of different acts that culminate in judgments made about what to say and what not to say on the basis of the needs of the context and the capacities of the hearers. Both of these poles need to be held in tension: on the one hand, there is Bonhoeffer's talk and practice of interpretation being bound to Scripture, and on the other hand is his talk and practice of freedom with respect to Scriptural interpretation.

One way to correlate these two—being bound and free—is to return to the doctrinal resource that formed Bonhoeffer's vision of interpretation in 1925, a resource that was helpfully reemphasized in 1935 as well. Rather than solely placing Bonhoeffer's conception of interpretation in proximity to Christ's eloquence that results from his Prophetic office, his conception can also be helpfully inflected by Pneumatology. Christ's clear speaking (a point Bonhoeffer is very happy himself to emphasize in "Vergegenwärtigung neutestamentlicher Texte" and elsewhere) has a correlate created by the Spirit. A robust vision of human action grounded in the Spirit can be construed as a responsive agency to Christ's speech in Scripture, a kind of appropriately active and engaged form of listening, attending to, and accepting.

A good, rich word to describe this, and a word with helpful resonances in both the doctrines of Creation and Sanctification (doctrines where Pneumatology is essential) is *dependence*. In the context of creaturely existence, to be dependent is to have the source of life outside oneself, to be in constant need. But, since the source of life is God, who administers life to creatures by his Spirit, dependence

been noted at several points in this book, the relationship of Barth and Bonhoeffer, while illuminating and fascinating, should not be given too much weight in assessing specific aspects of their theology, and especially their engagement with Scripture.

11. It is important to note that Webster's own theological project, as a whole, does emphasize both passive and active elements, as well as their relation dogmatically construed. My criticism is only directed at his account of Bonhoeffer in this specific essay.

is not a matter of diminishment but rather an establishment of creaturely life and action. This means that dependence is not a passive notion, even though it is often misunderstood in precisely this way.[12] Rather, genuine creaturely action is compatible with total dependence on God since creatures are dependent on him for the capacity to act at all. Creaturely action does not limit dependence because this relationship includes within itself the permission and obligation to freely chosen action, which is made concrete through individual acts. Dependence on God includes the concept of creaturely action within it, and in fact, it is the precondition of it. For example, praying is the quintessential *act* of dependence, because when we pray we ask for something, which is an act, but it is an act that at the same time acknowledges need.

Interpretation is a matter of dependence on the Spirit because an interpreter prays for the Spirit to reveal Christ in Scripture as it is actively interpreted for the benefit of others. Revelation of Christ is not going to come in any other way than by the Spirit as the interpreter is bound to Scripture, but that also implies that revelation will be accessed through the means available to a particular interpreter, that is, his or her specific choices, interests, reading strategies, resources, contexts, etc. An interpreter is therefore dependent on the Spirit to speak in Scripture while he or she actually utilizes the freedom given by the Spirit to interpret the texts of Scripture as a real act of engagement established and sustained by the Spirit.

For Bonhoeffer, interpretation is then, in answer to the question above, a form of Spirit-established (or pneumatological) freedom, a walking by the Spirit bound to Scripture that is evidenced in real interpretive, responsible acts before God demonstrated as a person reads and presents biblical texts in certain places and times for specific purposes. It is in this sense that Bonhoeffer himself can be called a biblical interpreter, who, in his specific case, expresses this dependence in a confessional, intentional, Christocentric, contextual, careful, and detailed way that is bound to Scripture in the Spirit, while working with a vision of Scripture's unity but acknowledging its diverse witnesses to Christ. In Bonhoeffer we find a practitioner of an expansive view of biblical interpretation, a way of thinking about and doing biblical interpretation that cannot be easily contained in any one method or approach, because the task calls for every available resource in order to communicate to people.

Dietrich Bonhoeffer interprets biblical texts theologically and historically, and it is difficult, to say the least, to determine where any one of these begins or ends in his work on the Bible. He does interpret Scripture theologically, but that adjective is descriptive rather than programmatic, and it points in a number of directions. It indicates the sphere of his activity as accomplished under God, the purpose of it as undertaken to construct theology, preach to congregations, or train seminarians and pastors, and the mode of his engagement with Scripture as carried out in the Spirit. This is Bonhoeffer's lowercase "t" version of interpreting Scripture

---

12. For a helpful argument along these lines, see Rowan Williams, "On Being Creatures," in *On Christian Theology* (Oxford: Blackwell, 2000), 63–78.

theologically.[13] But since this is an expansive vision of biblical interpretation, it is a vision that affords him significant flexibility as he works with biblical texts; theological is not, therefore, the only helpful adjective.

He also interprets historically. Bonhoeffer's biblical interpretation is not defined over-against historical interpretation. His mature vision of biblical interpretation includes the fluid and diverse tradition of academic biblical interpretation broadly conceived. As we have seen many times, Bonhoeffer assumes and presupposes many of the results of modern biblical scholarship, even if he does not emphasize them very often. His interpretation of the Bible would not have been possible if he had not gone through regular, academic training. This does not serve as a limit for him, forcing him into a fixed method that one either does or does not practice. This training served, rather, as a precondition for what he does when he interprets Scripture. Using whatever resources are at his disposal—resources like commentaries, lexicons, critical editions of Hebrew and Greek texts, and modern translations, all of which help to improve one's understanding of the biblical texts—he gets down to the task of interpreting Scripture.

And when he does so, it is clear that different jobs call for different tools. This means that he exploits opportunities each text itself generates and responds to what is in front of him and to whom he is speaking. Bonhoeffer's activity with biblical texts is an interpretive eclecticism: whether utilizing a Lutheran-influenced reading of Pauline theology that arises from and is applied to Jeremiah, or ordering (and reordering) Matthew in order to prioritize certain emphases, or reflecting on the theological significance of source criticism in relation to Genesis, or drawing out Paul's implicit rationale in 1 Corinthians, or employing a theology of divine address, or using a Law-Gospel hermeneutic that proceeds through negation and affirmation. It must be emphasized that this approach to interpreting Scripture is, as these examples make clear, both a by-product of his involvement with the text (interpreted, again, in a context and for a purpose and with specific intellectual and spiritual gifts and for specific people), as well as a result of the biblical text's own form and content (a point driven home very clearly in the relationship between his 1935 lecture on unity and diversity in Scripture and in his original approach to reading the Synoptic Gospels and Paul in *Nachfolge*). He thoughtfully, responsibly and creatively interprets the biblical text in specific

---

13. I mean the lowercase "t" in contrast to the uppercase "T" of the so-called "Theological Interpretation of Scripture" movement, if that's the right term for it. In an early stage of this book, I had planned to enter into substantive conversation with various proposals about theological interpretation of Scripture, but it became more and more clear to me that my main contribution to that discussion, which I care about, could be to demonstrate how Bonhoeffer, often taken to be an exemplar of theological interpretation of Scripture, interpreted the Bible. It seems to me that future conversations about how to interpret the Bible theologically will be served well by studying examples of people working with texts (as here) as well as developing programmatic and theoretical resources to clarify our conceptualities. May the numbers of both groups increase!

contexts and with certain interests, and because this is biblical interpretation
conducted by a Christian and concerned with Scripture's witness to Jesus, then
it is concerned with history and theology, and because this is a hermeneutical
framework on the basis of the Spirit, then the Spirit creates freedom to respond
in the wholeness of Bonhoeffer's person before God. The result is that a number
of diverse conversation partners have their voices blended together by the Spirit
into the unique form of biblical interpretation that becomes Bonhoeffer's text.
His distinct voice retains the integrity of an agent that is attentive to the voice of
the Spirit at work through the biblical text as it witnesses to God's action in Jesus
Christ. Bonhoeffer's hermeneutic consists of a self-reflective form of interpretation
in which the ecclesial context is taken for granted, shaping and thus creating a
closely related hermeneutical framework and interpretive practice. This is a form
of expansive, eclectic biblical interpretation worth attending to as we continue to
read Scripture and to think about how to read Scripture theologically, historically
and responsibly.

This book has shown that Bonhoeffer has a clearly developed and articulated
hermeneutical framework and the interpretive practice that goes along with it.
The two are correlated very closely. He is consistent in his approach and the results
follow from it. Over time, in 1925 and again in 1935, he reflected on these issues
and continued to interpret biblical texts for various reasons and in a variety of
contexts, opening himself up to critical questions that continued to refine his
engagement with Scripture. Evaluating Bonhoeffer's biblical interpretation is not
really as simple as asking, "Is it good or bad?" but rather a matter of seeking to
understand the relationship he proposed between an interpretive framework and
interpretive practice so that a consistent hermeneutic and practice, albeit a different
version, can arise in new contexts today. The main thing, in other words, is to go
on actually interpreting biblical texts in interesting and imaginative and creative
and life-giving ways, using the many resources available to us (commentaries,
lexicons, critical editions of Hebrew and Greek texts, modern translations, works
of history and philosophy and theological texts like ancient creedal formulations,
confessional statements, and systematic theologies) in order to continue to
improve our thinking and practice as it moves along. To say that, though, is simply
to say that Christian biblical interpretation needs to be in a relation of dependence
on the Spirit. So, it is probably the case that the most interesting thing to say about
Bonhoeffer's biblical interpretation is that it brings Pneumatology and interpretive
acts into relation, inviting interpreters of Scripture to depend on the Spirit in order
to encounter Christ for the benefit of others.

In the words of Bonhoeffer's student paper, which helpfully situate all his
biblical interpretation, theological work, prayerful devotion, and ethical action in
the years after 1925:

> Hier sind wir beim Letzten, Tiefsten, es lag in allem Vorhergesagten
> verborgen: jeder pneumatische Auslegungsversuch ist Gebet, ist Bitte um den
> Heiligen Geist, der sich allein Gehör und Verständnis schafft nach seinem
> Gefallen, ohne den auch geistvollste Exegese zu nichts wird. Schriftverständnis,

Auslegung, Predigt, d. h. Erkenntnis Gottes ist beschlossen in der Bitte: „Veni creator spiritus."[14]

Here we are at the end, the deepest point, which lies hidden in everything that has been said previously: every pneumatological interpretive attempt is a prayer, it is a request for the Holy Spirit, who alone—as he wills—creates hearing and understanding, without which even the most brilliant exegesis comes to nothing. Scriptural understanding, interpretation, preaching, that is, the knowledge of God, is incorporated in the request: "Come, Creator Spirit."

The language used here shows that Bonhoeffer's understanding of the interpreter includes action. It is an *Auslegungsversuch* [interpretive attempt], *Gebet* [prayer], and *Bitte* [request]. The Spirit creates hearing and understanding, but this cannot be taken for granted. Instead, it must take the form of an action, a request. Divine action establishes the possibility of dialogue. In other words, prior divine action creates a dialogical relationship, a relationship in which an action can be initiated from the human side, so that an act of asking really does invite a response. In these interpretive attempts, human action, itself established by God, precedes divine action, not ontologically but chronologically. The major emphasis of Bonhoeffer the biblical interpreter is that interpretation is a practice, an act or set of acts in relation to the biblical text for the benefit of others.

14. DBW 9:322.

BIBLIOGRAPHY

Andrews, James. *Hermeneutics and the Church: In Dialogue with Augustine*. Notre Dame, IN: University of Notre Dame Press, 2012.

Barclay, John. "Interpretation, Not Repetition: Reflections on Bultmann as a Theological Reader of Paul." *Journal of Theological Interpretation*, 9:2 (2015): 201–9.

Barker, Gaylon H. *The Cross of Reality: Luther's Theologia Crucis and Bonhoeffer's Christology*. Minneapolis, MN: Fortress, 2015.

Barnett, Victoria. *For the Soul of the People: Protestant Protest against Hitler*. Oxford: Oxford University Press, 1992.

Barth, Karl. *Church Dogmatics* I.1, *The Doctrine of the Word of God*. Translated by Geoffrey W. Bromiley, G. T. Thomson, and Harold Knight. London: T&T Clark Continuum, 2010.

Barth, Karl. *The Epistle to the Romans*. Translated by Sir E. Hoskyns. Oxford: Oxford University Press, 1933.

Barth, Karl. "No!" In *Natural Theology: Comprising "Nature and Grace" by Professor Dr. Emil Brunner and the Reply "No!" by Dr. Karl Barth*. Translated by Peter Fraenkel. London: Centenary Press, 1946, 65–128.

Barth, Karl. *The Word of God and Theology*. Translated by Amy Marga. New York: T&T Clark, 2011.

Bethge, Eberhard. *Dietrich Bonhoeffer: A Biography*. Rev. ed. Edited by Victoria Barnett. Translated by Eric Mosbacher, Peter Ross, Frank Clarke, and William Glen-Doepel. Minneapolis, MN: Augsburg Fortress, 2000.

Brock, Brian. *Singing the Ethos of God: On the Place of Christian Ethics in Scripture*. Grand Rapids, MI: Eerdmans, 2007.

Burnett, Richard E. *Karl Barth's Theological Exegesis: The Hermeneutical Principles of the* Römerbrief *Period*. Grand Rapids, MI: Eerdmans, 2004.

Chandler, Andrew. "The Quest for the Historical Bonhoeffer." *Journal of Ecclesiastical History*, 54:1 (2003): 89–96.

Clements, Keith W. *Bonhoeffer and Britain*. Church Together in Britain and Ireland: London, 2006.

Clements, Keith W. "'This Is My World' The Intentionality of Bonhoeffer's Preaching in London 1933–35." In *Dietrich Bonhoeffers Christentum: Festschrift für Christian Gremmels*. Edited by Florian Schmitz and Christiane Tietz. Germany: Gütersloher Verlagshaus, 2011, 17–36.

de Gruchy, John W. *The Cambridge Companion to Dietrich Bonhoeffer*. Cambridge: Cambridge University Press, 1999.

de Lange, Frits. *Waiting for the Word: Dietrich Bonhoeffer on Speaking about God*. Translated by Martin N. Walton. Grand Rapids, MI: Eerdmans, 2000.

DeJonge, Michael. *Bonhoeffer's Reception of Luther*. Oxford: Oxford University Press, 2017.

Dickens, W. T. *Hans Urs Von Balthasar's Theological Aesthetics: A Model for Post-critical Biblical Interpretation*. Notre Dame, IN: University of Notre Dame Press, 2003.

Feil, Ernst. *The Theology of Dietrich Bonhoeffer*. Philadelphia, PA: Fortress, 1985.

Ford, David F. *Barth and God's Story: Biblical Narrative and the Theological Method of Karl Barth in the Church Dogmatics*. Frankfurt am Main: Peter Lang, 1981.

Ford, David F. *Self and Salvation: Being Transformed*. Cambridge: Cambridge University Press, 2009.

Fowl, Stephen, and Gregory Jones. *Reading in Communion: Scripture and Ethics in Christian Life*, London: SPCK, 1991.

Frick, Peter (ed.). *Bonhoeffer's Intellectual Formation*. Tübingen: Mohr Siebeck, 2008.

Fulford, Ben. *Divine Eloquence and Human Transformation: Rethinking Scripture and History through Gregory of Nazianzus and Hans Frei*. Minneapolis, MN: Fortress Press, 2013.

Godsey, John D. *The Theology of Dietrich Bonhoeffer*. London: SCM Press, 1960.

Green, Clifford. *Bonhoeffer. A Theology of Sociality*. Grand Rapids, MI: Eerdmans, 1999.

Green, Clifford, and Michael DeJonge (eds.). *The Bonhoeffer Reader*. Minneapolis, MN: Fortress Press, 2013.

Greenman, Jeffrey P., Timothy Larsen, and Stephen R. Spencer (eds.). *The Sermon on the Mount through the Centuries: From the Early Church to John Paul II*. Grand Rapids, MI: Brazos Press, 2007.

Grunow, Richard. "Dietrich Bonhoeffers Schriftauslegung." In *Die Mündige Welt* 1. Munich: Kaiser, 1955.

Hamilton, Nadine. *Dietrich Bonhoeffers Hermeneutik Der Responsivität: Ein Kapital Schriftlehre im Anschluss an* "Schopfung und Fall." Göttingen: Vandenhoeck & Ruprecht, 2016.

Hamilton, Nadine. "Dietrich Bonhoeffer and the Necessity of Kenosis for Scriptural Hermeneutics." *Scottish Journal of Theology*, 71:4 (2018): 441–59.

Harrellson, Walter. "Bonhoeffer and the Bible." In *The Place of Bonhoeffer*. Edited by Martin E. Marty. London: SCM Press, 1963, 113–42.

Hays, Richard. *Echoes of Scripture in the Letters of Paul*. New York: Yale University Press, 1989.

Kahl, Werner. "Evangeliumsvergegenwärtigung." In *Dietrich Bonhoeffers Christentum: Festschrift für Christian Gremmels*. Edited by Florian Schmitz and Christiane Tietz. Gütersloh: Gütersloher Verlagshaus, 2011, 134–55.

Kelsey, David. *Proving Doctrine: Uses of Scripture in Modern Theology*. Harrisburg, PA: Trinity Press International, 1999.

Kuske, Martin. *The Old Testament as the Book of Christ*. Philadelphia, PA: Westminster Press, 1976.

Levering, Matthew. *Scripture and Metaphysics: Aquinas and the Renewal of Trinitarian Theology*. Hoboken, NJ: John Wiley, 2004.

Marsh, Charles. *Strange Glory: A Life of Dietrich Bonhoeffer*. New York: Alfred A. Knopf, 2014.

Mawson, Micheal. *Christ Existing as Community: Bonhoeffer's Ecclesiology*. Oxford: Oxford University Press, 2018.

Mawson, Micheal. "Scripture." In *The Oxford Handbook of Dietrich Bonhoeffer*. Edited by Michael Mawson and Philip G. Ziegler. Oxford: Oxford University Press, 2019.

McKim, Donald K. *Calvin and the Bible*. Cambridge: Cambridge University Press, 2006.

Moberly, Walter. "*Creation and Fall* and Biblical Exegesis for the Church." A presentation delivered at a conference held at St. John's College in Durham, UK in 2017 called Reading Bonhoeffer for the Life of the Church.

Müller, Hanfried. *Von der Kirche zur Welt: Ein Beitrag zu der Beziehung des Wort Gottes auf die societas in Dietrich Bonhoeffers theologische Entwicklung* [*From the Church to the World: A Contribution to the Relation of the Word of God to Society in Dietrich Bonhoeffer's Theological Development*]. Leipzig and Hamburg-Bergstedt: Reich, 1966.

Numada, Jonathan D. "Dietrich Bonhoeffer's Lutheran Existentialism in Theological Interpretation." In *Pillars in the History of Biblical Interpretation: Prevailing Methods after 1980*, vol. 2. Edited by Stanley E. Porter and Sean A. Adams. Eugene, OR: Pickwick Publications, 2016, 71–95.

Pasquerello III, Michael. *Dietrich: Bonhoeffer and the Theology of a Preaching Life*. Waco, TX: Baylor University Press, 2017.

Phillips, J. A. *The Form of Christ in the World*. New York: Collins, 1967.

Plant, Stephen J. "God's Dangerous Gift: Bonhoeffer, Luther, and Bach on the Role of Reason in Reading Scripture." In *God Speaks to Us*. Edited by Ralf K. Wüstenberg and Jens Zimmermann. Frankfurt am Main: Peter Lang, 2013, 37–54.

Plant, Stephen J. *Taking Stock of Bonhoeffer: Studies in Biblical Interpretation and Ethics*. Farnham: Ashgate, 2014.

Plant, Stephen J. "Uses of the Bible in the 'Ethics' of Dietrich Bonhoeffer," PhD Cambridge University, 1993.

Pribbenow, Brad. *Prayerbook of Christ: Dietrich Bonhoeffer's Christological Interpretation of the Psalms*. Lanham, MD: Rowman and Littlefield, 2018.

Quash, Ben. *Found Theology: History, Imagination and the Holy Spirit*. London: T&T Clark, 2013.

Rieger, Julius. *Bonhoeffer in England*. Germany: Lettner-Verlag, 1966.

Robertson, Edwin. *The Shame and the Sacrifice: The Life and Preaching of Dietrich Bonhoeffer*. London: Hodder and Stoughton, 1987.

Robinson, James M. (ed.). *The Beginnings of Dialectical Theology*, vol. 1. Translated by K. R. Crim, L. De Grazia. Louisville, KY: John Knox Press, 1968.

Rochelle, Jay C. "Bonhoeffer and Biblical Interpretation: Reading Scripture in the Spirit." *Currents in Theology and Mission*, 22:2 (1995): 85–95.

Sanders, Fred. *The Image of the Immanent Trinity: Implications of Rahner's Rule for a Theological Interpretation of Scripture*. New York: Peter Lang, 2004.

Sarisky, Darren. *Scriptural Interpretation: A Theological Exploration*. Hoboken, NJ: Wiley-Blackwell, 2012.

Schleiermacher, Friedrich. *Christian Faith: A New Translation and Critical Edition*. 2 vols. Edited and translated by Terrence N. Tice, Catherine L. Kelsey and Edwina Lawler. Louisville, KY: Westminster John Knox Press, 2016.

Schlingensiepen, Ferdinand. *Dietrich Bonhoeffer 1906–1945: Martyr, Thinker, Man of Resistance*. New York: T&T Clark, 2012.

Scholder, Klaus. *The Churches and the Third Reich*. 2 vol. English translation by John Bowden. London: SCM Press, 1987.

Steiner, Robert, and Helen Hacksley. "Enticing Otherness in Barcelona—Dietrich Bonhoeffer's Retelling of the Gospel like 'a Fairy Tale about a Strange Land.'" In *God Speaks to Us: Dietrich Bonhoeffer's Biblical Hermeneutics*. Edited by Ralf K. Wüstenberg and Jens Zimmermann. Peter Lang: Frankfurt am Main, 2013, 55–84.

Taylor, Derek. *Reading Scripture as Church: Dietrich Bonhoeffer's Hermeneutic of Discipleship*. Downers Grove, IL: IVP Academic, 2020.

Tietz, Christiane. *Theologian of Resistance: The Life and Thought of Dietrich Bonhoeffer*. Translated by Victoria J. Barnett. Minneapolis, MN: Fortress Press, 2016.

Vanhoozer, Kevin. "Lost in Interpretation? Truth, Scripture and Hermeneutics." *Journal of the Evangelical Theological Society*, 48:1 (2005): 89–114.

van't Slot, Edward. "The Freedom of Scripture—Bonhoeffer's Changing View of Biblical Canonicity." In *God Speaks to Us: Dietrich Bonhoeffer's Biblical Hermeneutics*. Edited by Ralf K. Wüstenberg and Jens Zimmermann. Frankfurt am Main: Peter Lang, 2013, 101–22.

Vischer, Wilhelm. *The Witness of the Old Testament to Christ*. Translated by A. B. Crabtree. London: Lutterworth Press, 1949.

Webster, John. "Reading the Bible: The Example of Barth and Bonhoeffer." In *Word and Church: Essays in Christian Dogmatics*. New York: T&T Clark, 2001, 87–110.

Wendel, Ernst Georg. *Studien Zur Homiletik Dietrich Bonhoeffers: Predigt—Hermeneutik—Sprache*. Mohr Siebeck: Heidelberg, Germany, 1985.

Westerholm, Stephen, and Martin Westerholm. *Reading Sacred Scripture: Voices from the History of Biblical Interpretation*. Grand Rapids, MI: Eerdmans, 2016.

Williams, Rowan. *On Christian Theology*. Oxford: Blackwell, 2000.

Winter, Sean F. "Bonhoeffer and Biblical Interpretation: The Early Years." *Bonhoeffer Legacy: Australasian Journal of Bonhoeffer Studies*, 1 (2013): 1–15.

Winter, Sean F. "Presenting the Word: The Use and Abuse of Bonhoeffer on the Bible." *Bonhoeffer Legacy: Australasian Journal of Bonhoeffer Studies*, 2:2 (2014): 19–35.

Winter, Sean F. "Word and World: Dietrich Bonhoeffer and Biblical Interpretation." *Pacifica*, 25 (2012): 137–50.

Woefel, James W. *Bonhoeffer's Theology. Classical and Revolutionary*. Nashville, TN: Abingdon Press, 1970.

Wüstenberg, Ralf K., and Jens Zimmermann (eds.). *God Speaks to Us*. Frankfurt am Main: Peter Lang, 2013.

Ziegler, Philip G. "Dietrich Bonhoeffer: A Theologian of the Word of God." In *Bonhoeffer, Christ and Culture*. Edited by Keith L. Johnson and Timothy Larsen. Downers Grove, IL: Intervarsity Press, 2013, 17–37.

Ziegler, Philip G. "Listening to *Discipleship's* 'B-Side.'" A presentation delivered at a conference held at St. John's College in Durham, UK in 2017 called Reading Bonhoeffer for the Life of the Church.

Ziegler, Philip G. *Militant Grace: The Apocalyptic Turn and the Future of Christian Theology*. Grand Rapids, MI: Baker, 2018.

Zimmermann, Jens. "Reading the Book of the Church: Bonhoeffer's Christological Hermeneutics." *Modern Theology*, 28:4 (2012): 763–80.

INDEX

Lightning Source UK Ltd.
Milton Keynes UK
UKHW020922140223
416919UK00002B/8